The Ethics of Confucius

The Sayings of the Master – Confucian Teachings of Chinese Wisdom, Philosophy and Morality

By Miles Menander Dawson

PANTIANOS
CLASSICS

Published by Pantianos Classics

ISBN-13: 978-1-78987-205-7

First published in 1915

Confucius, as depicted in a 1687 Latin translation of three of the
"Four Books" of Qing Confucianism.

Contents

Foreword

WHEN Confucius died, it is recorded that his last words were regrets that none among the rulers then living possessed the sagacity requisite to a proper appreciation of his ethical philosophy and teachings. He died unhonoured, — in his seventy-third year, 479 B.C., feeling in the flickering beats of his failing heart that his inspiring pleas for truth and justice, industry and self-denial, moderation and public duty, though then without having awakened men's impulses, would yet stir the depths of the social life of his land.

Only the future will tell how far his staunch guide-ropes to correct conduct will be extended within China, and even be threaded through the dark and dangerous passages of existence in the lands of the Occident to lead humanity safely to that elevated plane which the lofty ideals of the philosopher aimed at establishing. Not yet has the world, sagacious as it is, appreciated the wealth of gentleness, the profound forces for good, the uplifting influences embodied in the teachings of the ancient sage, whose aim, reduced to its simplest definition, was to show "how to get through life like a courteous gentleman."

A great step forward in the dissemination of the doctrine in foreign lands is taken in "The Superior Man." Lofty as appear the ideals, in the usual translations, they lose the effect on the average reader that the application which Mr. Dawson has now given them must create. Driving home the principles by careful compilation under different headings, the author causes the scheme of ethical conduct to attract and appeal; and the blessings it has bestowed in the vast expanses of China may yet give comfort to many people in many other lands.

Confucius strove to make the human being good—a good father, a good mother, a good son, a good daughter, a good friend, a good citizen. Though his truths were unpalatable at the time of their enunciation, they have lived to bear good fruit, despite the desperate efforts of Emperor Tsin Shi-hwang to destroy them by fire, and it is gratifying to see that a still wider sphere is being more and more developed for them in the West.

The movement that is now being energized in China to make the doctrine more familiar to the people, may also find reflection in foreign lands. "The Superior Man" will surely help the struggler in the mire of complexity to find his way out to the clean, substantial foothold of manliness and integrity.

Introduction

THE ethical and political precepts of Confucius are not well known in Occidental countries, even to most of those who give special attention to these subjects; and of what is known, much, indeed most, is confused with the notion that Confucius taught a religion in our sense of that term.

Yet these ethical teachings, which are almost purely secular, have for more than 2000 years been accepted by a larger number of human beings than those of any other teacher. This, also, notwithstanding that the peoples who so receive Confucian morals as their guide are of the most various views concerning religion, i.e., for instance, are Buddhists, Mahometans, Taoists, Shintoists, etc. No other ethical system, whether of religious origin, or of secular, has ever been acceptable to persons professing religious convictions so diverse.

And his political maxims have been regarded as fundamental, and knowledge of them, as well as of his ethics, has been insisted upon as a prime essential to political preferment, in a nation which, despite the not infrequent shifting of ruling dynasties, has the unparalleled record of continuing from prehistoric times to the present without a single break.

In view of their obvious importance and of the availability of translations of the Chinese classics, the question naturally arises: Why the prevailing want of information concerning the works of Confucius, his disciples and followers?

Though due in part, no doubt, to Confucianism not being a religion and so receiving but scant attention from students of comparative religions, to the relatively small interest of Occidentals, until very recently, in things Chinese, and to the somewhat expensive editions in which alone the best translation is available, the want of information concerning these teachings is, in my opinion, chiefly due to this: They are found in large volumes consisting of ancient Chinese classics which Confucius edited, of a collection of his sayings, of certain books by his disciples that purport to give his precepts accurately, in one book by his great apostle, Mencius, [1] who more than a century later led the revival of Confucian ethics which has continued to this day, and in certain books by later followers; and these books consist, in varying proportions, ranging from a minimum of more than half to a maximum of at least nineteen-twentieths, of discourses upon ceremonies, customs, and the like, possibly of great interest to dwellers in China or Japan, but almost absolutely devoid of interest to most Occidentals.

These ceremonies and customs, already firmly intrenched when Confucius was born, doubtless constitute a very rich and expressive language, crystallized into conduct; but it is one which is wholly unintelligible and even repellent to persons of Western origin.

The only form, other than this, in which the ethical teachings of Confucius and his followers have been presented, is through books about these teachings, *i.e.*, presenting, in the language of these modern authors, what they consider Confucius and his followers have taught.

The aim in preparing this book is to put before Occidental readers, in the words of the Chinese sage and his followers, as translated, everything concerning ethics and statecraft contained in the Confucian classics which is likely to interest them, omitting nothing of importance. This has been undertaken in the following fashion:

Every such passage has been extracted from all the works comprising the Confucian classics and several from the more important works of early Confucian scholars.

These have been arranged by topics in accordance with a scheme laid down as that of Confucius himself in "The Great Learning."

The passages, so quoted, have been thrown into the order deemed most effective to demonstrate and illustrate the doctrine of Confucius.

To sustain the interest unbroken, the passages quoted are connected by a running narrative, showing briefly the relationship of one with the other, stating from what bock taken and by whom enunciated, and most sparingly accompanied by quotations from other moralists, ancient or modern.

This book makes no claim to be an exhaustive study of the text, or of the commentaries on the text, of the Chinese sage; and much less to epitomize a critical investigation and collation of original texts. It accepts the generally received canon of the sayings and writings of Confucius as authentic, and deals exclusively with their significance as viewed scientifically in these days. Thus considered, the sayings of Confucius are seen to exhibit wonderful foresight and insight.

Indeed, it is a continual marvel that, like Socrates, Plato, and Aristotle, Confucius should have come so near to laying down, formally, the lines which scientific investigation must pursue; and yet that, as generation after generation passed away, the attitude of many of the disciples of each of these should have become more and more that of blind and even superstitious imitation of the great teacher, and almost scrupulous avoidance of the application of his principles in the never-ending search for truth. This seems to have commenced with the immediate disciples of the sage, and by the time of Mencius it was already a species of idolatry, expressed in such sayings as this: "Since first there were living men until now, there has never been another Confucius." (Bk. ii., pt. i., c. ii., v. 23.)

"From the birth of mankind till now, there has never been another like our Master." (Bk. ii., pt. i., c. ii., v. 27.)

So also, among the Greeks and Romans, the very name, "philosopher," *i.e.*, "lover of wisdom," which Socrates gave to himself as one who did not pretend to be wise already, but who merely sought wisdom earnestly, soon lost its true meaning, as veneration for Socrates, Plato, or Aristotle took the place of the child-like, simple, open-minded search for truth which they inculcated as the obvious duty of intelligent beings. In other words, the positive teaching of these great minds became in due time prescriptive authority in the view of their followers, while the essential factor in the thought of each of the great teachers, that the mind should be open—should, in the words of St. Paul, "try all things and hold fast that which is good"—gave way to a prohibition against questioning any declaration of the Master, and later against questioning any of the accepted derivations and corollaries of the authoritative sayings.

It is to be remembered that Confucius never made claim to be inspired; to be sure, he said of himself, "If Heaven had wished to let this cause of truth perish, then I, a mortal yet to be born, should not have got such a relation to that cause, but this was rather a declaration of the universality of divine providence than a claim of special inspiration.

Later, however, the commentators virtually claimed it for him, *i.e.*, that he was "divinely sent," as in the Annotation of Kung-Yang quoting the Adjunct of the Spring and Autumn and also in the Adjunct of the Hsiâo King, in which Confucius is represented as reporting to Heaven the completion of his writings and as receiving divine approval in the form of a red rainbow arching down and becoming transformed into yellow jade with words carved upon it.

This book is written to afford others opportunity for the same inspiring understanding of the true nature of the Confucian conception of good conduct as an encouragement of independent, clear thinking concerning the purposes of life and what may be done with it, which met so warm a welcome in my own mind when I first fortunately chanced upon a really good translation of the Analects of Confucius. What is here attempted is but an unworthy recognition of the great benefit, which, across twenty-five centuries, the Chinese sage conferred upon me.

My thanks are due to various persons who have aided me with criticisms and suggestions; but very especially to Chen Huan Chang. Ph.D. (Columbia), Chin Shih of 1904 A.D. (*i.e.*, winner of the prize in the highest competitive examination in China on the teachings of Confucius), formerly Secretary of the Grand Secretariat at Pekin, now President of the Confucian Society in China and leader of the successful movement there to restore public recognition of Confucian ethics and observances. Dr. Chen has looked up for me all doubtful interpretations of texts, advising me of the variant views and enabling me to choose among them. In general, and with almost no exceptions, the commonly accepted meaning is given.

[1] Mencius said of himself: "Although I could not be a disciple of Confucius myself, I have endeavoured to cultivate my virtue by means of others who were." (Bk. iv., pt. ii., c. xxii., v. 2.)

The Works of Confucius, His Disciples, and Most Important Followers

Including Ancient Books Edited by Him, Books of His Sayings, and Accounts of His Teachings by His Disciples and by Early Apostles and Commentators.

Confucius was born in 552 B.C. and died in 479 B.C. His name was Kung Ch'in Chung-ni, of which K'ung was the family name, Ch'in the personal (*i.e.*, what we call Christian) name, and Chung-ni the special name given upon reaching full age. He was called K'ung Fu Tse later, the appellation Fu Tse meaning "Master"; and this has been Latinized into Confucius.

1. The actual authorship of but one book is ascribed to him, viz: Ch'un Ch'in, "Spring and Autumn" (English Edition, vol. v., "Chinese Classics").

This book is said to have been written by Confucius himself, in his seventy-second year, and to have been designed by him to serve as an epitome of his teachings upon all ethical, social, and religious subjects. At least, Mencius so speaks of it. The book, in a different form and known as "The Annals of Lu," was in existence before Confucius, and his task seems, after all, to have been to edit and amplify it. The work as it has come down to us, however, undoubtedly unchanged since the Han dynasty, is a bare record of events, almost utterly devoid of instruction and even of interest.

2. A collection of conversations with Confucius, containing many of his most important sayings, was made by his disciples after his death. It is known as:

Lun Yü, "The Analects," translated by James Legge, and published in "The Sacred Books of the East."

Several important books or collections of books, already ancient when Confucius was born and regarded as classics, were edited by Confucius and further edited by his early disciples. These are:

3. Yi King, the "Book of Changes."

4. Hsiâo King, the "Book of Filial Piety."

5. Shu King, the "Book of History."

6. Shi King, the "Book of Poetry," also called "The Odes."

7. Li Ki, the "Book of Ceremonies."

All of these were translated by James Legge and published in "The Sacred Books of the East."

The last mentioned is also often called "Younger Tai's Record of Rites," and it is affirmed that the "Li-Ching," said to be an older and greatly variant edition, should be accepted instead. In this book or collection of books are comprised two of very special importance:

8. "The Great Learning," said to have been committed to writing by Tse-Tse, the grandson of Confucius, from his recollections of the teachings of his grandfather and from reports of the same by his father and other disciples of Confucius. His text is elucidated by commentaries in the "Li Ki." This book has also come down separately.

9. "The Doctrine of the Mean," also the work of disciples of Confucius and their early successors. This has also come down separately.

There is also the very valuable volume of the sayings of Meng Tse, the great apostle of Confucianism in the second century later—whose name is Latinized into:

10. Mencius.

This Book of Mencius was also translated by James Legge and is published in "The Sacred Books of the East."

"The Four Books," meaning thereby the elements and very core of Confucian doctrine, is the name given to "The Analects," "The Great Learning," "The Doctrine of the Mean," and "Mencius."

"The Five Classics" or "The Five Canons" is the name applied to the "Yi King," "Hsiâo King," "Shu King," "Shi King," and "Ch'un" (or "Ch'in King"), collectively. The word "King" means "classic" or "canon."

Other works of Confucian commentators and scholars which are occasionally quoted from, are:

11. Shuo Yuan ("Park of Narratives").

12. Hsun Tze.

13. Ku-hang Chuan ("Ku-liang's Commentary").

14. "Many Dewdrops of the Spring and Autumn."

15. Pan-Ku.

16. "History of Han Dynasty."

17. "History of Latter Han Dynasty."

18. "Narratives of Nations."

19. Kung-Yang Chuan ("Kung-Yang's Commentary").

The citations of this book are for the most part given by the name of the work, the name or number of the chapter and other grand division of the work and the verse, to the end that any edition in Chinese or any translation into English or into another language may be conveniently referred to.

M. M. D.

Confucius

K'ung Fu-tsze, "the philosopher K'ung," whose name has been Latinized into Confucius, was born in the year 551 (or 552) B.C. His father, Shuh-hang Heih was an officer in charge of the district of Tsow in the State of Lu and had been famous for his strength and daring; he was of the Kung family and lineally descended from Hwang-Ti, an almost legendary character of ancient China.

At the age of seventy, Shuh-liang Heih, the father of ten children of whom but one was a son and he a cripple, sought a wife in the Yen family where there were three daughters. The two elder of them demurred when apprised by their father of the old man's suit; but the youngest, Ching-tsai, only seventeen years of age, offered to abide by her father's judgment. The following year Confucius was born and three years later she was a widow.

Confucius was married, in accordance with Chinese custom, at nineteen and accepted public employment as a keeper of stores and later as superintendent of parks and herds. At twenty-two, however, he commenced his life-work as a teacher, and gradually a group of students, eager to be instructed in the classics and in conduct and government, gathered about him.

He was a contemporary of Lao-tsze, the founder of Taoism, who, however, was of the next previous generation. Confucius is said to have had several interviews with him about 517 B.C.

Up to the age of fifty-two, he was not much in public life. He was then made chief magistrate of the city of Chung-tu, which so thrived and improved under his care, that the Duke of Lu appointed him minister of crime which resulted in a great reduction of wrongdoing. The Duke accepting a present of female musicians and giving himself over to dissipation, Confucius withdrew and wandered among the various states, giving instruction as opportunity offered.

His disciples during his lifetime rose to three thousand and of these some seventy or eighty were highly esteemed by him.

Confucius when he set forth on his wanderings was fifty-six; it was thirteen years before he returned to Lu.

In 482 B.C., he lost his only son; in 481 B.C., his favourite student, Yen Hwuy, and in 478 B.C. Tsze-lu, another of his favourites, passed away, and the same year Confucius himself died at the age of seventy-two (or seventy-three).

He was buried in the K'ung cemetery outside the gates of K'iuh-fow, where most of his descendants, said to number more than forty thousand, still live. His tomb is yet preserved and is annually visited by vast numbers of his followers.

Chapter One - What Constitutes the Superior Man

THE central idea of Confucius is that every normal human being cherishes the aspiration to become a superior man—superior to his fellows, if possible, but surely superior to his own past and present self. This does not more than hint at perfection as a goal; and it is said of him that one of the subjects concerning which the Master rarely spoke, was "perfect virtue." (Analects, bk. ix., c. i.) He also said, "They who know virtue, are few" (Analects, bk. xv., c. iii.), and was far from teaching a perfectionist doctrine. It refers rather to the perpetually relative, the condition of being superior to that to which one may be superior, be it high or low,—that hopeful possibility which has ever lured mankind toward higher things.

This accords well with the ameliorating and progressive principle of evolution which in these days offers a substantial reward, both for a man and for his progeny, if he will but cultivate higher and more useful traits and qualities. The aim to excel, if respected of all, approved and accepted by common consent, would appeal to every child and, logically presented to its mind and enforced by universal recognition of its validity, would become a conviction and a scheme for the art of living, of transforming power and compelling vigour.

In various sayings Confucius, his disciples, and Mencius present the attributes of the superior man, whom the sage adjures his disciples to admire without ceasing, to emulate without turning, and to imitate without let or hindrance. These are some of them:

Purpose: "The superior man learns in order to attain to the utmost of his principles." (Analects, bk. xix., c. vii.)

Poise: "The superior man in his thought does not go out of his place." (Analects, bk. xiv., c. xxviii.)

Self-sufficiency: "What the superior man seeks, is in himself; what the ordinary [1] man seeks, is in others." (Analects, bk. xv., c. xx.)

Earnestness: "The superior man in everything puts forth his utmost endeavours." (Great Learning, ii., 4.)

Thoroughness: "The superior man bends his attention to what is radical. That being established, all practical courses naturally grow up." (Analects, bk. i., c. ii., v. 2.)

Sincerity: "The superior man must make his thoughts sincere." (Great Learning, vi., 4.) " Is it not his absolute sincerity which distinguishes a superior man?" (Doctrine of the Mean, c. xiii., 4.)

Truthfulness: "What the superior man requires is that in what he says there may be nothing inaccurate." (Analects, bk. xiii., c. iii., v. 7.)

Purity of thought and action: "The superior man must be watchful over himself when alone." (Great Learning, vi., 2.)

Love of truth: "The object of the superior man is truth." (Analects, bk. xv., c. xxxi.) "The superior man is anxious lest he should not get truth; he is not anxious lest poverty come upon him." (Analects, bk. xv., c. xxxi.)

Mental hospitality: "The superior man is catholic and not partisan; the ordinary man is partisan and not catholic." (Analects, bk. ii., c. xiv.) " The superior man in the world does not set his mind either for anything or against anything; what is right, he will follow." (Analects, bk. iv., c. x.)

Rectitude: "The superior man thinks of virtue; the ordinary man thinks of comfort." (Analects, bk. iv., c. xi.) " The mind of the superior man is conversant with righteousness; the mind of the ordinary man is conversant with gain." (Analects, bk. iv., c. xxi.) " The superior man in all things considers righteousness essential." (Analects, bk. xv., c. xvii.)

Prudence: "The superior man wishes to be slow in his words and earnest in his conduct." (Analects, bk. iv., c. xxiv.)

Composure: "The superior man is satisfied and composed; the ordinary man is always full of distress." (Analects, bk. vii., c. xxxvi.) "The superior man may indeed have to endure want; but the ordinary man, when he is in want, gives way to unbridled license." (Analects, bk. xv., c. i., v. 3.)

Fearlessness: "The superior man has neither anxiety nor fear." (Analects, bk. xii., c. iv., v. i.) "When internal examination discovers nothing wrong, what is there to be anxious about, what is there to fear?" (Analects, bk. xi., c. iv., v. 3.) " They sought to act virtuously and they did so; and what was there for them to repine about?" (Analects, bk. vii., c. xiv., v. 2.)

Ease and dignity: "The superior man has dignified ease without pride; the ordinary man has pride without dignified ease." (Analects, bk. xiii., c. xxvi.) "The superior man is dignified and does not wrangle." (Analects, bk. xv., c. xxi.)

Firmness: "Refusing to surrender their wills or to submit to any taint to their persons." (Analects, bk. xviii., c. viii., v. 2.) "The superior man is correctly firm and not merely firm." (Analects, bk. xv., c. xxxvi.) "Looked at from a distance, he appears stern; when approached, he is mild; when he is heard to speak, his language is firm and decided." (Analects, bk. xix., c. ix.)

Lowliness: "The superior man is affable but not adulatory; the ordinary man is adulatory but not affable." (Analects, bk. xiii., c. xxiii.)

Avoidance of sycophancy: "I have heard that the superior man helps the distressed, but he does not add to the wealth of the rich." (Analects, bk. vi., c. iii., v. 2.)

Growth: "The progress of the superior man is upward, the progress of the ordinary man is downward." (Analects, bk. xiv., c. xxiv.) "The superior man is distressed by his want of ability; he is not distressed by men's not knowing him." (Analects, bk. xv., c. xviii.)

Capacity: "The superior man cannot be known in little matters but may be entrusted with great concerns." (Analects, bk. xv., c. xxxiii.)

Openness: "The faults of the superior man are like the sun and moon. He has his faults and all men see them. He changes again and all men low look up to him." (Analects, bk. xix., c. xxi.)

Benevolence: "The superior man seeks to develop the admirable qualities of men and does not seek to develop their evil qualities. The ordinary man does the opposite of this." (Analects, bk. xii., c. xvi.)

Broadmindedness: "The superior man honours talent and virtue and bears with all. He praises the good and pities the incompetent." (Analects, bk. xix., c. iii.) "The superior man does not promote a man on account of his words, nor does he put aside good words on account of the man." (Analects, bk. xv., c. xxii.)

Charity: "To be able to judge others by what is in ourselves, this may be called the art of virtue." (Analects, bk. vi., c. xxviii., v. 3.)

Moderation: "The superior man conforms with the path of the mean." (Doctrine of the Mean, c. xi., vi. 3.)

The Golden Rule: "When Gm cultivates to the utmost the capabilities of his nature and exercises them on the principle of reciprocity, he is not far from the path. What you do not want done to yourself, do not do unto others." (Doctrine of the Mean, c. xiii., v. 3.)

Reserve power: "That wherein the superior man cannot be equalled is simply this, his work which other men cannot see." (Doctrine of the Mean, c. xxxiii., v. 2.)

The Art of Living. " The practice of right-living is deemed the highest, the practice of any other art lower. Complete virtue takes first place; the doing of anything else whatsoever is subordinate." (Li Ki, bk. xvii., sect. iii., 5.)

These words from the "Li Ki" are the keynote of the sage's teachings.

Confucius sets before every man, as what he should strive for, his own improvement, the development of himself,—a task without surcease, until he shall "abide in the highest excellence." This goal, albeit unattainable in the absolute, he must ever have before his vision, determined above all things to attain it, relatively, every moment of his life—that is, to "abide in the highest excellence" of which he is at the moment capable. So he says in "The Great Learning": "What one should abide in being known, what should be aimed at is determined; upon this decision, unperturbed resolve is attained; to this succeeds tranquil poise; this affords opportunity for deliberate care; through such deliberation the goal is achieved." (Text, v. 2.)

This speaks throughout of self-development, of that renunciation of worldly lusts which inspired the cry: "For what shall it profit a man if he shall gain the whole world and lose his own soul?"; but this is not left doubtful—for again in "The Great Learning" he says: "From the highest to the lowest, self-development must be deemed the root of all, by every man. When the root is neglected, it cannot be that what springs from it will be well-ordered." (Text, v. 6, 7.)

Confucius taught that to pursue the art of life was possible for every man, all being of like passions and in more things like than different. He says: "By

14

nature men are nearly alike; by practice, they get to be wide apart." (Analects, bk. xvii., c. ii.)

Mencius put forward this idea continually, never more succinctly and aptly than in this: "All things are already complete in us." (Bk. vii., pt. i., c. iv., 1.)

Mencius also announced that the advance of every man is independent of the power of others, as follows: "To advance a man or to stop his advance is beyond the power of other men." (Bk. i., pt. ii., c. xvi., 3.)

It has already in these pages been quoted from the "Analects" that "the superior man learns in order to attain to the utmost of his principles."

In the same book is reported this colloquy: "Tsze-loo asked 'What constitutes the superior man?' The Master said, 'The cultivation of himself with reverential care'" (Analects, bk. xiv., c. xlv.); and in the " Doctrine of the Mean," "When one cultivates to the utmost the capabilities of his nature and exercises them on the principle of reciprocity, he is not far from the path." (C. xiii., 3.).

In "The Great Learning," Confucius revealed the process, step by step, by which self-development is attained and by which it flows over into the common life to serve the state and to bless mankind.

"The ancients," he said, "when they wished to exemplify illustrious virtue throughout the empire, first ordered well their states. Desiring to order well their states, they first regulated their families. Wishing to regulate their families, they first cultivated themselves. Wishing to cultivate themselves, they first rectified their purposes. Wishing to rectify their purposes, they first sought to think sincerely. Wishing to think sincerely, they first extended their knowledge as widely as possible. This they did by investigation of things.

"By investigation of things, their knowledge became extensive; their knowledge being extensive, their thoughts became sincere; their thoughts being sincere, their purposes were rectified; their purposes being rectified, they cultivated themselves; they being cultivated, their families were regulated; their families being regulated, their states were rightly governed; their states being rightly governed, the empire was thereby tranquil and prosperous." (Text, 4, 5.)

Lest there be misunderstanding, it should be said that mere wealth is not to be considered the prosperity of which he speaks, but rather plenty and right-living. For there is the saying: "In a state, gain is not to be considered prosperity, but prosperity is found in righteousness." (Great Learning, x., 23.) The distribution of wealth into mere livelihoods among the people is urged by Confucius as an essential to good government, for it is said in "The Great Learning": "The concentration of wealth is the way to disperse the people, distributing it among them is the way to collect the people." (X., 9.)

The order of development, therefore, Confucius set forth as follows:

Investigation of phenomena.

Learning.

Sincerity.

Rectitude of purpose.

Self-development.

Family discipline.

Local self-government.

Universal self-government.

The rules of conduct, mental, spiritual, in one's inner life, in the family, in the state, and in society at large, which will lead to this self-development and beyond it, Confucius conceived to be of universal application, for it is said in the "Doctrine of the Mean" (c. xxviii., v. 3): "Now throughout the empire carriages all have wheels with the same tread, all writing is with the same characters, and for conduct there are the same rules."

How this may be, is set forth in the same book (c. xii., v. 1, 2): "The path which the superior man follows extends far and wide, and yet is secret. Ordinary men and women, however ignorant, may meddle with the knowledge of it; yet, in its utmost reaches, there is that which even the sage does not discern. Ordinary men and women, however below the average standard of ability, can carry it into practice; yet, in its utmost reaches, there is that which even the sage is not able to carry into practice."

It is, indeed, a true art of living which is thus presented, a scheme of adaptation of means to ends, of causes to produce their appropriate consequences, with clear and noble purposes in view, both as regards one's own development and man's, both as regards one's own weal and the common weal.

For the completion of its work, it requires, also, the whole of life, every deflection from virtue marring by so much the perfection of the whole. Its saintliness lies not in purity alone, but in the rounded fulness of the well-planned and well-spent life, the more a thing of beauty if extended to extreme old age. Confucius thus modestly hints how slowly it develops at best, when he says: "At fifteen I had my mind bent on learning. At thirty I stood firm. At forty I was free from doubt. At fifty I knew the decrees of Heaven. At sixty my ear was an obedient organ for the reception of truth. At seventy I could follow what my heart desired without transgressing what was right." (Analects, bk. ii., c. iv.)

That it is not finished until death rings down the curtain upon the last act, is shown in the "Analects" by this aphorism attributed to his disciple, Tsang: "The scholar may not be without breadth of mind and vigorous endurance. His burden is heavy and his course is long. Perfect virtue is the burden which he considers it his to sustain; is it not heavy? Only with death does his course stop; is it not long?" (Analects, bk. viii., c. vii.)

Mental Morality. "When you know a thing, to hold that you know it, and when you do not know a thing, to acknowledge that you do not know it—this is knowledge." (Analects, bk. ii., c. xvii.)

In these words Confucius set forth more lucidly than any other thinker, ancient or modern, the essential of all morality, mental honesty, integrity of the mind—the only attitude which does not close the door to truth.

16

The same thing is put forward in a different way in the "Li Ki," thus: "Do not positively affirm when you have doubts; and when you have not, do not put forth what you say, as merely your view." (Bk. i., sect. i., pt. i., c. iii., 5.)

The Chinese sage had no delusions about the real nature of the art of living, the rules of human conduct; he knew and understood that ethics are of the mind, that sticks and stones are neither moral nor immoral but merely un-moral, and that the possibilities of good and evil choices come only when the intelligence dawns which alone can choose between them.

Mencius considerably extended this view, starting from the position: "If men do what is not good, the blame cannot be imputed to their natural pow-ers." (Bk. xi., pt. i., c. vi., v. 6.)

Not that he did not recognize the perils of unrestrained animal passions, ministered to, instead of guided and controlled by, a human mind which ac-cordingly becomes their slave instead of master; for he says: "That whereby man differs from the lower animals is little. Most people throw it away, the superior man preserves it." (Bk. iv., pt. ii., c. xix., v. 1.)

And again he refers to this inexcusable reversal of the natural order, thus: "When a man's finger is deformed, he knows enough to be dissatisfied; but if his mind be deformed, he does not know that he should be dissatisfied. This is called: 'Ignorance of the relative importance of things.'" (Bk. vi., pt. i., c. xii., v. 2.)

The "Li Ki" says of this, more explicitly: "It belongs to the nature of man, as from Heaven, to be still at his birth. His activity shows itself as he is acted on by external things, and develops the desires incident to his nature. Things come to him more and more, and his knowledge is increased. Then arise the manifestations of liking and disliking. When these are not regulated by any-thing within, and growing knowledge leads more astray without, he cannot come back to himself, and his Heavenly principle is extinguished.

"Now there is no end of the things by which man is affected; and when his likings and dislikings are not subject to regulation (from within), he is changed into the nature of things as they come before him; that is, he stifles the voice of Heavenly principle within, and gives the utmost indulgence to the desires by which men may be possessed. On this we have the rebellious and deceitful heart, with licentious and violent disorder." (Bk. xvii., sect. i., v. 11, 12.)

Therefore, with acumen and discernment never excelled, Confucius divined that the mind must first be honest with itself. This indicates the essential im-morality of the mind which clings to that which it does not know, with ferven-cy and loyalty more devoted than that with which it holds to that which it does know. That one should not be swayed by what he prefers to believe, is again asserted in these words of the "Shu-King," ascribed to I Yin (pt. iv., bk. v., sect. iii., v. 2.):

"When you hear words that are distasteful to your mind, you must inquire whether they be not right; when you hear words that accord with your own views, you must inquire whether they be not contrary to right."

17

It is consonant with the spirit and teaching of Confucius that the philosopher Ch'ing should have said of the "Doctrine of the Mean": "This work contains the law of the mind which was handed down from one to another"; and that Confucius himself has said: "In the Book of Poetry are three hundred pieces, but the design of them all may be embraced in one sentence: Have no depraved thoughts.'" (Analects, bk. ii., c. ii.)

It was thus that Confucius conceived the art of living, as a thing thought out, a response purposive, instead of automatic, to every impulse from without. He says of himself, meaning thereby to instruct his disciples and inspire them to emulation: "I have no course for which I am predetermined and no course against which I am predetermined." (Analects, bk. xviii., c. viii., v. 5.)

And, as already quoted, these are among his most striking attributes of the superior man: "The superior man is catholic and not partisan; the ordinary man is partisan and not catholic." (Analects, bk. ii., c. xiv.) "The superior man in the world does not set his mind either for anything or against anything; what is right, he will follow." (Analects, bk. iv., c. x.) "The superior man is anxious lest he should not get truth; he is not anxious lest poverty should come upon him." (Analects, bk. xv., c. xxxi.)

In yet more glowing and enthusiastic terms he sang the praises of the open mind, its need, its utility, its essential beauty and sure promise, saying: "They who know the truth are not equal to them that love it, and they who love it are not equal to them that find pleasure in it." (Analects, bk. vi., c. xviii.)

Socrates said something akin to this when he rebuked the "sophists," *i.e.*, the "wise," and modestly called himself "philosophos," *i.e.*, only a lover of wisdom and one who devoutly wishes to learn.

Confucius sets before his disciples the apprehension and ascertainment of the bald truth concerning the phenomena of nature, as the thing first to be desired; for he says: "The object of the superior man is truth." (Analects, bk. xv., c. xxxi.)

Of himself, his disciples present this portrayal: "There were four things from which the Master was entirely free: He had no foregone conclusions, no arbitrary predeterminations, no obstinacy, and no egoism." (Analects, bk. ix., c. iv.)

The Investigation of Phenomena. "Wishing to think sincerely, they first extended their knowledge. This they did by investigation of things. By investigation of things, their knowledge became extensive. Their knowledge being extensive, their thoughts became sincere."

These words from "The Great Learning" (Text, v. 4, 5) are meant to show how the mind, holding itself in resolution, its conclusions ready to take whatever form the compelling logic of the ascertained facts may require, must, as an essential prerequisite of a normal and well-rounded life, investigate the phenomena which are around it. These are its world, with which it must cope, and which, in order that it may cope therewith, it must also understand. Confucius says: "To this attainment"—*i.e.*, perfect sincerity—"there are requisite extensive study of what is good, accurate inquiry into it, careful consideration of it, clear distinguishing about it, and earnest practical application of it." (Doctrine of the Mean, c. xx., v. 19.)

That there must be this ardent spirit of inquiry, this insatiable thirst after knowledge, or the man is lost, is indicated by Confucius in many sayings. One of the aptest of these is: "When a man says not, 'What shall I think of this? What shall I think of this?', I can indeed do nothing with him." (Analects, bk. xv., c. xv.)

On another occasion he announced: "I do not reveal the truth to one who is not eager to get knowledge, nor assist any one who is not himself anxious to explain." (Analects, bk. vii., c. viii.)

The apprehension that effect follows cause, was rightly regarded by him the first office of the human mind and the primary moral act of an intelligent being. This was made the foundation of "The Great Learning" (Text, v. 3): "Things have their root and their fruition. Affairs have their end and their beginning. To know what goes first and what comes after, is near to what is taught in the Great Learning."

As the followers of Socrates, Plato, and Aristotle soon lost the real point of view of the great lover of wisdom, by reason of their devotion to what they understood to be the positive teaching of himself and his disciples, and built up a system of prescriptive and authoritative learning which in fact stifled original investigation of phenomena, while encouraging mere speculation and dialectics, so in like manner the investigation of phenomena, enjoined by Confucius, soon degenerated into scholasticism, and the mere conning and memorizing of texts. The neglect of the true significance of his injunction was so complete that, though apparently no other sentences are missing, the chapter of "The Great Learning" in which was given the early author's version of what is meant by "investigation of things" is lost. Only these words are still extant: "This is called knowing the root. This is called the perfecting of knowledge."

Views, ascribed to the commentator Ch'ing, are usually supplied to fill this hiatus. They are here quoted to show how the true function of investigation, which is not the duty merely of the young and untutored mind but yet more the duty of the trained and experienced, was distorted into something altogether contrary, by passing through the intellect of the adoring scholiast: "The meaning of the expression, 'The perfecting of knowledge depends upon the investigation of things' is this: If we wish to carry our knowledge to the utmost, we must investigate the principles of all things we come into contact with; for the intelligent mind of man is certainly formed to know and there is not a single thing of which its principles are not a part. But so long as all principles are not investigated, man's knowledge is incomplete. On this account, the 'Learning for Adults,' in its opening chapters, instructs the learner in regard to all things in the world, to proceed from what knowledge he has of their principles and pursue his investigations of them until he reaches the extreme point. After exerting himself in this way for a long time, he will suddenly find himself possessed of a wide and far-reaching penetration. Then the qualities of all things, whether external or internal, subtle or coarse, will be apprehended and the mind, in its whole substance and its relations to things, will be perfectly intelligent. This is called the investigation of things, this is called the perfection of knowledge."

But, while it may have been, and indeed was, called "the investigation of things," by Ch'ing and by many of the scholiasts since his day, it is obviously far from that enduring open-mindedness and spirit of impartial inquiry which Confucius held to be the first essential to the art of living. The words of Confucius, therefore, have clearer and higher significance in this scientific age than in all the centuries during which Asiatic students have memorized them in the schools.

That Confucius meant no such blind following of authority is clear from this saying: "Hwuy gives me no assistance. There is nothing that I say, in which he does not delight." (Analects, bk. xi., c. iii.)

Investigation and the spirit of free investigation, in order that knowledge may ever be subjected to repeated tests, are "the root," according to the reasoning of Confucius, from which the conduct of life must proceed. Therefore and referring thereto, the philosopher Yew is quoted as saying: "The superior man bends his attention to what is radical. That being established, all practical courses naturally grow up." (Analects, bk. i., c. ii., v. 2.)

This is set forth at length in yet more enthusiastic language: "When we minutely investigate the nature and reasons of things till we have entered into the inscrutable and spiritual in them, we attain to the largest practical application of them; when that application becomes quickest and readiest and personal poise is secured, our virtue is thereby exalted. Proceeding beyond this, we reach a point which it is hardly possible to comprehend; we have thoroughly mastered the inscrutable and spiritual and understand the processes of transformation. This is the fulness of virtue." (Yi King, appendix iii., sect. ii., v. 33, 34.)

Learning. "Learning without thought is labour lost; thought without learning is perilous." (Analects, bk. ii., c. xv.)

The emphasis is put upon thinking in this statement of the Duke of Kau, quoted in the "Shu King," by Confucius with approval: "The wise, through not thinking, become foolish; and the foolish, by thinking, become wise." (Pt. v., bk. xviii., 2.)

To the idea expressed in these astute words thus adopted by Confucius, he has added a personal application elsewhere, emphasizing the emptiness of mere speculation: "I have been the whole day without eating and the whole night without sleeping, occupied with thinking. It was of no avail. The better plan is to learn." (Analects, bk. xv., c. xxx.)

The idleness of thought, desire, and conduct proceeding upon insufficient data is set forth by the sage in great detail, in the following: "There is the love of being benevolent without the love of learning;—the beclouding here leads to a foolish simplicity. There is the love of knowing without the love of learning;—the beclouding here leads to dissipation of mind. There is the love of being sincere without the love of learning;—the beclouding here leads to an injurious disregard of consequences. There is the love of straightforwardness without the love of learning;—the beclouding here leads to rudeness. There is the love of boldness without the love of learning;—the beclouding here leads to insubordination. There is the love of firmness without the love of learning;—the beclouding here leads to extravagant conduct." (Analects, bk. xvii., c. viii., v. 3.)

Therefore the necessity for patient, unremitting study, not merely of books but of men, animals, and things, of the phenomena of animate and inanimate nature, is urged by the great teacher again and again: "Learn as if you might not attain your object and were always fearing lest you miss it." (Analects, bk. viii., c. xvii.) "Is it not pleasant to learn with constant perseverance and application?" (Analects, bk. i., c. i., v. 1.)

In this regard, he leaves this picture of himself, in words which he spoke to one of his disciples: "The Duke of She asked Tsze-loo about Confucius and Tsze-loo did not answer him. The Master said, 'Why did you not say to him: He is simply a man who in his eager pursuit of knowledge forgets his food, who in the joy of attaining it forgets his sorrows, and who does not perceive that old, age is coming on?'" (Analects, bk. vii., c. xviii.)

And this is also declared to be an essential characteristic of the superior man: "The superior man learns and accumulates the results of his learning; puts questions and discriminates among those results; dwells magnanimously and unambitiously in what he has attained to; and carries it into practice with benevolence." (Yi King, appendix iv., c. vi., v. 31.)

That one must be modest as to his ability and acquirements, in order to learn, was as obvious to the mind of Confucius, as to that of Socrates. These words of Yueh in the "Shu King" are illustrative of this: "In learning there should be a humble mind and the maintenance of constant earnestness." (Pt. iv., bk. viii., sec. iii., i.)

And these are the words of Tsang, referring to his friend, Yen Yuan: "Gifted with ability and yet putting questions to those who were not so; possessed of much and yet putting questions to those possessed of little; having, as though he had not; full, and yet counting himself as empty; offended against, and yet entering into no altercation." (Analects, bk. viii., c. v.)

Though the mentor of princes, Confucius did not himself depart from such modesty in giving instruction, even as he adjured his disciples to observe it always in receiving t; for he gives this testimony concerning his course: "From the man bringing his bundle of dried flesh upwards, I have never refused instruction to any one." (Analects, bk. vii., c. vii.)

There comes before the mind of the modern student of Confucius, therefore, the same picture of humble companionship with the lowly as with the great, which the sojourn of Jesus, of Socrates, or of Epictetus among men also conjures forth. That such would be the universal consequence, were there universal instruction, i.e., that learning is essentially democratic and not a respecter of rank, riches, or even of persons, he affirms in this sentence: "There being instruction, there will be no distinction of classes" (Analects, bk. xv., c.

xxxviii.), which declaration, accepted and followed, has preserved China from that stifling death into which the caste system of India has forced its unhappy people.

Yet by no means unto all, the scoffer as well as the earnest student, the dull as well as the discerning, did Confucius consider that all knowledge should be imparted; instead he said: "To those whose talents are above mediocrity, the highest subjects may be announced. To those who are below mediocrity, the highest subjects may not be announced." (Analects, bk. vi., c. xix.)

The course which he who would learn must follow is given by Tsze-hea in these words: "He who from day to day recognizes what he has not yet attained to, and from month to month remembers what he has attained to, may be said to love to learn." (Analects, bk. xix., c. v.)

And that thoroughness and completion of all tasks are absolutely requisite, in these: "The prosecution of learning may be compared with what may happen in raising a mound. If there lack but one basket of earth to complete the work, and I there cease, the cessation is my own act." (Analects, bk. ix., c. xviii.)

That gravity and earnestness are requisite, he thus affirms: "If the scholar be not grave, he will not call forth any veneration, and his learning will not be solid." (Analects, bk. i., c. viii., v. 1.)

The reward of learning he declares to be: "It is not easy to find a man who has learned for three years, without coming to be virtuous." (Analects, bk. viii., c. xii.)

If observation in these twentieth-century days does not confirm this, is it not because of this, that investigation and study are but too often undertaken only in support of propositions to which the students are already committed, or, to put it otherwise, that such are rather the labours of the special advocate to establish his cause than of the impartial seeker after truth? And, if so, how could the result be as Confucius said? Moreover, in which of our schools are the rules of mental ethics, of correct study and thought, imparted? Is not the fault rather that education is not what it should be, than that there is education?

One of the disciples of Confucius testified concerning his instruction, "He enlarged my mind with learning and taught me the restraints of propriety" (Analects, bk. ix., c. x., v. 2), by which is meant the rules of conduct, mental and within one's self, as well as mental though outwardly expressed. Another disciple said: "There are learning extensively and having a firm and sincere aim, inquiring with earnestness, and reflecting with self-application; virtue is in such a course." (Analects, bk. xix., c. vi.)

Confucius himself remarked: "By extensively studying all learning and keeping himself under the restraint of the rules of propriety, one may thus likewise not err from what is right." (Analects, bk. xii., c. xv.)

And in the "Li Ki" this is found: "To acquire extensive information and remember retentively while yet modest; to do earnestly what is good and not become weary in so doing—these are characteristics of him whom we call the superior man." (Bk. i., sect. i., pt. iv., v. 27.)

By emphasizing that learning should be extensive, he did not mean to advise serious study of every idle speculation which the invention and ingenuity of human intellects can produce. Instead, the course which he marked out is that of close and careful observation of facts and pains-taking, cautious reasoning about them. Of the perils of the other, he says: "The study of strange doctrines is injurious indeed." (Analects, bk. ii., c. xvi.)

Notwithstanding this, he did not subordinate, and much less did he eliminate the need for, attention to the broad conception of the universe, while keeping one's eye upon the particle of dead matter or the infinitesimal forms of life. That the laws which operate in the phenomena of nature are the very laws of God, was ever present in his mind, and that narrow views of these phenomena, as if they were unrelated and independent, are not and cannot be true knowledge. Therefore is it, as he said, that "in order to know men," one "may not dispense with a knowledge of Heaven." (Doctrine of the Mean, c. xx., v. 7.)

That everything cognizable is the field of learning is suggested in the words: "Accordingly, the sage, looking up, contemplates the brilliant phenomena of the heavens and, looking down, examines the definite arrangements of the earth; thus he knows the causes of darkness and of light. He traces things to their beginning and follows them to their end; thus he knows what can be said about death and life." (Yi King, appendix iii., c. iv., v. 21.)

The great utility to him who would round out his own life by knowledge of the achievements of ancient worthies was enforced as follows: "The scholar lives and associates with men of his own dime; but the men of antiquity are the subjects of his study." (Li Ki, bk. xxxviii., v. ii.)

The great, the all-important place of learning, so defined as a moving force in the scheme of life, and, within the measure of his capacity, its claim upon every human being, he thus affirmed: "Knowledge, magnanimity, and energy, these three are the virtues which are universally binding." (Doctrine of the Mean, c. xx., v. 8.)

The union of a sublime trust and an earnest struggle to learn is thus praised by the sage himself: "With sincere trust he unites the love of learning; holding firm unto death, he is perfecting the excellence of his course." (Analects, bk. viii., c. xiii., v. i.)

Genius and Inspiration. It is characteristic of Confucius that, where he did not know, he did not affirm. His saying, "When you do not know a thing, to acknowledge that you do not know it, is knowledge " (Analects, bk. ii., c. xvii.), is far from being: "If you do not know a thing, affirm that it is not true."

Therefore, especially since, as all candid souls must ever have been, he was impressed with the marvellous insight which the minds of some of earth's children had shown, he was not a doctrinaire concerning the possibility of quicker, surer, and deeper discernment of facts and truths than that of which ordinary human beings are capable. Accordingly he says of this: "Those who

23

are born in the possession of knowledge, are the highest class of men. Those who learn and so acquire knowledge, are next. The dull and stupid who yet achieve knowledge, are a class next to these. Those who are dull and stupid and yet do not learn, are the lowest of the people." (Analects, bk. xvi., c. ix.)

Though he is now reverenced by millions in the Asiatic world as the greatest mind that has been incarnate among them, Confucius makes no claim to such inspiration and internal perception of knowledge without external observation, for himself; instead, he says: "I am not one who was born in the possession of knowledge; I am one who is fond of antiquity and earnest in seeking it there." (Analects, bk. vii., c. xix.)

In view of the fact that others were not able in his day to find what he set forth, in the archives of mankind or even in the contemplation of nature, and the further undeniable fact of his wonderful penetration and clarity, it may be questioned whether, in addition to his tireless industry, there was not present also the full measure of illumination from without and, let us reverently say, from above, which has attended others of the world's great moral teachers and leaders in all time.

That it was not all pure grind—nay, more, that it should never be all pure grind—but, instead, the organic absorption of knowledge into himself and as inherent parts of himself, blending into a harmonious, developed whole, these words indicate: "The Master asked, 'Tsze, you think, I suppose, that I am one who learns many things and keeps them in his memory?' Tsze-kung replied, 'Yes, but perhaps it is not so?' 'No,' was the answer, 'I seek unity, all pervading.'" (Analects, bk. xv., c. ii.)

That there might not be foolish reliance upon internal light as a means of escaping the onerous labour of learning, he spoke this parable: "The mechanic who wishes to do his work well must first sharpen his tools." (Analects, bk. xv., c. ix.)

Preparation for the practice of the art of living, he taught, is necessary unto all men, saying: "Let every man consider virtue as what devolves upon himself; he may not yield the performance of it even to his teacher." (Analects, bk. xv., c. xxxv.) And also that perfection is a plant of slow growth, matured only by steady progress in development, in this saying as in many others: "I saw his constant advance. I never saw him halt in his progress." (Analects, bk. ix., c. xx.)

Sincerity. "Their knowledge being extensive, their thoughts became sincere."

The foregoing from "The Great Learning" (Text, v. 5) is challenged more frequently, perhaps, than any other of its propositions; for the mind immediately recurs to the remembrance of many Machiavellian characters who were well-informed, even erudite, and yet insincere. And, although Confucius here speaks of sincerity within a man's self and toward himself, as counter-distinguished from sincere speech and action, yet, notwithstanding that one cannot read the inmost thoughts and purposes of another, few there are who have pondered deeply and observed widely and closely, that do not know that sincerity of thought must itself be cultivated or at least be preserved.

Confucius had no mind to say otherwise for he puts it thus in "The Great Learning" at the very outset: "Wishing to think sincerely, they first extended their knowledge as widely as possible. This they did by the investigation of things"; and he himself says, elsewhere: "Leaving virtue without proper cultivation; not thoroughly discussing what is learned; not being able to move toward righteousness of which knowledge has been gained; and not being able to change what is not good: these are the things which occasion me solicitude." (Analects, bk. vii., c. iii.)

He also said, referring to knowledge: "A man can enlarge his principles; the principles do not [*i.e.*, of themselves] enlarge the man." (Analects, bk. xv., c. xxviii.) The same is also implied, as well as that a man of character, while ready to serve, will not permit himself to be used, by this saying (Analects, bk. ii., c. xii.): "The superior man is not an utensil," *i.e.*, his usefulness is not confined to one thing.

Therefore, not to one who must as a matter of mere consequence comply, but to one who may exercise a choice whether to obey or not, learned though he may be, he directs this injunction: "Hold faithfulness and sincerity as first principles and be moving continually toward what is right." (Analects, bk. xii., c. x.)

Mencius puts it, beautifully, thus: "There is no greater delight than to be conscious of sincerity upon self-examination." (Bk. vii., pt. i., c. iv., v. 2.)

In the "Doctrine of the Mean," Confucius says: "Is it not just entire sincerity which marks the superior man?" (c. xiii., v. 4); and in "The Great Learning": "The superior man must make his thoughts sincere." (C. vi., 4.)

The same idea Mencius presents in this pleasing trope: "The great man is he who does not lose his child's heart." (Bk. iv., pt. ii., c. xii.)

This sincerity of thought, as of action, Confucius included among the five qualities essential to perfect virtue, saying: "To be able to practise five things everywhere under heaven constitutes perfect virtue: Gravity, magnanimity, sincerity, earnestness, and kindness." (Analects, bk. xvii., c. vi.)

That it should not be found in every man, however imperfect and however unstable, was incomprehensible to him, since to his view it is the very breath of life for an intelligent being. This he declares in these terms: "Ardent and yet not upright; stupid and yet not attentive; simple and yet not sincere: such persons I do not understand." (Analects, bk. viii., c. xvi.)

Yet that he did not expect those who were uninstructed to be sincere, is plain from this expression in the "Doctrine of the Mean": "If a man do not understand what is good, he will not attain sincerity in himself." (C. xix., v. 17.)

This is but a negative statement of what has already been quoted (Doctrine of the Mean, c. xx., v. 19): "To this attainment"—*i.e.*, of sincerity" there are requisite extensive study of what is good, accurate inquiry concerning it, careful consideration of it, clear distinguishing about it, and earnest practical application of it"—many things, in short, besides and beyond mere knowledge, essential as the intelligent perception of things as they are, may be. As much is also implied in: "He who attains to sincerity chooses the good and firmly holds it fast." (Doctrine of the Mean, c. xxi., v. 8.)

That the attainment of sincerity is an essential prerequisite to self-development, this book strongly asserts. "Sincerity," it says, "is that whereby self-development is effected and the path by which a man must direct himself " (Doctrine of the Mean, c. xxv., v. 1); and again: "It is only he who is possessed of the completest sincerity that can exist under Heaven, who can give full development to his nature." (Doctrine of the Mean, c. xxii.) In the "Yi King" (appendix iv., sect. i., c. ii., v. 3), it is said: "He is sincere even in his ordinary words and earnest in his everyday conduct. Guarding against depravity, he preserves his sincerity. His goodness is recognized in the world but he does not boast of it."

This beneficent power he is also not confined to exerting upon himself and for his own development only. Instead, it is of broader and even universal application; for Confucius says: "The possessor of sincerity develops not himself only; with it, he also develops others." (Doctrine of the Mean, c. xxv., v. 3.)

By means of sincerity, it is taught in the " Doctrine of the Mean," and by it alone, man becomes, and is welcomed as, the co-operator with Heaven, and may thus beneficially influence and even transform others. There is psychological import in the words: "It is only he who is possessed of the completest sincerity that can exist under Heaven, who can transform." (Doctrine of the Mean, c. xxiii.)

This is but one of the many alluring rewards that the sage saw to attend sincerity, which is, besides, sufficiently its own reward. Insight and foresight are others, concerning which it is said in the "Doctrine of the Mean": "He who has sincerity without effort hits what is right and discerns without laborious thought; he is a sage who naturally and readily follows the path." (C. xx., v. 18.) "It is characteristic of the completest sincerity to be able to foreknow." (C. xxiv.) "When calamities or blessings are about to befall, the good or the evil will surely be foreknown by him. He, therefore, who is possessed of the completest sincerity, is like a spirit." (C. xxiv.)

Extreme as these statements may appear, who is there among earnest thinkers and students that has not seen or experienced something very like this? It is obvious that the mind can the better fulfil its highest offices, if steadily applied thereto and never to the grovelling arts of deception or, lower yet, of self-deception. If gross self-deception, as by cowardice, self-seeking, prejudice, or superstition, renders the mind incapable of perceiving the simplest truths concerning the phenomena of nature, it may well be that complete absence of the wish to deceive or to be deceived bespeaks clarity of vision and of -prevision—which is, perhaps, only clear reasoning from the known and now, to the unknown and to be—though it otherwise seem impossible.

"The Great Learning" teaches that a large measure of this clear vision may be attained; for, immediately after saying, "The superior man is watchful over himself, when alone," it is added: "There is no evil to which the inferior man will not proceed, when alone. When he beholds a superior man, he tries at once to disguise himself, concealing his evil under a display of virtue. The other penetrates him as if he saw his heart and reins" (Text, vi., v. 1, 2).

And this is said (Great Learning, vi., v. 2) to warn the inferior man and encourage the superior: "What is in fact within, will show without"; and the Master is quoted in the "Doctrine of the Mean" (c. xx., v. 18), as saying with an enthusiasm no more than commensurate with the subject: "Sincerity is the path of Heaven. The attainment of sincerity is the path for men," and the "Doctrine of the Mean" adds yet more rapturously in its praise: "Sincerity is the end and the beginning of all things; without sincerity, there is nothing. Therefore, the superior man regards the attainment of sincerity the highest excellence." (C. xxv., v. 2.)

This eloquent passage in the "Shu King" (pt. v., bk. ix., v. 2) is evidently at one with the view of Confucius: "Awful though Heaven be, it yet helps the sincere."

Rectification of Purpose. "Their thoughts being sincere, their purposes were rectified."

In "The Great Learning," from which this is taken (Text, v. 5), the following brief explanation of it is given: "This is meant by 'Self-development depends upon rectifying one's purposes': If a man be swayed by passion, his conduct will be wrong; and so also if he be swayed by terror, by fondness, by sorrow, by distress. When the mind is not dominant, we look but see not, we hear but comprehend not, we eat but taste not." (C. vii., v. 1, 2.)

The same thought Confucius expresses at another time when addressing one of his disciples: "Ch'ang is under the influence of his passions; how can he be pronounced firm and unbending?" (Analects, bk. v., c. x.)

Rarely in any of the books edited by Confucius, composed of his sayings or purporting to set forth his views, is anything advanced as the very word of God. Yet upon this topic the following is found in the "Shi King" (Major Odes, decade i., ode 7): "God said to King Wan: 'Be not like them who reject this and cling to that! Be not like them who are ruled by their likes and desires!'"

And in the "Li Ki" is found this account of the methods and purposes of the ancient kings, already once quoted: "It belongs to the nature of man, as from Heaven, to be still at his birth. His activity shows itself as he is acted on by external things, and develops the desires incident to his nature. Things come to him more and more, and his knowledge is increased. Then arise the manifestations of liking and disliking. When these are not regulated by anything within, and growing knowledge leads more astray without, he cannot come back to himself, and his Heavenly principle is extinguished.

"Now there is no end of the things by which man is affected; and when his likings and dislikings are not subject to regulation (from within), he is changed into the nature of things as they come before him; that is, he stifles the voice of Heavenly principle within, and gives the utmost indulgence to the desires by which men may be possessed. On this we have the rebellious and deceitful heart, with licentious and violent disorder." (Li Ki, bk. xvii., sect. i., v. 11, 12.)

The starting-point for such rectification is vividly portrayed by the sage in the following passage, also from the "Li Ki" (bk. vii., sect. ii., v. 20): "The things which men greatly desire are comprehended in meat, drink, and sexual pleasure; the things which they greatly dislike are comprehended in death, exile, poverty, and suffering. Likes and dislikes are the great elements of men's minds."

If to the three things desired by all men were added "air," the four primal animal requisites to self-preservation and race-preservation would have been named, each good and well adapted for its own purposes and not one of them subject to any abuses by the unthinking beast.

That the mind of man, in possessing which he differs from his brother animals, should fail to subordinate each of these and at the same time more perfectly and accurately to adapt it to its own purposes, constitutes abandonment by him of his highest heritage; and such abuses of normal appetites as are involved in feasting, drinking, abandoned venery, or snuff-taking, or tobacco or opium smoking, each an exercise in an abnormal way of a special function for its own sake and without design that the consequences of its healthful exercise should follow, obviously are perversions of the mind and well illustrate that saying of the sage: "The progress of the superior man is upward; the progress of the ordinary man is downward." (Analects, bk. xiv., c. xxiv.)

The destructive results of setting the heart upon blind indulgence in these refinements of sensual pleasure were sung in "The Odes" by one of the ancient bards:

"He who loves hunting and women
 Abandons his state to ruin."
    (Li Ki, bk. ix., sect. ii., v. 12.)

And this bald fact, abundantly shown in this age by the vital statistics of every country, was spoken by the Duke of Kau and handed down in the "Shu King" (pt. v., bk. xv., v. 2): "They sought for nothing but excessive pleasure and so not one of them had long life."

The greater longevity of men who were earnest students and vigorous, forceful thinkers, not given to dissipation of their energies in any of the ways described, had already been remarked, indeed, centuries before the time of Confucius. Yet he had more respect for misguided seekers after pleasure, at bottom, than for the smug lovers of safe comfort; the former at least lived, however mistaken their view of life's true aim, the strenuous existence, making sacrifices to obtain that which they desired. He would not have been ready to go so far, perhaps, as Ibsen who says through the lips of Brand:

"Let be, ye are the serfs of pleasure;
 Be such, then, with no let nor measure!
 Not one thing merely for today

And quite another thing tomorrow.
The Bacchants were ideal. They
Kept up a constant round of revel.
The sot who swings 'twixt drink and sorrow
Is but a 'pitiable devil.'
Silenus was a fine *figure*,
The tippler but his caricature."

But much more clearly than any of the other great ethical teachers of ancient times, Confucius recognizes the true opposite of lofty purpose when he puts the contrast thus: "The superior man thinks of virtue; the ordinary man thinks of comfort." (Analects, bk. iv., c. xi.)

He thus sets one against the other the highest and the lowest aims of which man is capable; for all other low aims involve at least some sacrifice, while he who seeks comfort only, thinks that he would be happier as a mere parasite. Of such, Confucius says: "Hard is the case of him who will stuff himself with food the whole day, without applying his mind to anything. Are there not gamesters and chessplayers? Even to be one of these would be better than doing nothing at all." (Analects, bk. xvii., c. xxii.)

In this age, when comfort is the sole god of the many, who also deem themselves good and virtuous and even superior, surely these truths need to be held before all men without surcease, lest the race degenerate and perish— degenerate because of low aim and its successful attainment, and perish because they whose god is comfort tend to cease to propagate. Was it not to this the sage referred when he said, "Your good, careful people of the villages are the thieves of virtue" (Analects, bk. xvii., c. xiii.), and, as quoted by Mencius, "I hate your good, careful men of the villages, lest they be confounded with the virtuous"? (Bk. vii., pt. ii., c. xxxvi., v. 12.)

The Duke of Kau is represented in the "Shu King " (pt. v., bk. xv., v. 1) to have said of old: "The superior man rests in this, that he will indulge in no injurious ease."

Confucius was ever insistent upon contrasting the love of virtue with the love of comfort as in these sayings: "The scholar who cherishes the love of comfort is not fit to be deemed a scholar." (Analects, bk. xiv., c. iii.) "A scholar, whose mind is set on truth and who is ashamed of poor clothes and poor food, is not fit to be discoursed with." (Analects, bk. iv., c. ix.)

Scarcely less apposite to the conditions of the present day is this contrast which he makes: "The mind of the superior man is conversant with righteousness; the mind of the ordinary man is conversant with gain." (Analects, bk. iv., c. xxi.)

Yet he holds that one may receive and welcome his reward, albeit that to secure it should not be his purpose in doing an excellent thing or service. Indeed, one must not even set before him the purpose to secure rewards which are real, though not material, such as fame or even success and self-approbation. The course of virtue, leading to singleness of purpose and thoroughness of work, is thus marked out: "The man of virtue makes the difficulty to be overcome his first business, and success only a subsequent consideration." (Analects, bk. vi., c. xx.)

This he adverts to again, saying: "If doing what is to be done be made the first business, and success a secondary consideration, is not this the way to exalt virtue?" (Analects, bk. xii., c. xxi., v. 3.)

And repeatedly in the "Li Ki" this idea is presented in such varied and beautiful forms as these: "The Master said: 'The superior man will decline a position of high honour, but not one that is mean; will decline riches, but not poverty. . . . The superior man, rather than be rewarded beyond his desert, will have his desert greater than the reward.'" (Bk. xxvii., v. 7.) "The Master said: 'There is only now and then a man under heaven who loves what is right without expectation of reward, or hates what is wrong without fear of consequences.'" (Bk. xxix., v. 13.) "A superior man will not for counsel of little value accept a great reward, nor for counsel of great value a small reward." (Bk. xxix., v. 36.)

Yet more reprehensible, if possible, he deems it that in learning the purpose be not solely the attainment of truth and the acquisition of know- ledge, but also or even exclusively the praise or favours of others; for he says: "In ancient times men learned with a view to their own improvement. Nowadays men learn with a view to the approbation of others." (Analects, bk. xiv., c. xxv.)

From the book of Mencius the following is taken: "Yang Hoo said: 'He who seeks to be rich will not be benevolent; he who seeks to be benevolent will not be rich.'" (Bk. ii., pt. i., c. iii., v. 5.)

The following inspiring saying from the "Li Ki" (bk. xxix., v. 27) points out the goal to attain which the sincere mind must perforce direct all its power: "The services of Hau Ki were the most meritorious of all under heaven. . . . But all he longed for was that his actions should be better than the fame of them, and so he said of himself that he was simply 'a man who is useful to others.'"

Mencius supplies these infallible indications that one's purpose is not unmixed with selfish designs, and therefore that it requires careful scrutiny and rectification: "If a man love others and that love is not returned, let him examine himself as to his love of others. If he rules others but his government is not successful, let him examine himself as to wisdom. If he is polite to others but they impolite to him, let him examine himself as to real respect for them. When by what we do we do not achieve our aim, we must examine ourselves at every point. When a man is right, the whole empire will turn to him." (Bk. iv., pt. i., c. iv., v. 1, 2.)

Rectified Purpose. "Exalted merit depends on high aim."

This precept, taken from the "Shu King" (pt. v., bk. xxi., v. 4), in altered form and otherwise applied, runs through these sentences of Confucius: "Do not be desirous of having things done quickly. Do not look at small advantages. Desire to have things done quickly prevents their being done thoroughly. Looking at small advantages prevents great affairs from being accomplished." (Analects, bk. xiii., c. xvii.)

Stern self-examination is inculcated in the "Li Ki" as the first duty of him who aspires to be of service, or who assumes responsibilities: "For one who wished to serve his ruler, the rule was first to measure his abilities and duties and then enter upon the responsibilities; he did not first enter and then measure. The same rule applied when one begged or borrowed from others or sought to enter their service." (Bk. xv., v. 19.)

And yet more pointedly in this from the "Shi King" (Major Odes, decade iii., ode 6): "He was always anxious lest he should not be equal to his task."

Thoroughness, continuity of purpose and persistence are strongly urged; but, above all things, that rigorous judgment of a man's self which alone can keep his effort directed toward the goal. On this point, Confucius sadly and repeatedly warns his disciples against over-confidence that these things will come of themselves, saying: "I have not seen one who loves virtue as he loves beauty." (Analects, bk. ix., c. xvii., bk. xv., c. xii.) And again: "I have not yet seen one who could perceive his faults and inwardly accuse himself." (Analects, bk. v., c. xxvi.)

Nevertheless the necessity for constant self-inspection was held before his disciples, as in this parable (Great Learning, c. ii.): "On the bathtub of Tang the following words were engraved: 'If you can purify yourself a single day, do so every day. Let no day pass without purification!'"; and the same he said, even more vigorously, thus: "To assail one's own wickedness and not assail that of others, is this not the way to correct cherished evil?" (Analects, bk. xii., c. xxi., v. 3.)

On another occasion Confucius illustrated it by referring to archery and saying: "In archery, we have something like the way of the superior man. When the archer misses the centre of the target, he turns around and seeks the cause of his failure within himself." (Doctrine of the Mean, c. xiv., v. 5.)

His disciple, Tsang, thus describes the scrutiny to which he habitually and daily submitted his own thoughts and conduct: "I daily examine myself on three points: whether, in transacting business for others I may not have been faithful; whether, in intercourse with friends, I may not have been sincere; and whether I may not have mastered and practised the instructions of my teacher." (Analects, bk. i., c. iv.)

This the "Doctrine of the Mean" enjoins as necessary in order that one may justly cherish true self-respect, saying: "The superior man examines his heart that there may be nothing wrong there and that he may have no cause for dissatisfaction with himself." (C. xxxiii., v. 2.)

Both emulation of the virtues of superior men and this unrelenting introspection are urged in this counsel: "When we see men of worth, we should think of equalling them; when we see men of the contrary character, we should turn inwards and examine ourselves." (Analects, bk. iv., c. xvii.)

Mencius illustrates this and enlarges upon it thus: "To support the resolution, there is nothing better than to make the desires few. Here is a man whose desires are few; in some things he may not be able to maintain his resolution, but they will be few. Here is a man whose desires are many; in some things he may be able to maintain his resolution, but they will be few." (Bk. vii., pt. ii., c. xxxv.)

The emphasis which the sage thus puts upon desire and purpose, does not imply that he deems the act good or bad, only according as the motive is virtuous or evil. The act will be judged by its effect and the motive also by its result. The act may affect for weal or woe the man or others or both, entirely independently of the purpose; but the wish and intention immediately affect the development of the man himself, and make him more or less a man.

Therefore is it that from earliest youth one must be careful about that which he most earnestly desires, not because he will not obtain it, but because he will, to his making or his undoing; and the teachers of the young have greater reason to direct with care their wishes, longings, and ambitions than merely their present application to study and work.

Mencius refers to this when he aptly says: "Let a man stand fast in the nobler part of himself and the meaner part will not be able to take it from him." (Bk. vi., pt. i., c. xv., v. 2.)

He also points out how men are distinguished by the loftiness or lowness of their purposes, thus: "Those who follow that part of themselves which is great, are great men; those who follow that part of themselves which is little, are little men." (Bk. vi., pt. i., c. xv., v. 1.)

The intimate and immediate connection between sincerity and purity of purpose is self-evident; only by the most searching sincerity can the human intellect be prevented from deceiving itself, where elemental appetites, useful for the purposes for which they exist but destructive if unrestrained, plead for freedom from restraint and even for stimulation as ends in themselves and not in furtherance of the cosmic purposes of self-preservation and race-preservation for which they were given.

This glorious picture of achievement Confucius puts before those of his disciples who will preserve in thought and action unswerving integrity of purpose and of aim: "Contemplating good and pursuing it as if they could not attain to it, contemplating evil and shrinking from it as they would from thrusting the hand into boiling water—I have seen such men as I have heard such words." (Analects, bk. xvi., c. xi., v. 1.)

There may, then, be such men; no impossible standard is here set up. Confucius had long held his conduct up to it and says of himself: "With coarse rice to eat, with water to drink and my bended arm for a pillow, I still have joy in the midst of these things. Riches and honours, acquired by unrighteousness, are to me as a. floating cloud." (Analects, bk. vii., c. xv.)

[1] I have been much concerned about the word which should be given for the Chinese word appearing here. Legge renders it "mean," meaning thereby "average." I discard his word as ambiguous and choose "ordinary" as nearest to the idea, which is "the average among men who are not superior." This expression must not, however, be taken as a term describing the common people; as will be seen, Confucius reverenced them, as in our age did Abraham Lincoln.

Chapter Two - Self-Development

THE characteristics of the superior man having been presented, it is in logical order to examine the faculties and qualities which Confucius would have one cultivate to attain this ideal state. First in importance is the will.

The Will. "Their purposes being rectified, they cultivated themselves."

By these words in "The Great Learning" (Text, v. 5) it is meant that when there is no conflict of aims, of duties and desires, when one wills what he wishes, and with all his heart singly and clearly wishes what he wills, then and not till then does the will become clear and firm and strong.

The man is his will; back of his will is his purpose; and back of his purpose, his desire. If his knowledge enable him to make right choices, he should be sincere, his desires should be disciplined, his purpose lofty, and, resting thereupon as on a rock, his will fixed and immovable. That is character.

Confucius puts it: "If the will be set on virtue, there will be no practice of wickedness." (Analects, bk. iv., c. iv.) True; for when the will rests upon set purpose, based upon purified desire, born of knowledge and discriminating investigation of phenomena, nothing can undermine it!

This rectification of the antecedent conditions is what the sage refers to when he says: "To subdue one's self and return to propriety is perfect virtue" (Analects, bk. xii., c. 1), and again: "The firm, the enduring, the simple, and the unpretentious are near to virtue." (Analects, bk. xiii., c. xxvii.)

That the will is proved by its resistance rather than its impelling force, Mencius says in this: "Men must be resolute about what they will not do and then they are able to act with vigor." (Bk. iv., pt. ii., c. viii.)

The same is meant, *i.e.*, that if one's trust is thus grounded, nothing external can shake his determination, when Confucius says: "The commander of the forces of a large state may be carried off, but the will of even a common man cannot be taken from him." (Analects, bk. ix., c. xxv.) So speaks Ibsen who puts into the mouth of Brand:

"That one cannot him excuses,
But never that he does not will."

Confucius refuses to accept the excuse of inability unless one actually expires in a supreme effort to achieve. Therefore, when his disciple, Yen K'ew, said: "It is not that I do not delight in your doctrines, but my strength is insufficient," he admonished him: "They whose strength is insufficient give over in the middle of the way, but now you do but set limits unto yourself." (Analects, bk. vi., c. x.)

The scorn of craven compromise is well voiced in this: "Tsze-Chang said, 'When a man holds fast virtue, but without seeking to enlarge it, and credits right principles, but without firm sincerity, what account can be made of his existence or non-existence?'" (Analects, bk. xix., c. ii.)

That the path of duty leads to the very brink of the grave—and beyond it—Confucius says in no uncertain language: "The determined scholar and the man of virtue will not seek to live at the expense of injuring their virtue. They will even sacrifice their lives to preserve their virtue complete." (Analects, bk. xiv., c. viii.) "The man who in the view of gain thinks of righteousness, who in the view of danger is prepared to give up his life, and who does not forget an old agreement, however far back it extends—such a man may be reckoned a complete man." (Analects, bk. xiv., c. xiii., v. 2.)

His disciple, Tsze-Chang, said of this: "The scholar, beholding threatened danger, is prepared to sacrifice his life. When the opportunity for gain is presented to him, he thinks of righteousness." (Analects, bk. xix., c. i.)

This picture, which to uninstructed mortals may seem dark and forbidding,—it should not seem so, since to die is before every man and few can hope to have so noble an end,—Confucius did not always hold before the eyes of his disciples, however, but on the contrary justly declared, in the face of their craven dread: "Virtue is more to man than either fire or water. I have seen men die by treading upon fire or water, but I have never seen a man die by treading the path of virtue." (Analects, bk. xv., c. xxxiv.)

It costs really nothing to will that which is good and beneficial; the cost is all on the other side. That one sacrifices, is pure delusion; the pleasure as well as the solid benefit is to be found where the enlightened will would bear us. Such conduct is heroic to contemplate; but it is simple truth and not merely personal praise which Confucius spake of another: "With a single bamboo dish of rice, a single gourd dish of drink, and living in a mean, narrow lane, while others could not have endured the distress, he did not allow his joy to be affected by it." (Analects, bk. vi., c. ix.)

It might, indeed it ought and would, be true of any other, if unspoiled; and, as he has well said: "For a morning's anger, to wreck one's life and involve the lives of his parents, is not this a case of delusion?" (Analects, bk. xii., c. xxi., v. 3.)

And, while not so strikingly and obviously true, this statement holds for every aberration from the path of duty, into which one may believe himself led by reason of the greater pleasure and satisfaction that it seems to offer, be it what it may. The beauty, the compensations and relaxations of the upward course are thus set forth by the sage: "Let the will be set on the path of duty! Let every attainment of what is good be firmly grasped! Let perfect virtue be emulated! Let relaxation and enjoyment be found in the polite arts!" (Analects, bk. vii., c. vi.)

To the instructed mind there is nothing uninviting in this prospect; and low and mind-destroying pleasures and comforts which are in fact, though not apparently, lower and more destructive are well abandoned for these higher, simpler, keener, and more abiding satisfactions. Confucius puts it also more explicitly thus: "To find enjoyment in the discriminating study of ceremonies and music; to find enjoyment in speaking of the goodness of others; to find enjoyment in having many worthy friends:—these are advantageous. To find enjoyment in extravagant pleasures; to find enjoyment in idleness and sauntering; to find enjoyment in the pleasures of feasting: these are injurious." (Analects, bk. xvi., c. v.)

Even reverses and hardships have their lesson and reward if one but meet them with resolution; for as Mencius says: "When Heaven is about to confer a great office on any man, it first disciplines his mind with suffering and his bones and sinews with toil. It exposes him to want and subjects him to extreme poverty. It confounds his undertakings. By all these methods it stimulates his mind, hardens him, and supplies his shortcomings." (Bk. vi., pt. ii., c. xv., v. 2.)

This development of the will, which is the development of the man, is therefore not a thing to terrify or repel. Instead, it is mastery, power, sway, achievement—that for which the mind of man longs unceasingly. And it comes of itself, if the basis for it has been safely and carefully laid in purified desires and righteous aims, without effort, without strain, without pain or penalty.

"Is virtue a thing remote?" asked the sage; and answered: "I wish to be virtuous, and lo, virtue is at hand!" (Analects, bk. vii., c. xxix.)

What, then, is this will? What, this virtue? The disciples of Confucius handed the secret of it down from one to another, in these words: "The doctrine of our master is to be true to the principles of our nature and the benevolent exercise of them to others." (Analects, bk. iv., c. xv., v. 2.)

That the joy of well-doing is more than comparable with the pleasure of abandonment to sensual playing with elemental appetites, is said in these words of Wu, reported in the "Shu King": "I have heard that the good man, doing good, finds the day insufficient; and that the evil man, doing evil, also finds the day insufficient." (Pt. v., bk. i., sect. 2)

Fortitude. When the will accords completely with the purpose and the desire, courage follows necessarily; for, if one desires a given result, designs to compass it, and wills to achieve it, it can only mean that he is not fearful about it but instead is cool and determined. As it costs nothing to will, when the purpose are rectified; so, when the will is clear and firm, it costs nothing to be brave. Therefore in "The Great Learning" it is said that by this course, "unperturbed resolve is attained." Confucius elsewhere puts it: "To see what is right and not to do it, is want of courage." (Analects, bk. ii., c. xxiv., v. 2.)

For if one see what is right, he should think sincerely about it, without self-delusion; and, thinking thus, his desires and his purposes should be rectified and therefrom the will to do right will flow. And if he see the truth and do not do these things, it is plainly want of courage—the courage to cast aside comfortable delusions, to think sincerely and be undeceived. When undeceived and with desire and resolve purified, the will and courage follow inevitably.

Confucius again refers to this, saying: "When you have faults, do not fear to abandon them." (Analects, bk. i., c. viii., v. 4.) This is also the gist of the following injunction from the "Li Ki" (bk. xv., v. 22): "Do not try to defend or conceal what was wrong in the past."

So also speaks Yueh in the "Shu King": "Do not be ashamed of mistakes and so proceed to make them crimes!" (Pt. iv., bk. viii., sect. v. I.)

The fear here referred to is doubtless both the fear of discomfort and the fear of the prying eyes and the caustic tongues of others. To this craven dread, reference is made when Tsze-Hea says: "The inferior man is sure to gloss his faults." (Analects, bk. xix., c. viii.) The remedy for it, Confucius demonstrates in these brave words: "I am fortunate! If I have any faults, people are sure to know them." (Analects, bk. vii., c. xxx., v. 3.)

Thus Mencius puts it: "When any one told Tsze-loo that he had a fault, he rejoiced." (Bk. ii., pt. i., c. viii., v. 1.)

Again speaking in the "Yi King" in praise of the son of the Yen family, Confucius says: "If anything that he did was not good, he was sure to become conscious of it; and, when he knew it, he did not do the thing again." (Appendix iii., v. 42.)

So, also, King Thang is represented in the "Shu King" as saying: "The good in you I will not dare to keep concealed; and for the evil in me, I will not dare to forgive myself." (Pt. iv., bk. iii., v. 3.)

And in the "Shu King," also, the great Shun is reported to have said: "When I am doing wrong, it is yours to correct me. Do not concur to my face and when you have retired, speak otherwise!" (Pt. ii., bk. iv., I.)

Fearlessness Confucius ever named as an attribute of the superior man, saying (Analects, bk. xiv., c. xxx., v. 1): "The way of the superior man is threefold, but I am not equal to it. Virtuous, he is free from anxieties; wise, he is free from perplexities; bold, he is free from fear"; and he presents this opposite picture (Analects, bk. iv., c. ii.): "They who are without virtue cannot abide long either in a condition of poverty and hardship or in a condition of enjoyment."

This is even more strikingly presented in the following: "Having not and yet affecting to have, empty and yet affecting to be full, straitened and yet affecting to be at ease! It is difficult with such characteristics to have constancy." (Analects, bk. vii., c. xxv., v. 3.)

And in this contrast: "The superior man is satisfied and composed, the ordinary man is always full of distress." (Analects, bk. vii., c. xxxvi.)

The cowardice of such concern about the future as sets one to speculating and worrying is condemned in the "Li Ki" (bk. xv., 22) as follows: "Do not try . . . to fathom what has not yet arrived."

The sage was not unaware that boldness may be the result of ignorance as well as of knowledge, that it may be madness and folly instead of clear sanity and wisdom. It was concerning such that Confucius spoke when he said of the superior man: "He hates those who have valour only and are unobservant of propriety. He hates those who are forward and determined and at the same time of contracted understanding." (Analects, bk. xvii., c. xxiv., v. 2.)

That the bravery of the superior man and the bravado of the inferior should be distinguished, is the gist of the following saying: "Men of principle are sure to be bold, but those who are bold may not always be men of principle." (Analects, bk. xiv., c. v.)

The absolute need of fearlessness, Mencius enjoins in this which he puts into the mouth of Mang She-Shay: "I look upon not conquering and conquering in the same way. To measure the enemy and then advance, to calculate the chances of victory and then engage—this is to stand in dread of the opposing force. How can I make certain of conquering? But I can rise superior to all fear." (Bk. ii., pt. i., c. ii., v. 5.)

The shame of moral cowardice is well set forth by Confucius in the " Yi King, "thus: "If one be distressed by what need not distress him, his name is sure to be disgraced." (Appendix iii., sect. ii., c. v.)

What, then, may the superior man fear? The answer, disclosing that upon which the courage of the superior man rests securely, is in this query: "They sought to act virtuously and they did so; and what was there for them to repine about?" (Analects, bk. vii., c. xiv., v. 2.)

The freedom from fear which is here referred to costs no effort; if the precedent conditions have been fulfilled, it is their natural and necessary consequence and appears in the noble attributes of the superior man, to which Confucius often adverted, as thus: "The superior man has neither anxiety nor fear." (Analects, bk. xii., c. iv., v. t.) "When internal examination discovers nothing wrong, what is there to be anxious about, what is there to fear?" (Analects, bk. xii., c. iv., v. 3.)

Poise. "To this"—*i.e.*, to unperturbed calm—"succeeds tranquil poise. In this poise is found deliberation."

This passage from "The Great Learning" (Text, v. 2) aims to enforce that it is not enough that one should be resolute and composed in the presence of danger; he must ever be calm and resolute. Thus the sage has said: "What the superior man seeks, is in himself; what the ordinary man seeks, is in others." (Analects, bk. xiv., c. xxviii.) And his disciple, Tsang, says: "The superior man in his thoughts does not go out of his place." (Analects, bk. xiv., c. xxviii.)

In the "Yi King" (appendix ii., c. iii.), it is put thus: "The superior man does not in his thoughts go beyond the position in which he is."

And thus, also: "The influence of the world would make no change in him; he would do nothing merely to secure fame. He can live withdrawn from the world without regret; he can experience disapproval without a troubled mind. . . . He is not to be torn from his root." (Appendix iv., c. ii., v. 41.)

In the "Li Ki" this is much expatiated upon, in part only as follows: "The scholar keeps himself free from all stain; . . . he does not go among those who are low, to make himself seem high, nor set himself among those who are foolish, to make himself seem wise; . . . he does not approve those who think as he, nor condemn those who think differently; thus he takes his stand alone and pursues his course, unattended." (Bk. xxxviii., v. 15.)

The reward for this attainment of perfect poise is described in the "Yi King" (appendix iii., sect. i., c. i., v. 8), in these words: "With the attainment of such ease and such freedom from laborious effort, the mastery is had of all principles under the sky."

And the mode and manner of it are portrayed in the same book (appendix iii., sect. ii., c. v., v. 44) by this saying attributed to Confucius: "The superior man composes himself before trying to move others; makes his mind at rest and easy, before he opens his mouth; determines upon his method of intercourse with others, before he seeks anything of them."

The central conception is that the man should be so balanced that, instead of giving unconscious reactions or semi-conscious responses to stimuli from without, every response, however promptly delivered in speech or act, should be purposive—the consequence of intelligent understanding and resolve.

Mencius said of himself (bk. ii., pt. i., c. ii., v. 1): "At forty I attained to an unperturbed mind"; and Confucius of himself (Analects, bk. vi., c. xxvii.): "There may be those who do this or that, without knowing why. I do not do so."

The sage also eulogizes the balanced, self-centred man in no uncertain terms, as follows: "He with whom neither calumny which slowly soaks into the mind, nor insults that startle like a wound to the flesh, are successful, may indeed be called intelligent; yea, he with whom neither soaking calumny nor startling insults are successful may be called far-seeing." (Analects, bk. xii., c. vi.)

Here are yet other words of penetrating wisdom concerning the advantages of this perfect poise and calm: "He who does not anticipate attempts to deceive him nor think beforehand of his not being believed, and yet apprehends these things readily when they occur, is he not a man of superior worth?" (Analects, bk. xiv., c. xxxviii.)

Mencius also characterizes such a man as follows: "When he obtains the desired position to practise virtue for the good of the people; when disappointed in that ambition to practise virtue for himself; to be above the power of riches and honours to corrupt, of poverty and a mean condition to swerve and of might and sway to bend—these characterize the great man." (Bk. iii., pt. ii., c. ii., v. 3.)

Confucius deemed it indispensable for a ruler to thus possess his soul. Alone it would make a ruler good, if not indeed great. Therefore, he says: "May not Shun be instanced as having governed efficiently without exertion? What did he do? He did nothing but gravely and reverently occupy his imperial seat." (Analects, bk. xv., c. iv.)

And again in these enthusiastic words: "How majestic was the manner in which Shun and Yu held possession of the empire, as if it were nothing to them!" (Analects, bk. viii., c. xviii.)

How this singleness of purpose and this perfect poise of soul, unsuspected during an uneventful life, when great occasion arises, stand forth and reveal the man, is the burden of this saying: "The superior man cannot be known in little matters but he may be entrusted with great concerns." (Analects, bk. xv., c. xxxiii.)

Self-Control. " Want of forbearance in small matters confounds great plans." (Analects, bk. xv., c. xxvi.)

The need for constancy and self-control is often urged by the sage, as thus: "Inconstant in his virtue, he will be visited with disgrace." (Analects, bk. xiii., c. xxii., v. 2.) In the "Shu King," I Yin is represented as expressing this sentiment: "Be careful to strive after the virtue of self-restraint and to cherish far-reaching plans." (Pt. iv., bk. v., sect. 1, 2.)

What is emphasized in these passages, is that he who has formed worthy conceptions of the significance of life and correct designs for accomplishing its ends must not permit himself, at unguarded moments, to be surprised into revelations of deeper-seated longings, by the unexpected presentation of opportunities for the safe enjoyment of sensual delights or by the excitement of rage or terror or other unworthy emotion.

It is well said in the "Shi King" (Minor Odes of the Kingdom, decade v., ode 2): "Men who are grave and wise, though they drink, are masters of themselves. Men who are benighted and ignorant become slaves of drink and more so, daily. Be careful, each of you, of your conduct! What Heaven confers, when once lost, will not be regained."

The necessity for reflection and consideration, though it be but momentary, before responding to any impulse from without, either in speech or in action, instead of the automatic, animal response of a curse or a blow, a smile or a caress, or whatever it may be when one is played upon, is always present in the mind of the sage. It is significantly expressed thus: "Ke Wan Tze thought thrice and then acted. When the Master was informed of it, he said: 'Twice may do.'" (Analects, bk. v., c. xix.)

That even greater prudence in speech is desirable, is indicated by this reply to the inquiry of Tsze-kung: "What constitutes the superior man? " "He acts before he speaks and afterwards speaks in accordance with his act." (Analects, bk. ii., c. xiii.)

Reasons for reticence are given in several passages, from which these are culled: "The Master said, 'The superior man is modest in his speech but exceeds in his actions.'" (Analects, bk. xiv., c. xxix.) "This man seldom speaks; when he does, he is sure to hit the point." (Analects, bk. xi., c. xiii., v. 3.) "When a man feels the difficulty of doing, can he be otherwise than cautious and slow in speaking?" (Analects, bk. xii., c. iii., v. 3.) "The reason why the ancients did not readily give utterance to their words was because they feared lest their deeds should not come up to them." (Analects, bk. iv., c. xxii.)

The prudence of this course is illustrated in the "Shi King" (Major Odes, decade iii., ode 2) by this apt comparison: "A flaw in a mace of white jade may be ground away, but a word spoken amiss cannot be mended."

This is expatiated upon by the sage as follows: "Hear much and put aside the points of which you are in doubt, while you speak cautiously at the same time of others;—then you will afford few occasions for blame. See much and put aside the things which seem perilous, while you are cautious at the same time in carrying the others into practice;—then you will have few occasions for repentance." (Analects, bk. ii., c. xvii., v. 2.)

And when Fan Ch'e asked about perfect virtue, Confucius replied in practical terms: "It is, in retirement, to be sedately grave; in the management of business, to be reverently attentive; in intercourse with others, to be strictly sincere." (Analects, bk. xiii., c. xix.)

The portrait of such a man is well drawn in these outlines: "Looked at from a distance, he appears stern; when approached, he is mild; when he is heard to speak, his language is firm and decided." (Analects, bk. xix., c. ix.)

By this is not meant mere obstinacy, but firmness, based upon resolve, resting in turn on rectified purpose, that in turn upon clarified and illuminated desire, and all upon intelligent investigation and determination of facts. Therefore, he has also said: "The superior man is correctly firm, and not firm merely." (Analects, bk. xv., c. xxxvi.)

Dignity also accompanies this aplomb or mental and moral balance, as a consequence and not as a thing which must be thought about and striven for—simple dignity which comes as naturally as the bloom upon the peach or upon the cheek of youth or maiden—never to be confounded with arrogance. Of this, we learn: "The superior man has dignified ease without pride. The ordinary man has pride without dignified ease." (Analects, bk. xiii., c. xxvi.)

Moderation. "Sincerely hold fast the due mean." (Analects, bk. xx., c. i., v. 1.)

"The Master said: 'Alas, how the path of the mean is not walked in!'" (Doctrine of the Mean, c. v.)

An entire book, bearing the title: "The Doctrine of the Mean," consisting chiefly of sayings of Confucius upon this subject, survives. The following account of its origin is found in the introduction: "This work contains the law of the mind which was handed down from one to another in the Confucian School till Tsze-tsze (the grandson of Confucius), fearing lest in the course of time errors should arise about it, committed it to writing and delivered it to Mencius."

What is meant by "the mean" is the virtue which the ancient Greeks especially praised under the name of temperance. It is defined in the "Li Ki" as follows: "Pride should not be allowed to grow. The desires should not be indulged. The will should not be gratified to the full. Pleasure should not be carried to excess." (Bk. i., sect. i., pt. i., c. ii.)

Confucius attached great importance to this idea, saying: "Perfect is the virtue which is according to the mean. They have long been rare among the people who could practise it." (Doctrine of the Mean, c. iii.)

He also said: "I know how it is that the path of the mean is not walked in; the knowing go beyond it and the stupid do not come up to it. I know how it is that the path of the mean is not understood; the men of talents and virtue go beyond it, and the worthless do not come up to it." (Doctrine of the Mean, c. iv., v. 1.)

The difficulty, indeed the well-nigh impossibility, of attaining this perfect self-control was appreciated by Confucius, who often spoke of it, saying: "All men say, 'We are wise'; but happening to choose the path of the mean, they are not able to keep it for a round month." (Doctrine of the Mean, c. vi.)

And again: "The empire, its states, and its families may be perfectly ruled, dignities and emoluments may be declined, naked weapons may be trampled under the feet, but the course of the mean cannot be attained to." (Doctrine of the Mean, c. ix.)

And in another place he says: "The good man tries to proceed according to the right path, but when he has gone half-way he abandons it." (Doctrine of the Mean, c. xi., v. 2.)

Yet he does not overemphasize this nor fail to recognize that this path is as frequently found by the lowly and humble as by those who are conscious of greatness. He says, instead: "The path is not far from man. When men try to pursue a course which is far from the common indications of consciousness, this course cannot be considered the path." (Doctrine of the Mean, c. xiii., v. 1.)

Mencius in two places reverently echoes this sentiment, as follows: "The path of duty lies in what is near and men seek for it in what is remote; to follow it is easy and men seek it among arduous undertakings." (Bk. iv., pt. i., c. xi.) "The way of truth is like a great road. It is not hard to find it. The trouble is only that men will not look for it. Go home and seek it and you will find many ready to point it out." (Bk. vi., pt. ii., c. ii., v. 7.)

This strange but necessary combination of simplicity and complexity, of things easy and things difficult to understand, is well set forth in the following cryptic language: "The way of the superior man may be found in its simple elements in the intercourse of common men and women, in its utmost reaches it shines brightly through Heaven and earth." (Doctrine of the Mean, c. xii., v. 4.)

Confucius finds the starting point for following the path of the mean in this, that one should be natural, should be himself. The whole picture of what is fundamentally necessary and of what result may be hoped for is in the following from the "Doctrine of the Mean" (c. xiv.):

"The superior man does what is proper to the station in which he is, he does not desire to go beyond this. In a position of wealth and honour he does what is proper to a position of wealth and honour; in a poor and low position, he does what is proper to a poor and low position; situated among barbarous tribes, he does what is proper to a situation among barbarous tribes; in a position of sorrow and difficulty, he does what is proper to a position of sorrow and difficulty.

"The superior man can find himself in no position in which he is not himself. In a high situation he does not treat with contempt his inferiors, in a low situation he does not court the favour of his superiors. He rectifies himself, and seeks for nothing from others, so that he has no dissatisfaction.

"He does not murmur against Heaven nor grumble against men. Thus it is that the superior man is quiet and calm, waiting for the appointments of

41

Heaven, while the inferior man walks in dangerous paths, looking for lucky occurrences."

This path, according to Confucius, lies before every man. It is put thus in the "Doctrine of the Mean" in a passage deemed by Chinese scholars to refer to Confucius only: "It waits for the proper man, and then it is trodden. Hence it is said, 'Only by perfect virtue can the perfect path in all its courses be realized.' Therefore the superior man honours his virtuous nature and maintains constant inquiry and study, seeking to carry it out to its breadth and greatness, so as to omit none of the most exquisite and minute points which it embraces, and to raise it to its greatest height and brilliancy, so as to pursue the course of the mean." (C. xxvii., v. 4, 5, 6.)

The qualities of the man who follows the path of the mean are matters about which the author of the "Doctrine of the Mean" becomes enthusiastic, indulging in declarations such as these: "It is only he, possessed of all sagely qualities that can exist under Heaven, who shows himself quick in apprehension, clear in discernment, of far-reaching intelligence and all-embracing knowledge, fitted to exercise rule; magnanimous, generous, benign and mild, fitted to exercise forbearance; impulsive, energetic, firm and enduring, fitted to maintain a firm grasp; self-adjusted, grave, never swerving from the mean and correct, fitted to command reverence; accomplished, distinctive, concentrative, and searching, fitted to exercise discrimination; all-embracing is he, and vast, deep, and active as a fountain, sending forth, in their due seasons, his virtues." (Doctrine of the Mean, c. xxxi., v. 1, 2.)

Confucius rarely held out any actual, earthly reward, external to the man, for any line of conduct; and indeed above all other attitudes of mind, he praised that which considered solely the thing to be done and not the reward for doing it. Yet as to certain consequences which flow from following the path of the mean, the "Doctrine of the Mean" was not silent, but said of him who follows it consistently: "Wherever ships and carriages reach, wherever the strength of man penetrates, wherever the heavens overshadow and the earth sustains, wherever the sun and moon shine, wherever frost and dew fall, all who have blood and breath unfeignedly honour and love him." (C. xxxi., v. 3.)

Righteousness. "Such deliberation results in achievement of the ends of being."

These words from "The Great Learning" (Text, v. 2) raise the question: What is life's object? Confucius elsewhere answers it: "Man is born for uprightness. If a man lose his uprightness and yet live, his escape is the result of mere good fortune." (Analects, bk. vi., c. xvii.)

Tsang Tze, according to Mencius, attributes this also to Confucius: "If on self-examination, I find I am not upright, shall I not be in fear even of a poor man in his loose garments of hair-cloth? If on self-examination I find that I am upright, I will go forward against thousands and tens of thousands." (Mencius, bk. ii., pt. i., c. ii., v. 7.)

It is to this, also, that Confucius refers when he says: "Let every man consider virtue as what devolves upon himself; he may not yield the performance of it even to his teacher." (Analects, bk. xv., c. xxxv.)

That it comes naturally and easily if the purpose has been rectified and the will is clear and strong, he says in these words: "If the will be set on virtue, there will be no practice of wickedness." (Analects, bk. iv., c. iv.)

The life which is devoid of purity and rectitude, he regards as thrown away. Righteousness should reign in men's hearts and in their lives. Its name and how desirable a thing it is should be upon their lips every day; for of this he speaks as follows: "When a number of people are together for a whole day without their conversation turning on righteousness, and when they are fond of carrying out a narrow shrewdness, theirs is indeed a hard case." (Analects, bk. xv., c. xvi.)

Cunning shrewdness he regarded as utterly inconsistent with rectitude, saying: "Who says of Wei-chang Kao that he is upright? One begged some vinegar of him and he begged it of a neighbour and gave it to him." (Analects, bk. v., c. xxiii.)

That righteousness is of the man and not only of his deed, Mencius thus affirms: "Kao Tze has never understood righteousness. He makes it a thing external." (Bk. ii., pt. i., c. ii., v. 15.)

The attainment of righteousness of thought and conduct, then, is the aim of all who wish, in conformity with the art of living, to achieve a well-spent life. Perfect and complete rectitude is, of course, not a *sine qua non* in order that one should be a superior man; for the word "superior" is relative. Confucius says: "Superior men, and yet not always virtuous, there have been, alas! But there has never been an inferior man who was at the same time virtuous." (Analects, bk. xiv., c. vii.)

Among the descriptions of the superior man, we find these which bear upon the same subject; for the most part they have already been quoted, but it is necessary to reconsider them here: "The superior man thinks of virtue, the ordinary man thinks of comfort. The superior man thinks of sanctions of law, the ordinary man of favours." (Analects, bk. iv., c. xi.) "The mind of the superior man is conversant with righteousness, the mind of the ordinary man is conversant with gain." (Analects, bk. iv., c. xvi.) "The superior man holds righteousness to be of the highest importance." (Analects, bk. xvii., c. xxiii.) "The superior man in all things considers righteousness essential." (Analects, bk. xv., c. xvii.)

Mencius thus identifies righteousness as the normal attribute of man: "Benevolence is the tranquil habitation of man and righteousness his straight path. Alas for them who leave the tranquil habitation tenantless and dwell not therein and who turn away from the straight path and pursue it not!" (Bk. iv., pt. i., c. x., v. 2, 3.)

Nine things, as regards which one must keep watch over himself, are enumerated by Confucius as follows: "The superior man has nine things which are subjects with him of thoughtful consideration. In regard to the use of his eyes, he is anxious to see clearly. In regard to the use of his ears, he is anxious to hear distinctly. In regard to his countenance, he is anxious that it should be benign. In regard to his demeanour, he is anxious that it should be respectful. In regard to his speech, he is anxious that it should be sincere. In regard to his doing of business, he is anxious that it should be reverently careful. In regard to what he doubts about, he is anxious to question others. When he is angry, he thinks of the difficulties his anger may involve him in. When he sees gain to be got, he thinks of righteousness." (Analects, bk. xvi., c. x.)

Some of the qualities which go to make up rectitude of demeanour and conduct are recorded in this passage, with appropriate statements as to their advantages: "If you are grave, you will not be treated with disrespect. If you are generous, you will win all. If you are sincere, people will repose trust in you. If you are earnest, you will accomplish much. If you are kind, this will enable you to employ the services of others." (Analects, bk. xvii., c. vi.)

And in the "Li Ki" (bk. vii., sect. ii., 19), the following are given as essentials of right-living: "What are the things which men consider right? Kindness in a father, filial piety in a son; gentleness in an elder brother, obedience in a younger; righteousness in a husband, submission in a wife; kindness in elders, deference in juniors; benevolence in a ruler, loyalty in a minister. These ten are things which men consider right. To speak the truth and work for harmony are what are called things advantageous to men. To quarrel, plunder, and murder are things disastrous to men."

The philosophy, the sequence, even the causation of it are contained in this, from the same book: "He who knows how to exemplify what a son should be, can afterwards exemplify what a father should be. He who knows how to exemplify what a minister should be, can afterwards exemplify what a ruler should be. He who knows how to serve others, can afterwards employ them." (Bk. vi., sect. i., 20.)

Perhaps there are traces of an ancient freemasonry—or did they merely presage the newer symbolism?—in this, from the "Yi King" (appendix iv., sect. ii., c. ii., 6): "The plumb signifies correctness; the square, righteousness." There are several such passages in the ancient books of the Chinese.

Self-righteousness is far from what the sage has in mind. Indeed, such a conception could not be harboured by him who said: "I am fortunate. If I have any faults, people are sure to know them" (Analects, bk. vii., c. xxx., v. 3); and again: "In letters I am perhaps equal to other men, but the character of the superior man, carrying out in his conduct what he professes, is what I have not yet attained to." (Analects, bk. vii., c. xxxii.) As the sage puts it: "To have faults and not to reform them, this indeed should be pronounced having faults." (Analects, bk. xv., c. xxix.)

He also said concerning himself: "If some years were added to my life, I would give fifty to the study of the Yi, and then I might come to be without great faults" (Analects, bk. vii., c. xvi.); and he especially praised the selection by Keu Pih-yuh of a messenger who, when asked, "What is your master engaged in?" replied: "My master is anxious to make his faults few, but has not yet succeeded." (Analects, bk. xiv., c. xxvi.)

And the necessity for frequent introspection and unsparing criticism of self is thus enjoined: "Therefore, the superior man examines his heart that there may be nothing wrong there, and that he may have no cause for dissatisfaction with himself." (Doctrine of the Mean, c. xxxiii., v. 2.)

That righteousness may—and, indeed, must, in order to be practicable by mortals—coexist with the presence of many shortcomings and may even be reflected in them, Confucius indicates in this shrewd remark: "By observing a man's faults, it may be known that he is virtuous." (Analects, bk. iv., c. vii.)

Not that one is to hug this to his soul in self-justification and self-indulgence, for it is written: "Hold faithfulness and sincerity as first principles, and be moving continually toward what is right! " (Analects, bk. xii., c. x., v. 1.) He would not lightly excuse or condone the abandonment of virtue; for is it not he "who in the view of gain thinks of righteousness," that is pronounced "a complete man"? (Analects, bk. xiv., c. xiii., v. 2.) "The determined scholar and the man of virtue," he also said, "will not seek to live at the expense of injuring their virtue. They will even sacrifice their lives to preserve their virtue complete." (Analects, bk. xv., c. viii.) Mencius also puts forth this idea in another dress: "I prize life indeed but there is that which I prize more than life and therefore I will not seek to preserve it by improper means. I shrink from death indeed but there is that which I shrink from more than death, and therefore there are occasions when I will not avoid danger." (Bk. vi., pt. i., c. x., v. i.)

Confucius had no notion of palliating the offence of one who abandons right-doing; for he said of this: "If a superior man abandon virtue, how can he fulfil the requirements of the name? The superior man does not, even for the space of a single meal, act contrary to virtue. In moments of haste, he cleaves to it. In seasons of danger he cleaves to it." (Analects, bk. iv., v. 2, 3.)

And this constancy he again adverts to, sagely: "The virtuous rest in virtue; the wise desire virtue." (Analects, bk. iv., c. ii.) Yet he laments: "I have not seen a person who loved virtue, or one who hated what is not virtuous. He who loved virtue, would esteem nothing above it. He who hated what is not virtuous, would practise virtue in such a way that he would not allow anything that is not virtuous to approach his person. Is any one able for one day to apply his strength to virtue? I have not seen the case in which his strength would be insufficient. Should there possibly be such a case, I have not seen it." (Analects, bk. iv., c. vi.)

Yet he despairs of constant righteousness; for he says elsewhere: "To subdue one's self and return to propriety is perfect virtue. If a man for one day subdue himself and return to propriety, all under heaven will ascribe perfect virtue to him." (Analects, bk. xii., c. i., v. 1.) And likewise: "If a man in the morning hear the right way, he may die in the evening without regret." (Analects, bk. iv., c. viii.)

Earnestness. "Wheresoever you go, go with all your heart!" (Shu King, pt. v., bk. ix., 2.)

These words are ascribed to the illustrious Wu or to Khang, his son. The injunction which Ibsen puts into the mouth of Brand:

"Be what thou art, with all thy heart—
Not piecemeal, only, and in part!"

seems but a modern echo, or reaffirmation, of this sentiment of thousands of years ago.

In the "Shu King," also, I Yin is made to say: "What attainment can be made without anxious thought? What achievement without earnest effort?" (Pt. iv., bk. vi., sect. iii., 2.)

Mencius puts it strongly thus: "Now chess-playing is but a small art; but without giving his whole mind to it and bending his will to it, a man cannot excel in it." (Bk. vi., pt. i., c. ix., v. 3.)

The absolute sincerity of thought which has been found prerequisite to the acquisition of sound learning, the formation of right desires, and the planning of the art of life, must ripen into earnestness in conduct and candour of speech. Else were it fruitless and unavailing. As much is embraced in this primary injunction of Confucius: "Hold faithfulness and sincerity as first principles!" (Analects, bk. i., c. viii., v. 2.)

Among the nine things which are with the superior man subjects "of thoughtful consideration," he includes these: "In regard to his speech, he is anxious that it be sincere. In regard to his doing of business, he is anxious that it should be reverently careful." (Analects, bk. xvi., c. x.)

These resulting virtues of speech and action were two of the "four things which the Master taught: Letters, ethics, devotion of spirit, and truthfulness." (Analects, bk. vii., c. xxiv.) And urgently did he enjoin each of his disciples "to give one's self earnestly to the duties due to men." (Analects, bk. vi., c. xx.)

That this should come naturally and easily, without strain or striving, Mencius says in this: "The great man does not think beforehand of his words that they may be sincere nor of his actions that they may be resolute; he simply speaks and does what is right." (Bk. iv., pt. ii., c. xi.)

The opposite Mencius finds in this: "The disease of men is this:—that they neglect their own fields and go to weed the fields of others and that what they require from others is great, while what they lay upon themselves is light." (Bk. vii., pt. ii., c. xxxii., v. 3.)

The evil results of uninstructed earnestness in conduct, *i.e.*, earnestness unaccompanied by clear knowledge of what is aimed at, of consequences and causes and of the means by which one's real ends may be furthered, are set forth in this: "There is the love of being sincere without the love of learning; the beclouding here leads to an injurious disregard of consequences." (Analects, bk. xvii., c. viii., v. 3.)

Notwithstanding these obvious limitations, none of which goes to the root and all of which have to do only with what should accompany earnestness

46

and candour, Confucius enjoins both, upon the young as upon the old, as absolutely essential to right-living. Thus of the youth, he says: "He should be earnest and truthful" (Analects, bk. i., c. vi.), and of the superior man: "He who aims at complete virtue . . . is earnest in what he is doing and careful in his speech." (Analects, bk. i., c. xiv.) "The superior man wishes to be slow in speech and earnest in conduct." (Analects, bk. iv., c. xxiv.) " What the superior man requires, is just that in his words there may be nothing inaccurate." (Analects, bk. xiii., c. iii., v. 7.)

Twice in the "Analects," although Confucius spoke seldom about "perfect virtue," he referred, when replying to inquiries on this important subject, especially to sincerity of speech and faithfulness of conduct, the first time briefly thus: "Fan Ch'e asked about perfect virtue. The Master said, 'It is in retirement, to be sedately grave; in the management of business, to be reverently attentive; in intercourse with others, to be strictly sincere.'" (Analects, bk. xiii., c. xix.)

The second time, he did not content himself with mere categorical mention, but proceeded to expatiate upon the beneficent results of these virtues, in the following: "Tsze-chang asked Confucius about perfect virtue. Confucius said, 'To be able to practise five things everywhere under heaven constitutes perfect virtue.' He begged to inquire what they were, and was told: 'Gravity, generosity, sincerity, earnestness, and kindness. If you are grave, you will not be treated with disrespect. If you are generous, you will win all. If you are sincere, people will repose trust in you. If you are earnest, you will accomplish much. If you are kind, this will enable you to employ the services of others.'" (Analects, bk. xvii., c. vi.)

These results, he further taught, are independent of time and place and of the state of civilization of those among whom these virtues are practised, for he says: "Let his words be sincere and truthful, and his actions honourable and careful;—such conduct may be practised among the rude tribes of the South or of the North. If his words be not sincere and truthful, and his actions not honourable and careful, will he, with such conduct, be appreciated, even in his own neighbourhood?" (Analects, bk. xv., c. v., v. 2.)

Humility. "I am not concerned that I have no place; I am concerned how I may fit myself for one. I am not concerned that I am not known; I seek to be worthy to be known." (Analects, bk. iv., c. xiv.) "I will not be afflicted that men do not know me; I will be afflicted that I do not know men." (Analects, bk. i., c. xvi.) "I will not be concerned at men's not knowing me; I will be concerned at my own want of ability." (Analects, bk. xiv., c. xxxii.) "The superior man is distressed by his want of ability; he is not distressed by men's not knowing him." (Analects, bk. xv., c. xvii.)

These are but a few of the many expressions in the "Analects" of the spirit of humility which is essential to true self-development. It is not want of self-respect that is here inculcated; but, instead, that poise which demands not the acclaim of others. In the "Yi King" (appendix ii., sect. i., c. xxviii.) it is put thus:

"The superior man . . . stands alone and has no fear, and keeps retired from the world without regret."

Yet it is also far from encouraging the progress-destroying self-sufficiency of one who disregards others' opinions because placing too high an estimate upon his own. For in the "Shu King" (pt. iv., bk. vi., 4) the earnest injunction is found, accredited to I Yin: "Do not think yourself so large as to deem others small!"

And this, also, is found in the "Shu King" (pt. iv., bk. ii., 4): "He who says that others are not equal to himself, comes to ruin."

And in the same book (pt. iv., bk. viii., sect. ii., 1) the illustrious Yueh is reported to have said: "Indulging the consciousness of being good is the way to lose that goodness; being vain of one's ability is the way to lose it."

And in its pages also (pt. v., bk. xxvi.) King Mu is made to say of himself, in all humility: "I rise at midnight and think how I can avoid falling into errors."

The Duke of Khin, also in the "Shu King" (pt. v., bk. xxx.), thus describes how difficult, albeit salutary, it is to receive, welcome, and apply the reproof of others: "Reproving others is easy, but to receive reproof and allow it free course is difficult."

And in the "Li Ki" (bk. ii., sect. ii., pt. iii., 17) the ruinous consequences of false pride are depicted by means of a clever parable, as follows: "It is because I would not eat 'Poor man, come here!' food that I am come to this state."

In the same book (Li Ki, bk. xxvii., 9) it is related of Confucius: "The Master said, 'The superior man exalts others and abases himself; he gives the first place to others and takes the last himself.'"

Mencius applied this to himself in this famous colloquy: "The officer Ch'oo said, 'Master, the King sent persons to spy out whether you were really different from other men.' Mencius said, 'How should I be different from other men? Yaou and Shun were the same as other men.'" (Bk. iv., pt. ii., c. xxxii.)

This also does Confucius teach, that with admiration and appreciation a man should look upon superior men, rejoicing in their virtue, and emulating them; and that, on the contrary, when beholding persons with grave and glaring faults, he is not to rejoice that he is not like unto them, but instead, with deep humility, to search his own heart with microscopic care and remorseless earnestness, lest these very faults or errors be hiding there. Thus he says: "When we see men of worth, we should think of equalling them; when we see men of contrary character, we should turn inward and examine ourselves." (Analects, bk. iv., c. xvii.)

The difficulty of doing this, however, he did not minimize, knowing full well how prone the human mind is to justify its own aberrations. Indeed he more than once complained with sadness: "I have not yet seen one who could perceive his faults and inwardly accuse himself." (Analects, bk. v., c. xxvi.)

He counselled the greatest possible avoidance of the thought of personal success as a prime consideration of conduct, and inculcated the truth that unless the mind is devotedly bent to the achievement of its own purpose, to the accomplishment of the thing which it designs, the man's work will not be that which he desired to do but will merely be done in order that men might acclaim him.

He often emphasized even to a superlative degree the obstacles in the way of the formation of character and of living a well-spent and therefore successful life. Indeed, that this should ever come up to one's longings, or even to one's expectations, was, he frequently granted, quite impossible, meaning thereby not that the structure might not be imposing or beautiful, but that it would fall short of that perfect beauty which the mind is able to conjure up before it, and must so imagine to itself if the man is to be kept steadily on the path of progress.

It is true that in all this there is no departure from the notion that the man should be in fact self-sufficient. It is not the idea of the sage that he should abandon himself to despair but that his mind, beholding clearly and courageously the perfection that he cannot hope to equal, should do all that lies in its power to mould itself after that vision of beauty, which after all is but an imperfect attempt to reconstruct within itself the glories which it cannot fully apprehend. Thus he teaches that one should be at ease about himself, even though others should hold him of no account. This is not meant by Confucius to be mere self-abasement, affected in order to obtain an advantage in coping with others, but a genuine willingness that one's work be done year in and year out, without being visited with the acclaim of the multitude. He says: "Is he not a man of complete virtue who feels no discomposure though men may take no note of him?" (Analects, bk. i., c. i., v. 3.)

He thus pays his tribute of praise and appreciation to the great soul who compasses this: "Admirable, indeed, was the virtue of Hwuy! With a single bamboo dish of rice, a single gourd dish of drink, and living in his mean narrow lane, while others could not have endured the distress he did not allow his joy to be affected by it. Admirable, indeed, was the virtue of Hwuy!" (Analects, bk. vi., c. ix.)

Aspiration. "The scholar does not deem gold and jade precious, but loyalty and good faith. He does not crave broad lands and possessions, but holds the rectification of himself his domain. He asks not great wealth but looks upon many- sided culture as true riches." (Li Ki, bk. xxxviii., 6.)

Thus in the "Li Ki" Confucius indicates that for and unto which man should aspire. It is contrasted thus with the opposite and vainglorious but destructive course: "It is the way of the superior man to prefer the concealment of his virtue while it daily becomes more illustrious, and it is the way of the inferior man to seek notoriety while he daily goes more and more to ruin." (Doctrine of the Mean, c. xxxiii., v. 1.)

And in this passage perhaps even more discriminatingly and finely: "The thing wherein the superior man cannot be equalled is simply this, his work which other men cannot see." (Doctrine of the Mean, c. xxxiii., v. 2.)

Of the path which leads to this and which Confucius trod, it is said in this from the "Doctrine of the Mean," already once quoted: "It waits for the proper man, and then it is trodden. Hence it is said, 'Only by perfect virtue can the perfect path in all its courses be realized.' Therefore the superior man honours his virtuous nature and maintains constant inquiry and study, seeking to carry it out to its breadth and greatness so as to omit none of the most exquisite and minute points which it embraces and to raise it to its greatest height and brilliancy, so as to pursue the course of the mean." (C. xxvii., v. 4, 5, 6.)

This is the portrait, considered by Chinese scholars to be that of Confucius, which in a passage from the same book, already once quoted, presents the many-sided character to which men, striving for the right, are to aspire: "It is only he possessed of all sagely qualities that can exist under Heaven, who shows himself quick in apprehension, clear in discernment, of far-reaching intelligence and all-embracing knowledge, fitted to exercise rule; magnanimous, generous, benign, and mild, fitted to exercise forbearance; impulsive, energetic, firm, and enduring, fitted to maintain a firm grasp; self-adjusted, grave, never swerving from the mean and correct, fitted to command reverence; accomplished, distinctive, concentrative, and searching, fitted to exercise discrimination. All embracing is he, and vast, deep, and active as a fountain, sending forth in their due seasons his virtues." (Doctrine of the Mean, c. xxxi., v. 1, 2.)

In the "Li Ki," in more prosaic but not less striking fashion, the aspirations which are justifiable, honourable, and beneficial for a man are detailed, thus: "There are three things that occasion sorrow to a superior man. If there be a subject of which he has not heard, and he do not hear of it; if he hear of it, and do not come to learn it; if he learn it but have no chance to practise it. There are five things that occasion the superior man humiliation. If in office and unfamiliar with its duties; if familiar with them but not carrying them into practice; if once in office and then dismissed; if in charge of a large territory but not well populated; if anybody with the same duties do better than he." (Li Ki, bk. xviii., 20.)

In the "Yi King" (appendix iii., sect. ii., c. v., 37), Confucius sharply contrasts this with the sordid, self-destroying motives of the inferior man, thus: "The inferior man is not ashamed of what is not benevolent nor does he fear to do what is not righteous. Without the prospect of gain he does not stimulate himself to what is good, nor does he correct himself without being moved."

The attitude which should be taken toward these incentives, usually so powerful, the sage thus presents: "Riches and honours are what men desire. If it cannot be brought about in the proper way, they should not be held. Poverty and meanness are what men dislike. If it cannot be brought about in the proper way, they should not be avoided." (Analects, bk. iv., c. v., v. 1.)

Yet Confucius deemed it self-evidently a desirable thing that one's merit should be recognized and a thing almost incredible that true merit should go unrecognized. But he urged that this should be regarded as but an incident and not as the object to be aimed at and striven for. Instead, the labour must be primarily to serve one's fellowman and to develop one's self. Notoriety and genuine distinction he discussed in the following: "The Master said, 'What is it you call being distinguished?' Tsze-chang replied, 'It is to be heard of through the state, to be heard of through the family.' The Master said: 'That is notorie-ty, not distinction. The man of distinction is substantial and straightforward and loves uprightness. He examines people's words and looks into their coun-tenances. He is anxious to defer to others. Such a man will be distinguished in the country; he will be distinguished in the family. As to the man of notoriety, he assumes the appearance of virtue but his actions belie it, and he rests in this character without any doubts about himself. Such a man will be heard of in the country; he will be heard of in the family.'" (Analects, bk. xii., c. xx.)

There is one sort of aspiration for fame which Confucius said that he him-self did not possess: "To live in obscurity and to practise wonders, in order to be mentioned with honour in future ages—this is what I do not do." (Doctrine of the Mean, c. xi., v. i.)

Yet it is by no means his opinion that only they who by their virtues deserve to be known or even to be loved, receive the acclaim of the multitude. This but raises the question whether the man is really worthy or has merely deceived and misled the people. Confucius says that it but puts one upon inquiry, thus: "When the multitude hate a man, it is necessary to examine into the case. When the multitude like a man, it is necessary to examine into the case." (Analects, bk. xv., c. xxvii.)

This he explains more fully at another time in the following colloquy: "Tsze-kung asked, saying, 'What do you say of a man who is loved by all the people of his village?' The Master replied, 'We may not for that accord our approval of him.' 'And what do you say of him who is hated by all the people of his vil-lage?' The Master said, 'We may not for that conclude that he is bad. It is bet-ter than either of these cases that the good in the village love him, and the bad hate him.'" (Analects, bk. xiii., c. xxiv.)

Confucius could not enough condemn the doing of any act for the mere pur-pose of obtaining the approval of men or of winning the laurels of fame. The aim must be the accomplishment of the work or service, itself. This he has said in many passages, among them these: "If doing what is to be done be made the first business and success a secondary consideration, is not this the way to exalt virtue?" (Analects, bk. xii., c. xxi., v. 3.) "In ancient times men learned with a view to their own improvement. Nowadays, men learn with a view to the approbation of others." (Analects, bk. xiv., c. xxv.) "The man of vir-tue makes the difficulty to be overcome his first business and success only a subsequent consideration." (Analects, bk. vi., c. xx.)

The true spirit of the man with an exalted aim he thus depicts: "Though he may be all unknown, unregarded by the world, he feels no regret." (Doctrine of the Mean, c. xi., v. 3.)

In the "Yi King" (appendix iv., sect. i., c. ii., 6) Confucius recurs to it thus: "He occupies a high position without pride and a low position without anxiety."

And in the "Li Ki" with greater circumstantiality the indifference and un-concern of the superior man toward mere worldly rewards or failure to ob-tain them, and his complete immunity from evil result of either of these things, are thus portrayed: "The scholar is not cast down or uprooted by poverty and a mean condition; he is not elated or enervated by riches and an exalted condition." (Bk. xxxviii., 19.)

Yet, not utterly is ambition for worldly honours discouraged; for in the "Doctrine of the Mean," in a passage already once quoted, and which Chinese scholars deem to refer to Confucius himself, the prospect of the man who pursues the path of the mean is thus apostrophized: "Wherever ships and carriages reach, wherever the strength of man penetrates, wherever the heavens overshadow and the earth sustains, wherever the sun and moon shine, wherever frosts and dews fall, all who have blood and breath unfeignedly honour and love him." (Doctrine of the Mean, c. xxxi., v. 3.)

And, although the words, "I desire nothing but rightly to die," are ascribed to Tsang-tse, when dying (Li Ki, bk. ii., sect. i., pt. i., 18), Confucius himself has said: "The superior man dislikes the thought of his name not being mentioned after his death." (Analects, bk. xv., c. xix.)

Prudence. "If a man take no thought about what is distant, he will find sorrow near at hand." (Analects, bk. xv., c. xi.)

In the "Yi King" (appendix iii., sect. ii., c. v., 39), the wisdom of prudence and of foresight, thus vividly presented in the "Analects," is enforced by the Master in these maxims: "He who keeps danger in mind, is he who will rest safe in his seat; he who keeps ruin in mind, is he who will preserve his interests secure; he who sets the danger of disorder before him, is he who will maintain order."

And in the "Shu King" Yueh is represented as urging thoughtful care, by these words: "For all affairs let there be adequate preparation; with preparation there will be no calamitous issue." (Pt. iv., bk. viii., sect. ii., 1.)

Of the same nature is this injunction from the "Li Ki" (bk. xv., 22): "Do not commence or abandon anything hastily."

Though far from teaching that the aim of the superior man should be the acquisition of wealth, and though insistent upon the view that this depends so much more upon fortune than upon the desert, or even the scheming, of individuals, Confucius, as in the foregoing, pleads always for the use of foresight and prudence in the ordinary affairs of life. Thus he places among the cardinal qualities of the superior man reverent attention to business. (Analects, bk. xvi., c. x.) Yet he rarely discoursed upon this subject nor, indeed, upon the part of Heaven in determining the good or ill fortune which attends man; and that this is not true only of the sayings which have come down to us, is shown by this statement of his disciples: "The subjects of which the Master seldom spoke were: profitableness, also the appointments of Heaven and perfect virtue." (Analects, bk. ix., c. i.)

That the sordid pursuit of wealth is to be avoided he indicated in these words already quoted: "Riches and honour are what men desire. If it cannot be brought about in the proper way, they should not be held. Poverty and meanness are what men dislike. If it cannot be brought about in the proper way, they should not be avoided." (Analects, bk. iv., c. v., v. 1.)

This he also said again and again, as in this contrast: "The mind of the superior man is conversant with righteousness; the mind of the average man is conversant with gain " (Analects, bk. iv., c. xvi.); and in another place he names as one of the qualities of "the complete man" that, "in view of gain," he "thinks of righteousness." (Analects, bk. xiv., c. xiii., v. 2.)

He teaches that "riches and honours depend upon Heaven" (Analects, bk. xii., c. v., v. 3); notwithstanding which, prudence and industry will, in a well-governed country, insure a competence. Wherefore he says: "When a country is well governed, poverty and a mean condition are things to be ashamed of. When a country is ill governed, riches and honour are things to be ashamed of." (Analects, bk. viii., c. xiii., v. 3.)

To nothing would his proverb, "To go beyond is as bad as to fall short" (Analects, bk. xi., c. xiv., v. 3), apply more aptly than to expenditure, of which he also sagely remarks (Analects, bk. vii., c. xxxv.): "Extravagance leads to insubordination and parsimony to meanness. It is better to be mean than to be insubordinate"—though, obviously, best of all to be neither.

As regards the pursuit of wealth, Confucius spoke, for himself, thus: "If the search for riches were sure to be successful, though I should become a groom with whip in hand to get them, I would do so. As the search may not be successful, I will pursue that which I desire." (Analects, bk. vii., c. xi.)

Resignation to the appointments of Heaven in this regard, and the greater desirability that more worthy ambitions be dominant, are urged in this striking passage: "There is Hwuy! He has nearly attained to perfect virtue. He is often in want." (Analects, bk. xi., c. xviii.)

That riches is not that to which the soul of the superior man aspires, he affirms in these words, already quoted in another connection: "The superior man is anxious lest he should not get truth: he is not anxious lest poverty should come upon him." (Analects, bk. xv., c. xxxi.)

This version of "Riches takes unto itself wings" is given by the commentator in "The Great Learning": "Wealth, got by improper means, will take its departure in the same way." (C. x., v. 10.)

Among the "three things which the superior man guards against," he names avarice, saying: "In youth, when the physical powers are not yet settled, he guards against lust. When he is strong, and the physical powers are full of vigour, he guards against quarrelsomeness. When he is old, and the animal powers are decayed, he guards against covetousness." (Analects, bk. xvi., c. vii.)

Though duties, corresponding to their ill fortune or good fortune, rest upon the poor and upon the rich, Confucius deems it much harder for the impoverished man to possess his soul and act according to propriety; of this he says: "To be poor without murmuring is difficult. To be rich without pride is easy." (Analects, bk. xiv., c. xi.)

The imprudence, not to speak of the immorality, of acting in a purely selfish manner, is shown in this: "He who acts with a constant view to his own advantage will be much murmured against." (Analects, bk. iv., c. xii.)

This, however, is not limited to financial dealings, but applies as well to all other exactions; as to which the sage shrewdly observes: "He who requires much from himself and little from others, will keep himself from being the object of resentment." (Analects, bk. xv., c. xiv.)

It is also the part of prudence as early as possible to guard against speech and conduct which cause dislike; for, as the sage somewhat sweepingly asserts: "When a man at forty is the object of dislike, he will always continue what he is." (Analects, bk. xvii., c. xxvi.)

The same idea, but a different application of it, is presented in this wise saying from the "Shu King" (pt. v., bk. xxi., 2) attributed to King Khang: "Seek not every quality in one individual!"

And this vivid picture of the foredoomed failure of the ambitious but imprudent man Confucius gives in the "Yi King" (appendix iii., sect. ii., c. v., v. 40): "Virtue small and office high; wisdom small and plans great; strength small and burden heavy—where such conditions exist, it is seldom they do not end in evil."

The necessity for unflinching self-examination before engaging in any important undertaking or assuming any heavy obligation, not merely as a matter of personal honesty, but also as a matter of prudence, is thus enjoined in the "Li Ki" in a passage already quoted: "For one who wished to serve his ruler, the rule was first to measure his abilities and duties and then enter on the responsibilities; he did not first enter and then measure. The same rule applied when one begged or borrowed from others or sought to enter their service." (Bk. xv., 19.)

And in the "Yi King" (appendix ii., c. xxxiii., v. 4) this caution and this self-restraint are thus appreciated: "A superior man retires, notwithstanding his likings; an average man cannot attain to it."

This sketch of the superior man is elaborated further in the following passage in the "Analects": "He who aims to be a man of complete virtue, in his food does not seek to gratify his appetite, nor in his dwelling-place does he seek the appliances of ease; he is earnest in what he is doing, and careful in his speech; he frequents the company of men of principle that he may be rectified." (Analects, bk. i., c. xiv.)

Prudence is, of course, merely the application of the same calm clear-sightedness and study of cause and effect, which the sage enjoins as the very foundation of the investigation of phenomena, upon which in turn the entire superstructure of the art of life rests. To what advantage does one refuse to recognize the stubborn facts, whether as regards himself or as regards others? Or as the sage phrases it: "Who can go out but by the door? How is it that men will not walk according to these ways?" (Analects, bk. vi., c. xv.)

The need of patience and thoroughness he also repeatedly inculcates, as in this: "Do not be desirous of having things done quickly; do not look at small advantages! Desire to have things done quickly prevents their being done thoroughly. Looking at small advantages prevents great things being accomplished." (Analects, bk. xiii., c. xvii.)

And the slow but solid achievement which attends this course is thus portrayed: "The way of the superior man may be compared with what takes place in travelling, when to go to a distance we must first traverse the space that is near and when in ascending a height we must first begin from the lower ground." (Doctrine of the Mean, C. xv., v. 1.)

Chapter Three - General Human Relations

AFTER instruction in self-development, men need to know their relation to their fellows. First in importance of our social duties, and intimately connected with individual character, Confucius placed propriety.

The Rules of Propriety. "Let the superior man never fail reverentially to order his own conduct; and let him be respectful to others and observant of propriety. Then all within the four seas will be his brothers." (Analects, bk. xii., c. v., v. 4.)

Thus Confucius in the "Analects" emphasizes the importance of the due observance of propriety. The rules of propriety were, in the mind of the sage, of much the same order as the positive commands which make up the ordinary man's only system of morality. They were the things enjoined, which the superior man must observe, not in order to become or even to be a superior man, however, but because he is such. Therefore it is said: "If a man be without the virtues proper to humanity, what has he to do with the rites of propriety?" (Analects, bk. iii., c. iii.)

Yet propriety has its office, also, and that not a small one, albeit the real character, the open mind, sincerity, purity of purpose, will, courage, poise, and all the rest, must first have been attained; else mere outward conformity with propriety is nothing. Its office is thus described: "It is by the rules of propriety that the character is established." (Analects, bk. viii., c. viii., v. 2.) "Without an acquaintance with the rules of propriety, it is impossible for the character to be established." (Analects, bk. xx., c. iii., v. 3.)

This is indeed sufficiently obvious upon consideration since character can be evinced only in speech, conduct, deportment, and demeanour, each of which must have its own canons of propriety. The utility of these rules in this respect is adverted to in the "Li Ki," thus: "The rules of propriety serve as instruments to form men's characters. . . . They remove from a man all perversity and increase what is beautiful in his nature. They make him correct, when employed in the ordering of himself; they ensure for him free course, when employed toward others." (Bk. viii., sect. i., 1.)

In another place in the "Li Ki," the following is said concerning the depraved state of men who have no conception of propriety: "But if beasts and without the rules of propriety, father and son might have the same mate." (Bk. i., sect. i.. pt. i., c. v., v. 21.)

And in yet another place in that book the following tribute to the superlative utility of propriety and especially to its usefulness in forming character appears: "Therefore the rules of propriety are for man what the yeast is for liquor. By the use of them the superior man becomes better and greater. The inferior man by neglect of them becomes smaller and poorer. (Bk. vii., sect. iv., v. 7.)

Mencius thus laid bare the very foundation for the sense of propriety: "The sense of shame is of great importance to man." (Bk. vii., pt. i., c. vii., v. i.)

The Chinese tradition was that the rules of propriety had been established by the ancient kings and embodied their conception of right. The following account, also in the "Li Ki," which is devoted to a discussion of these rules, is given, both of their origin and of their construction: "The rules as instituted by the ancient kings had their radical element and their outward, elegant form. A true heart and good faith are their radical element. The characteristics of each according to the idea of what is right in it are its outward, elegant form. Without the radical element, they could not have been established; without the elegant form, they could not have been put in practice." (Bk. viii., sect. i., v. 2.)

That an observance is to be judged, not only by its general acceptance as "good form," but also and, if need be, exclusively by what is right, is urged in this passage from the same book: "Rules of ceremony are the embodied expression of what is right. If an observance stand the test of being judged by the standard of what is right, although it may not have been among the usages of the ancient kings, it may be adopted on the ground of its being right." (Bk. vii., sect. iv., v. 9.)

Mencius thus rebuked the notion, yet prevalent in more than one quarter, that mere "good form" is propriety although it be the cover for wanton cruelty and wrong: "Acts of propriety which are not proper and deeds of righteousness that are not righteous, the great man does not do." (Bk. iv., pt. ii., c. vi.)

The untoward consequences, if the rights of propriety are neglected, are strikingly set forth by Confucius in these words: "Respectfulness, without the rules of propriety, becomes laborious bustle; carefulness, without the rules of propriety, becomes timidity; boldness, without the rules of propriety, becomes insubordination; straightforwardness, without the rules of propriety, becomes rudeness." (Analects, bk. viii., c. ii., v. 1.)

Several of the nine things which he names as worthy "of thoughtful consideration" are of this nature. The pronouncement, already once quoted, will bear repetition: "The superior man has nine things which are subjects with him of thoughtful consideration: In regard to the use of his eyes he is anxious to see clearly. In regard to the use of his ears he is anxious to hear distinctly. In regard to his countenance he is anxious that it should be benign. In regard to his demeanour he is anxious that it should be respectful. In regard to his speech he is anxious that it should be sincere. In regard to his doing of business he is anxious that it should be reverently careful. In regard to what he doubts about he is anxious to question others. When he is angry he thinks of the difficulties his anger may involve him in. When he sees gain to be got he thinks of righteousness." (Analects, bk. xvi., c. x.)

In another place he says: "If you are grave, you will not be treated with disrespect; if you are generous, you will win all; if you are sincere, people will repose trust in you; if you are in earnest, you will accomplish much; if you are kind, this will enable you to employ the services of others." (Analects, bk. xvii., c. vi.)

Each of these has reference to a rule of propriety.

Again, when asked what constitutes perfect virtue, he said: "It is in retirement to be sedately grave, in the management of business to be reverently attentive, in intercourse with others to be strictly sincere." (Analects, bk. xiii., c. xix.)

Among the repulsive characters which he holds it the duty of the superior man to hate, is this: "He hates those who have valour merely and are unobservant of propriety." (Analects, bk. xvii., e. xxiv., v. 1.)

Perhaps in nothing are the real qualities of a man more frankly exhibited than in his conduct toward those who are subject to his orders and must obey him. The petty tyrannies which the small mind invents under such conditions are familiar to every observer, but few have had the penetration to discern what Confucius illustrates in the following passage: "The superior man is easy to serve and difficult to please. If you try to please him in any way which is not accordant with right, he will not be pleased. But in his employment of men he uses them according to their capacity. The inferior man is difficult to serve, and easy to please. If you try to please him, though it be in a way which is not accordant with right, he may be pleased. But in his employment of men he wishes them to be equal to everything." (Analects, bk. xiii., c. xxv.)

This is but a shrewd practical application of this observation from the "Li Ki": "Propriety is seen in humbling one's self and giving honours to others." (Bk. i., sect. i., pt. i., c. vi., v. 25.)

But this humility must be such as comports with true dignity; for, as the Duke of Shao says in the "Shu King" (pt. v., bk. vi., 2): "Complete virtue allows no contemptuous familiarity."

This combination of humility and dignity, which has ever characterized the Chinese conception of propriety, is cleverly adverted to in these significant and weighty sentences: "Gan P'ing Chung knew well how to maintain friendly intercourse. The acquaintance might be long, but he showed the same respect as at first." (Analects, bk. v., c. xvi.)

This combination of humility and dignity is yet more pointedly and convincingly outlined in this pithy sentence: "Condemning none, courting none, what can he do that is not good?" (Analects, bk. ix., c. xxvi., v. 2.)

Though Confucius was so insistent that his disciples should learn and practise the refinements of polite behaviour, he held the balance even, and at all times urged the greater importance of the real things of character. Complete sanity is in these discerning sentences: "Where the solid qualities are in excess of the accomplishments, we have rusticity; where the accomplishments are in excess of the solid qualities, we have the manners of a clerk; when the accomplishments and solid qualities are equally blended, we then have the man of complete virtue." (Analects, bk. vi., c. xvi.)

In the "Li Ki" the urgent need that one give reverent attention to propriety is thus phrased: "The superior man watches over the manner in which he maintains his intercourse with other men." (Bk. viii., sect. ii., v. 14.)

It is, however, not desirable that over-emphasis be laid upon unimportant details; for as Tsze-hea says in the "Analects": "When a person does not transgress the boundary-line of the great virtues, he may pass and repass it in the small virtues." (Analects, bk. xix., c. xi.)

There is, notwithstanding, something near to vehemence in this urgent adjuration that propriety is on no account to be neglected either in passive or in active moments: "Look not at what is contrary to propriety; listen not to what is contrary to propriety; speak not what is contrary to propriety; make no movement which is contrary to propriety!" (Analects, bk. xii., c. i., v. 2.)

This glowing picture of what the superior man, conversant with propriety and following its rules with discernment, sympathy, and enthusiasm, may become, already quoted from the " Doctrine of the Mean," is so illuminating in this connection that it is here repeated: "The superior man does what is proper to the station in which he is; he does not desire to go beyond this. In a position of wealth and honour he does what is proper to a position of wealth and honour; in a poor and low position, he does what is proper to a poor and low position; situated among barbarous tribes he does what is proper to a situation among barbarous tribes; in a position of sorrow and difficulty, he does what is proper to a position of sorrow and difficulty.

"The superior man can find himself in no position in which he is not himself. In a high situation he does not treat with contempt his inferiors, in a low situation he does not court the favour of his superiors; he rectifies himself, and seeks for nothing from others, so that he has no dissatisfaction." (Doctrine of the Mean, c. xiv.)

The influence and the value of such a man to his community he thus rates, when told that the tribes of the East, with whom he purposes to live, are rude: "If a superior man lived among them, what rudeness would there be?" (Analects, bk. ix., c. xiii., v. 2.)

Propriety of Demeanour. "Always and in everything let there be reverence, with the demeanour grave as when one is thinking deeply and with speech composed and definite." (Li Ki, bk. i., sect. i., pt. i., c. i.) "If the heart be for a moment without the feeling of harmony and joy, meanness and deceitfulness enter it. If the outward demeanour be for a moment without gravity and reverence, indifference and rudeness show themselves." (Li Ki, bk. xxi., sect. ii., 8.)

These two passages from the "Li Ki" illustrate the high estimate which the Chinese justly placed upon the value of grave demeanour. The idea is that between two superior men there is a communion of souls and a commerce one with another which results inevitably from virtuous purposes, high resolves, and the reflection of these in the attitude of one toward the other. This association the superior man values not merely for the opportunities for benevolence and influence which it affords, but also for that which it means for himself as well.

It was not for nothing that the Greek poets located the gods aloof from one another on the peaks of mountains, silent for the most part though in communion each with the others, and breaking the silence only when concerns of great import called for expression.

It is something like this which Confucius sets before the superior man, as the ideal. It is for this reason that he strongly affirms that the superior man should be grave and serious. Of this he says: "If the scholar be not grave, he will not call forth veneration, and his learning will not be solid." (Analects, bk. i., c. viii.)

By manners, it is almost needless to say, he did not mean anything at all similar to the mere gloss of one who is conversant with the rules of social behaviour, and who adroitly manipulates them to please this person or vent his spite on that; for one of his aptest texts runs: "Fine words and an insinuating appearance are seldom associated with true virtue." (Analects, bk. i., c. iii.)

Mencius thus illustrates the reward for frank demeanour and the sure detection of the contrary: "Of all the parts of a man's body there is none more excellent than the pupil of the eye. The pupil cannot hide a man's wickedness. If within the breast all be correct, the pupil is bright. If within the breast all be not correct, the pupil is dull. Listen to a man's words and look at the pupil of his eye. How can a man conceal his character?" (Bk. iv., pt. i., c. xv.)

This concerning the demeanour of Confucius is related in the "Analects": "The Master was mild but dignified; commanding but not fierce; respectful but easy." (Analects, bk. vii., c. xxxvii.)

Tsze-hea in the "Analects" thus depicts the demeanour of the superior man: "Looked at from a distance, he appears stern; when approached, he is mild; when he is heard to speak, his language is firm and decided." (Analects, bk. xix., c. ix.)

In another place Confucius contrasts the poise of the superior man with the pose of the man with low ideals, the one dignified without being conscious of it, the other constantly striving to show that control over himself and confidence in himself which he really does not possess. But the idea is better apprehended from the sage's own words: "The superior man has dignified ease without pride; the ordinary man has pride without dignified ease." (Analects, bk. xiii., c. xxvi.)

Propriety of Deportment. "It is virtuous manners which constitute the excellence of a neighbourhood. If a man in selecting a residence do not fix upon one where such prevail, how can he be wise?" (Analects, bk. iv., c. i.)

These words of the sage, taken from the "Analects," are characteristic. Confucius is more frequently accused of paying too much attention to propriety in manners than too little. Undoubtedly, he did place great stress both upon ceremonies and upon manners, but more upon the spirit that should inform them. How significant the ceremonies may have been in view of the traditions and customs of the people, it is impossible for men of this age living in Western countries to divine. But the canons of good manners which Confucius set up, although subjected to most critical examination, are found to be universal in scope and quite as valid today and in Western countries as in his day and in the East.

How universal and permanent they are, may be seen from this, taken from the "Li Ki": "Do not listen with head inclined on one side nor answer with a loud, sharp voice, nor look with a dissolute leer nor keep the body in a slouching position. Do not saunter about with a haughty gait nor stand with one foot raised. Do not sit with your knees wide apart nor lie face down." (Bk. i., sect. i., pt. iii., c. iv.)

This from the same book is so advanced that even in these modern days men in civilized Occidental countries have barely commenced to apprehend it: "When he intends to go to an inn, let it not be with the feeling that he must have whatever he asks for!" (Bk. i., sect. i., pt. ii., c. v., v. 2, 3.)

Undoubtedly he attached great importance to manners, in part because his whole system was one of breeding. It was his notion that a man should care about himself and therefore that his behaviour should comport with his real dignity and his sense of dignity.

One who so earnestly urged the necessity for absolute sincerity could scarcely be expected to praise that social polish which is both an affectation and a lie. He draws, indeed, a sharp distinction between the superior man, who is approachable and far from distant in manner but avoids flattery, and the man who behaves with hauteur, intended to wound and embarrass, toward all but those into whose favour he would ingratiate himself. He places them thus in contrast: "The superior man is affable but not adulatory; the inferior man is adulatory but not affable." (Analects, bk. xiii., c. xxiii.)

That by propriety in deportment is not meant subserviency, Confucius shows by his reply, when asked by his disciple, Tsze-loo, how a sovereign should be served: "Do not impose upon him, and moreover withstand him to his face." (Analects, bk. xiv., c. xxiii.) This counsel, it is worth remarking, was given by one who was the instructor of princes.

How minute, accurate, and well-taken were the rules of behaviour which he laid down is well illustrated by the following passages from the "Li Ki": "In all cases, looks directed up into the face denote pride, below the girdle grief, askance villainy." (Bk. i., sect. ii., pt. iii., c. vii.) "When a thing is carried with both hands, it should be held on a level with the heart; when with one hand, on a level with the girdle." (Bk. i., sect. ii., pt. i., c. i., v. 1.) "When sitting by a person of rank, if he begin to yawn and stretch himself, to turn round his tablet, to play with the head of his sword, to move his shoes about, or to ask about the time of day, one may ask leave to retire." (Bk. xv., 18.)

From a volume upon human conduct which betrays so fine and discriminating penetration, pit is not surprising that we may cull so choice an expression of good taste as this: "For great entertainments there should be . . . no great display of wealth." (Bk. i., sect. ii., pt. iii., c. ix.)

This acute perception of the most delicate distinctions was evidenced no more strongly, perhaps, in any of the marvellous sentences which have come down to this generation than in the following: "Of all people, girls and servants are the most difficult to behave to. If you are familiar with them, they lose their humility; if you maintain a reserve toward them, they are discontented." (Analects, bk. xvii., c. xxv.)

That youth, or rather childhood, is the period when development of character and therefore of deportment should commence, is ever in his thought. That the son should admire and imitate his father, and the father should make of himself a human being whom the son, without surrendering his power to see things as they are, might admire and imitate, was fundamental in the Confucian conception of the art of living.

Whatever indicated the contrary of admiration and respect of a son for his father was to him as to all right-minded men offensive and disgusting. He characterizes such a boy: "In youth not humble as befits a junior " (Analects, bk. xiv., c. xlvi.), and later excoriates him in the following burning sentences: "I observe that he is fond of occupying the seat of a full-grown man. I observe that he walks shoulder to shoulder with his elders. He is not one who is seeking to make progress in learning. He wishes quickly to become a man." (Analects, bk. xiv., c. xlvii., v. 2.)

That this might be avoided and that the manner as well as the purposes of the son might be directed into other and better channels, one of his disciples placed this requirement upon the father, whose parenthood vests him with responsibility for the manners of his offspring: "I have also heard that the superior man maintains a distant reserve toward his son." (Analects, bk. xvi., c. xiii., v. 5.)

Not one of the foregoing is inapplicable to the regrettable incivility of children in this buoyant but inconsiderate age; and surely no others are so sorely needed in these days of flippant disrespect for elders as these trenchant exposures of the inherent badness of the manners of Oriental youths of olden times.

It remained for Mencius to lay down the following obviously correct rule for the association of friends: "Friendship should be maintained without condescension on the ground of age, station, or family. Friendship with a man is friendship with his virtue and does not admit of assumptions of superiority." (Bk. v., pt. ii., c. iii., v. I.)

The views of the sage as to what constitutes the true spirit of polite deportment seem always to square with the maturest judgment of the most recent authorities. What trained gentleman of any school will fail to recognize, with a thrill of satisfaction, this expression of the fundamentally correct notion of sportsmanship, observable according to his disciples in the conduct of Confucius himself: "The Master angled, but did not use a net; he shot, but not at birds perching." (Analects, bk. vii., c. xxvi.)

Propriety of Speech. "They who meet men with smartness of speech, for the most part procure themselves hatred." (Analects, bk. v., c. iv., v. 2.)

That one should be most circumspect about his speech, Tsze-kung enforces, also in the "Analects," by saying: "For one word a man is often deemed to be wise and for one word he is often deemed to be foolish." (Bk. xix., c. xxv., v. 2.)

And especially that he should be cautious about making rash promises, Confucius thus enjoins: "He who speaks without modesty, will find it hard to make his words good." (Analects, bk. xiv., c. xxi.)

The same idea is more fully and explicitly developed in this passage of the "Li Ki": "The Master said: 'Dislike and reprisals will attend him whose promises from the lips do not ripen into fulfilment. Therefore the superior man incurs

rather the resentment due to refusal than the charge of breaking his promise. ' (Bk. xxix., 49.)

The need for caution in giving commands is urged in these apt words from the "Shu King" (pt. v., bk. xx., 4): "Be careful in the commands you issue; for, once issued, they must be carried into effect and cannot be retracted." And yet more generally, emphatically, and powerfully the reason for caution in speech in this striking passage of the " Shi King, "already quoted in another connection: "A flaw in a mace of white jade may be ground away, but a word spoken amiss cannot be mended." (Major Odes, decade iii., ode 2.)

The limits of proper admonition of a friend and the reasons therefor, Confucius also indicates thus: "Faithfully admonish your friend and try to lead him kindly. If you find him impracticable, stop; do not disgrace yourself!" (Analects, bk. xii., c. xxiii.)

This proverb furnishes yet another reason for great moderation in that respect: "Those whose courses are different cannot lay plans for one another." (Analects, bk. xv., c. xxxix.)

This also, which the "Analects" puts into the mouth of a madman, fixes the limits both of reproof and of the utility of reference to the past: "As to the past, reproof is useless, but the future may be provided against." (Bk. xviii., c. v., v. 1.)

Confucius dwells upon the same idea in another place: "Things that are done, it is needless to speak about; things that have had their course, it is needless to remonstrate about; things that are past, it is needless to blame." (Analects, bk. iii., c. xxi., v. 2.)

That one must watch carefully, lest he be misled by fair words, the sage shows, referring to his own experience: "At first, my way with men was to hear their words and give them credit for their conduct. Now my way is to hear their words and look at their conduct." (Analects, bk. v., c. ix., v. 2.)

Simplicity and directness of discourse are commended in all that Confucius says of sincerity of thought, candour of speech, and earnestness of conduct; but he rarely, if ever, put it better than in the following (Analects, bk. xvi., c. xl.): "In language it is sufficient that it convey the meaning"—*i.e.*, the precise meaning, not something other than what seems to be said or variant from it. To this, also, the sage refers, though to the part of the listener, rather than that of the speaker, when he says: "Without knowing the force of words, it is impossible to know men." (Analects, bk. xx., c. iii., v. 3.) That is, one must accurately understand what a man says, though it is, of course, necessary to look beneath the mere words in many cases in order to discover the true character of the man. To this, also, the sage gives expression thus: "The virtuous will be sure to speak aright; but not all whose speech is good are virtuous." (Analects, bk. xiv., c. v.)

In the "Li Ki," this is said of the superior men of old: "They did not peer into privacies nor form intimacies in matters aside from their proper business. They did not speak of old affairs nor wear an appearance of being in sport." (Bk. xv., 20.)

And the urgent reasons for care in speaking of important matters are thus presented in the "Yi King" (appendix iii., sect. i., c. viii., 47): "If important matters in the germ be not kept secret, that will be injurious to their accomplishment. Therefore the superior man is careful to maintain secrecy and does not allow himself to speak."

Regarding candour it was well said, not alone of worldly success, but yet more of self-development: "I know not how a man without truthfulness is to get on." (Analects, bk. ii., c. xxii.)

The craven character of deceit he often indicated and strongly condemned, as in these pregnant sentences: "Fine words, an insinuating appearance, and excessive respect; Tso-k'ew Ming was ashamed of them. I also am ashamed of them. To conceal resentment against a person and appear friendly with him; Tso-k'ew Ming was ashamed of such conduct. I also am ashamed of it." (Analects, bk. v., c. xxiv.)

The contempt with which such conduct is to be regarded, is thus described in the "Li Ki": "The Master said, The superior man does not merely look benign as if, while cold at heart, he could feign affection. That is of the inferior man and stamps him as no better than the sneak thief.'" (Bk. xxix., 50.) However covert such dissimulation may be, Confucius finds it equally reprehensible and degrading. Thus, again in the "Li Ki" it is written: "The Master said, 'When on light grounds a man breaks off his friendship with the poor, and only on weighty grounds with the rich and influential, his love of merit must be small and his contempt for meanness is not seen.'" (Bk. xxx., 21.)

And in the same book the more elusive hypocrisy of decrying what a man himself indulges in, is discovered and condemned, thus: "To disapprove of the conduct of another and yet to do the same himself, is contrary to the rule of instruction." (Bk. xxii., 12.)

Here is yet another unflattering picture, taken from the "Analects," of the unhappy and most undesirable state of the dissembler who is keeping up appearances: "Having not and yet affecting to have, empty and yet affecting to be full, straitened and yet affecting to be at ease, it is difficult with such characteristics to have constancy." (Bk. vii., c. xxv., v. 3.)

And here a picture of yet another type of man, going about deceiving himself, rather than others, because what he is shows through: "Ardent and yet not upright; stupid and yet not attentive; simple and yet not sincere: such persons I do not understand." (Analects, bk. viii., c. xvi.)

That such dissimulation must ever be unsuccessful in the end, Confucius asserted in many places, in no other perhaps more persuasively than in this: "See what a man does! Mark his motives! Examine in what things he rests! How can a man conceal his character?" (Analects, bk. ii., c. x.)

Or in this from "The Great Learning" (c. vi., v. 2): "There is no evil to which the inferior man, dwelling retired, will not proceed; but when he sees a superior man, he instantly tries to disguise himself, concealing his evil and displaying what is good. The other beholds him, as if he saw his heart and reins; of what use is his disguise? This is an instance of that saying, 'What truly is within will be manifested without.'"

That without being continually on his guard and therefore constantly the slave of suspicion, the superior man, with his own mind open and sincere, should readily detect the attempt to delude him, however cleverly designed and executed, Confucius advanced as follows: "He who does not anticipate attempts to deceive him, nor think beforehand of his not being believed, and yet apprehends these things readily when they occur, is he not a man of superior worth?" (Analects, bk. xiv., c. xxxiii.)

That the chief peril is to him who would deceive others, that is, that he will himself deceive, Confucius says in this: "Specious words confound virtue." (Analects, bk. xv., c. xxvi.)

Precisely as in all else, none the less, it is in earnestness and candour possible to go to excess; in this as in everything, to go too far is as bad as to fall short. Thus there are hidden things of life, intimate relations, tender ties, too private and sacred to be talked of. Of such, it is said: "I hate those who make secrets known and think that they are straightforward." (Analects, bk. xvii., c. xxiv.)

Candour may thus degenerate into indiscreet chattering. Obviously, when directed at the faults of others, it may also become incivility, unless tempered by considerate good-will and training in deportment. They, for instance, who would push their requirements as to frankness to a prohibition of the polite evasion, "Mr. So-and-so is not at home," will find little encouragement in the following revelations as to the ancient custom upon similar occasions, with which Confucius complied, as with all other ceremonies, such constituting a language of their own: "Joo Pei wished to see Confucius, but Confucius declined to see him on the ground of being ill. When the bearer of this message went out at the door, he took the harpsichord and sang to it, in order that Pei might hear him." (Analects, bk. xvii. c. xx.)

Mencius thus characterizes both the impropriety and the injudiciousness of over-candour: "What future misery do they have and ought they to have, who talk of what is not good in others!" (Bk. iv., pt. ii., c. ix.)

Confucius puts this in two ways, each illustrative of something which is wanting when such takes place: "There is the love of straightforwardness without the love of learning; the beclouding here leads to rudeness." (Analects, bk. xvii., c. viii., v. 3.) "Straightforwardness, without the rules of propriety, becomes rudeness." (Analects, bk. viii., c. ii., v. 1.)

Propriety of Conduct. "What I do not wish men to do to me, I also wish not to do to men." (Analects, bk. v., c. xi.)

This text from the "Analects" of Confucius is more widely known among English-speaking people than is any other; and is very generally understood to be a merely colourless, negative phase of the Golden Rule.

But even in the days of Confucius it had developed into a standard for human conduct, broad and of general application. Thus, when Tsze-kung asked, "Is there any one word which may serve as a rule of practice for all one's life?" the Master replied: "Is not 'Reciprocity' such a word? What you do not want done to yourself, do not do to others!" (Analects, bk. xv., c. xxiii.)

This is far indeed from being all that Confucius says upon the subject; for in "The Great Learning" (c. x., v. 10) is found this extended and thorough exposition of his views: "What a man dislikes in those who are over him, let him not display toward those who are under him; what he dislikes in those who are under him, let him not display toward those who are over him! What he hates in those who are ahead of him, let him not therewith precede those who are behind him; and what he hates in those who are behind him, let him not therewith pursue those who are ahead of him! What he hates to receive upon the right, let him not bestow upon the left; and what he hates to receive upon the left, let him not bestow upon the right! This is called the standard, by which, as by a measuring square, to regulate one's conduct."

Confucius, indeed, put the performance of the duties due to one's fellowman above all other duties, except that of self-development, with which he found it to be in no way inconsistent. Thus he placed it far above the duty of ancestor communion—miscalled "worship" by Occidentals—then as now the prevailing religious ceremony in China, in a memorable colloquy with one of his disciples: "Ke Loo asked about serving the spirits of the dead. The Master said: 'While you are not able to serve men, how can you serve spirits?'" (Analects, bk. xi., c. xi.)

The same, in a slightly different form, he repeated at another time, saying: "To give one's self earnestly to the duties due to men, and, while respecting spiritual beings, to keep aloof from them, may be called wisdom." (Analects, bk. vi., c. xx.)

The philosophy of human service and of duty to others, as a necessary means of self-development, was surely never better expressed than in these words: "Now the man of perfect virtue, wishing to be confirmed himself, confirms others; wishing to be enlarged himself, enlarges others." (Analects, bk. vi., c. xxviii., v. 2.)

The contrast between this obviously correct rule of human conduct and the unedifying spectacle of the brutal struggle for success which marks and mars the picture of modern business and social life, renders this moral enlightenment of the highest importance to men of the here and now. Confucius phrases it, however, even more beautifully and with added meaning, thus:

"The superior man seeks to develop the admirable qualities of men and does not seek to develop their evil qualities. The inferior man does the opposite of this." (Analects, bk. xii., c. xvi.)

In the "Li Ki," Tsang-tsze is represented as saying with his failing breath, when death had come upon him: "The superior man loves on grounds of virtue; the inferior man's love appears in his indulgence." (Bk. ii., sect. i., pt. i., 18.)

Mencius indicates, however, the limitations of this, namely, that one should not be urging that excellence of conduct upon others which he indulgently neglects himself: "The evil of men is that they like to be teachers of others." (Bk. iv., pt. i., c. xxiii.)

The discriminating and judicial character of the superior man's respect and regard for others is well put in the "Li Ki," thus: "Men of talents and virtue can be familiar with others and yet respect them; can stand in awe of others and yet love them. They can love others and yet recognize the evil that is in them." (Bk. i., sect. i., pt. i., c. iii.)

And Confucius has said in the "Analects": "Pih-e and Shuh-ts'e did not keep the former wickedness of men in mind, and hence the resentments directed towards them were few." (Analects, bk. v., c. xxii.)

The same sentiment of broad charity the sage displays in this declaration of his own personal policy: "If a man purify himself to wait upon me, I receive him, so purified, without endorsing his past conduct." (Analects, bk. vii., c. xxviii., v. 2.)

Confucius did not, however, concur in the view that charity should be so all-embracing as utterly to lose sight of distinctions between men. On the contrary he sturdily reprobated that notion. He often urged the recognition of the special ties of kinship and of friendship, as thus in the "Li Ki": "I have heard that relatives should not forget their relationship nor friends their friendship." (Bk. ii., sect. ii., pt. iii., 24.)

And in the "Yi King" (Appendix iii., sect. i., c. viii., v. 43) appears this beautiful tribute to friendship by Confucius:

"This in public office toils;
 That at home the time beguiles;
 One his lips with silence seals,
 One his inmost soul reveals.
 But when two are one at heart,
 Bolts will not keep them apart;
 Words they in communion use
 Orchids' fragrances diffuse."

In the time of Confucius, the religious teacher, Lao Tsze, was laying the foundations of Taoism, the most widely resorted to of all the forms of worship of Chinese origin other than reverence for and communion with departed ancestors. Lao Tsze urged the validity of the rule of conduct: "Love thine enemies!" Inquiry was made of Confucius regarding this, resulting in the following dialogue: "Some one said, 'What do you say concerning the principle that injury should be recompensed with kindness?' The Master said: 'With what then will you recompense kindness? Recompense injury with justice and recompense kindness with kindness!'" (Analects, bk. xiv., c. xxxvi.)

Confucius also went much further than this; for he taught that there is a duty to hate men who evince certain evil traits of character, wherever found, and that this duty is as binding as the other. He says (Analects, bk. iv., c. iii.): "It is only the truly virtuous man who can love, or who can hate, others," by which it is understood that he who is not of virtuous purpose loves only in order that he may selfishly enjoy, and hates on personal grounds; while the virtuous man loves because he finds that which should be loved, and in order to bless, and also hates that which is worthy of hate and not because of any personal offence.

In the following colloquy are a few specimens of the courses of conduct which one is privileged to hate, as Confucius sees it:

"Tsze-kung said, 'Has the superior man his hatreds also?' The Master said: 'He has his hatreds. He hates those who proclaim evil in others. He hates the man who, being of a low station, slanders his superiors. He hates those who have valour merely and are unobservant of the rules of propriety. He hates those who are forward and determined and, at the same time, of contracted understanding.'

"The Master then inquired, 'Tsze, have you also your hatreds?' Tsze-kung replied: 'I hate those who pry out matters and ascribe the knowledge to their wisdom. I hate those who are only not modest and think that they are brave. I hate those who reveal secrets and think that they are straightforward.'" (Analects, bk. xvii., c. xxiv.)

In another place, he has said: "I hate those who with their sharp tongues overthrow kingdoms and families." (Analects, bk. xvii., c. xviii.)

Yet Confucius said that a youth "should overflow with love for all." (Analects, bk. i., c. vi.)

The policy, even the necessity, for this course is thus indicated in the "Shu King": "To evoke love, one must love; to evoke respect, one must respect." (Pt. iv., bk. iv., 2.)

And Confucius was so far from intending that what he said of hatred for the wrong-doer should be interpreted as merely rancorous dislike of an unfortunate human being, the victim of evil influences, that, when asked by Fan-Ch'e about benevolence, he replied: "It is to love all men." (Analects, bk. xii., c. xxii., v. 1.)

Propriety of Example. "There are three friendships which are advantageous and three which are injurious. Friendship with the upright, friendship with the sincere, and friendship with the man of much observation—these are advantageous. Friendship with the man of specious airs, friendship with the insinuatingly soft, and friendship with the glib-tongued—these are injurious." (Analects, bk. xvi., c. iv.)

Confucius, in addition to the foregoing, numbered among "the three things men find enjoyment in, which are advantageous," this: "to find enjoyment in having many worthy friends"; and said that a youth "should . . . cultivate the friendship of the good." (Analects, bk. i., c. vi.) One of the traits, also, of him "who aims to be a man of complete virtue" is, he declares, that "he frequents the company of men of principle that he may be rectified." (Analects, bk. i., c. xiv.)

In the "Li Ki," the converse is remarked: "Friendship with the dissolute leads to the neglect of one's learning." (Bk. xvi., 12.)

And in the "Shu King" (pt. v., bk. xxvi.) Mu is recorded as voicing this warning: "Cultivate no intimacy with flatterers!"

The same ancient worthy is represented in the "Shu King" (bk. xxvi.) to have uttered this admonition: "Do not employ men of artful speech and insinuating looks!"

Confucius obviously intended to give the same counsel, when he said: "Fine words and an insinuating appearance are seldom associated with real virtue." (Analects, bk. i., c. iii.)

The contrast between the meritorious and the meretricious in human character and of the usefulness of one and the harmfulness of the other is most cleverly revealed in this saying of Confucius, taken from the "Li Ki" (bk. xxix., 47): "The superior man seems uninteresting but he aids to achievement, the inferior man winning but he leads to ruin."

Prudence as regards conversation and association with others is also variously recommended by Confucius, as thus: "When a man may be spoken with, not to speak with him is to waste opportunity. When a man may not be spoken with, to speak with him is to waste words." (Analects, bk. xv., c. vii.)

The last of these admonitions he elsewhere puts figuratively, thus: "Rotten wood cannot be carved; a wall of dirty earth will not receive the trowel." (Analects, bk. v., c. ix., v. 2.)

The same idea recurs in this counsel: "Faithfully admonish your friend and kindly try to lead him. If you find him impracticable, desist; do not disgrace yourself." (Analects, bk. xii., c. xxiii.)

Also in this warning against unnecessary admonitions: "In serving a prince, frequent remonstrances lead to disgrace. Between friends, frequent reproofs make the friendship distant." (Analects, bk. iv., c. xxvi.)

The three wishes, however, to which Confucius gave expression when interrogated by Tsze-loo, were: "In regard to the aged, to give them rest; in regard to friends, to show them sincerity; in regard to the young, to treat them tenderly." (Analects, bk. v., c. xxv.)

It therefore appears that he would not withhold his counsel or even reproof, if needed, although it might result in breaking the bonds of friendship; but would instead prefer to lose his friend, if need be, rather than fail of his full duty toward him. The attitude which the friend should take and the course, likewise, are indicated in these words: "Can men refuse assent to the words of just admonition? But it is reforming the conduct because of them, which is the thing." (Analects, bk. ix., c. xxiii.)

The great value of good example Confucius strikingly set forth in this question: "If there were not virtuous men in Loo, how could this man have acquired this character?" (Analects, bk. v., c. ii.)

So also when remonstrated with, upon expressing his intention to go and live among the nine wild tribes of the east, Confucius, answering, inquired: "If a superior man dwelt among them, what rudeness would there be?" (Analects, bk. ix., c. xiii., v. 2.)

In another place he says (Analects, bk. i., c. viii., v. 3): "Have no friends not equal to yourself!" meaning thereby of course not that they should be equal in abilities, necessarily, but equal in character and deportment. The same, very nearly, is the significance of this text: "When the persons on whom a man leans are proper persons for him to be intimate with, he can make them his guides and masters." (Analects, bk. i., c. xiii.)

This his disciples, with boundless admiration, asserted that they had themselves obeyed, when they had hung upon the lips of Confucius; for they leave this panegyric of their teacher: "Our Master cannot be attained to, precisely as the heavens cannot be scaled by the steps of a ladder." (Analects, bk. xix., c. xxv., v. 2.)

That the wisdom of this counsel is not confined to the case of a single associate, but instead extends to all associations both individual and communal, is shown by this additional text, already quoted in another connexion: "It is virtuous manners which constitute the excellence of a neighbourhood. If a man in selecting a residence do not fix on one where such prevail, how can he be wise?" (Analects, bk. iv., c. i.)

Yet the evil in man is useful for instruction, as well as the good; and he says of this: "When I walk along with two others, they may serve me as my teachers. I will select their good qualities and follow them, their bad qualities and avoid them." (Analects, bk. vii., c. xxi.)

And in another place he warns his disciples, saying: "When we see men of worth, we should think of equalling them; when we see men of a contrary character, we should turn inwards and examine ourselves." (Analects, bk. iv., c. xvii.)

This does not, however, necessarily imply that he advises association with the latter nor indeed does he, though he says of himself: "It is impossible for me to associate with birds and beasts, as if they were the same with us. If I associate not with these people—with mankind—with whom am I to associate?" (Analects, bk. xviii., c. vi., v. 4.)

In reply to doubts expressed by his disciples, however, Confucius on one occasion defended himself in a manner very like the response of Jesus, saying: "I admit people's approach to me without committing myself as to what they may do when they have retired. Why must one be so severe? If a man purify himself to wait upon me, I receive him, so purified, without endorsing his past conduct." (Analects, bk. vii., c. xxviii., v. 2.)

It is interesting and refreshing to find in Confucius something akin to the sage words of the Elder Edda: "Unwise is he who permits the grass to grow between his house and his friend's." It runs: "'How the flowers of the aspen-plum flutter and turn! Do I not think of you? But your house is distant.' The Master said: 'It is the want of thought over it. How is it distant?'"

(Analects, bk. ix., c. xxx.) That the truly virtuous man will not want for companionship, the sage thus declares: "Virtue is not left to stand alone. He who practises it, will have neighbours." (Analects, bk. iv., c. xxv.)

This is but another way of saying what is elsewhere so well said in these words: "Let the superior man never fail reverentially to order his own conduct, and let him be respectful to others and observant of propriety; then all within the four seas will be his brothers." (Analects, bk. xii., c. v., v. 4.)

Sexual Propriety. "The scholar keeps himself free from all stain." (Li Ki, bk. xxxviii., 15.) "The Master said, 'Refusing to surrender their wills or to submit to any taint to their persons; such, I think, were Pih-e and Shuh-ts'e.'" (Analects, bk. xviii., c. viii., v. 2.) These two passages illustrate the sage's insistence upon sexual continence, among other virtues.

While of course personal purity is a conception which, both in ancient China and in the modern Occident, embraces much more than this, and while abuses of the appetites for food or drink, or even of the more unconsciously exercised appetite for breathing, as in smoking, may contaminate in essentially the same fashion as the misuse of the function which reproduces the race of men, yet both in the days of Confucius and in these later days the superior seductiveness of the appeal of feminine beauty causes the mind to recur at once to chastity when personal purity is spoken of.

Confucius distinguished and understood all of these evil habits which were exigent in his day and condemned them, as thus: "To find enjoyment in extravagant pleasures, to find enjoyment in idleness and sauntering, to find enjoyment in the pleasures of feasting—these are injurious." (Analects, bk. xvi., c. v.)

And again: "Hard is the case of him who will stuff himself with food the whole day, without applying the mind to anything." (Analects, bk. xvii., c. xxii.)

As regards all the physical functions, Mencius puts at once the problem and the difficulties, thus: "The physical organs with their functions belong to our Heaven-conferred nature. But a man must be a sage before he can satisfy the design of his physical organism." (Bk. vii., pt. i., c. xxxviii.)

But especially as respects the greatest of all human relations, that of a man with a woman, and those which grow out of it, the sage urged such regard for the purity of both sexes as would assure the suppression of mere playing with the means of the greatest of all human ends, the bringing of new lives into being and the development of higher and yet higher orders of human beings upon the earth. In the "Li Ki" it is thus insisted that the distinction between men and women must be observed and preserved for the good of all: "If no distinction were observed between males and females, disorder would arise and grow." (Bk. xvii., sect. i., 32.)

King Wan, one of the most celebrated rulers of China, in the time of Confucius already a character of almost legendary antiquity, is said in the first Appendix to the "Yi King" (sect. ii., c. xxxviii., v. 3) to have given this reason for the necessary distinction and separation of men from women: "Heaven and earth are separate and apart, but the work which they do is the same. Male and female are separate and apart, but with a common will they seek the same objects."

This rule of separation did not withdraw woman into the absolute seclusion of a harem; it permitted innocent intercourse of mind with mind. But, according to the "Li Ki," it avoided all physical contact and, so far as possible, all opportunities for it.

These are some of the rules there laid down: "The Master said, 'According to the rules, male and female do not give the cup, one to the other, except at sacrifice. This was intended to guard the people.'" (Bk. xxvii., 35.) "Males and females should not sit on the same mat, nor have the same stand or rack for their clothes, nor use the same towel or comb, nor let their hands touch in giving and receiving." (Bk. i., sect. i., pt. iii., c. vi., v. 31.) "They should not share the same mat in lying down, they should not ask or receive anything from one another, and they should not wear upper or lower garments alike." (Bk. x., sect. i., 12.)

The following explanation of the reasons for such separation is attributed in the "Li Ki" to Confucius himself: "The Master said: 'The ceremonial usages serve as dykes for the people against evil excesses. They exemplify the separation between the sexes which should be maintained, that there may be no ground for suspicion and human relations may be clearly defined. . . . So it was intended to guard the people; yet there are women among them who offer themselves.'" (Bk. xxvii., 33.)

In a more extended passage, also attributed to Confucius, the reason for the strictness of the rules is more fully stated, together with illustrations of their application, as follows: "The Master said: 'The love of virtue should balance the love of beauty. Men of position should not be like anglers for beauty in those below them. The superior man withstands the allurements of beauty, to give an example to the people. Thus men and women, in giving and receiving, allow not their hands to touch; in driving even with his wife in his carriage, a husband holds forth his left hand; when a young aunt, a sister, or a daughter is wed and returns to her father's house, no male relative should sit with her upon the mat; a widow should not lament at night; in asking after a wife who is ill, the nature of her illness should not be referred to. Thus it was sought to guard the people. Yet there are those who become licentious and introduce disorder and confusion into their families.'" (Li Ki, bk. xxvii., 37.)

There was no relaxation of this separation before marriage. Thus Mencius says: "When a son is born, what is desired for him is that he may have a wife; when a daughter is born, that she may have a husband. All men as parents have this feeling. If, without awaiting the instructions of their parents and the arrangements of the intermediary, they bore holes to steal a sight of each other, or climb over a wall to be with each other, their parents and all others will despise them." (Bk. iii., pt. ii., c. iii., v. 6.)

In the "Yi King" (appendix iii., sect. i., c. viii., 48) the adornment of women so as to attract men is thus referred to: "Careless laying up of things excites to robbery, as a woman's adorning herself excites to lust."

Under the rules laid down in the "Li Ki" this delicacy about sex was carried so far that "a man was not permitted to die in the hands of women, nor a woman in the hands of men!" (Bk. xix., sect. i., I.)

Confucius and for centuries before his time the dominant persons in Chinese society were firm believers in the home as the sphere of woman. Within the home she was supreme; the privacies of her realm should not be revealed without, nor the hardships and worries of the outside world brought within to annoy and terrify her. In the "Li Ki" it is said: "The men should not speak of what belongs to the inside of the house, nor the women of what belongs to the outside." (Bk. x., sect. i., 12.)

And again: "Outside affairs should not be talked of inside the home, nor inside affairs outside of it." (Bk. i., sect. i., pt. iii., c. vi., v. 33.)

The severity of the rules enjoined by Confucius and his Chinese predecessors in the matter of avoiding temptation is well illustrated by the following, the enforcement of which must have rendered the childhood and youth of the sage, himself the only son of a widow, unusually and even painfully solitary at times:

"The Master said: 'One does not pay visits to the son of a widow. This may seem an obstacle to friendship, but the superior man, in order to avoid suspicion, will make no visits in such a case. Hence, also, in calling upon a friend, if the master of the house be not at home, unless there be some great cause for it, the guest does not cross the threshold.'" (Bk. xxvii., 36.)

Chapter Four - The Family

WITH the Chinese, as with the ancient Romans, the family is the social unit, and Confucius has much to say on this subject. As he connected propriety, the relation of a man to his fellows, with self-development, so he does even more intimately the relation of a man to the members of his household.

Prerequisites to its Regulation. "What is meant by 'The regulation of one's own family depends on his self-development' is this: Men are partial where they feel affection and love, partial where they despise and dislike, partial where they stand in awe and reverence, partial where they feel sorrow and compassion, partial where they are arrogant and harsh. Thus it is that there are few men in the world who love and at the same time know the bad qualities of them they love or who hate and yet know the excellences of them they hate. Hence it is said, in the common adage: 'A man does not know the wickedness of his son; he does not know the richness of his growing corn.'

This is what is meant by saying that if there is not self-development, a man cannot regulate his family." (Great Learning, c. viii.)

The idea expressed in this passage from "The Great Learning" seems to be that the love of an inferior man for his family is not really affectionate regard for the welfare of wife or child but merely an indulgent disposition, permitting them, partly through favour, partly because to take the trouble to regulate them is too great a detriment to his own personal comfort, to go their own way without restraint. Such, the sage conceives, is the conduct of the inferior man whose partiality so blinds him to the faults of those whom he loves, that he cannot bring himself to correct them. The superior man, he holds, should be, and indeed necessarily is, of the contrary view and practice. Of this it is said in the "Li Ki": "The superior man commences with respect as the basis of love. To omit respect is to leave no foundation for affection. Without love there can be no union; without respect the love will be ignoble." (Bk. xxiv., 9.)

Precisely the opposite of mere indulgent laxity is indicated as the course of the superior man in respect to his family; and it is asked by Confucius with full assurance as to what the reply must be if veracious: "Can there be love which does not lead to strictness with its objects?" (Analects, bk. xiv., c. viii.)

The essential mutuality and the prerequisites of that union of hearts upon which alone true marriage may rest, and by means of which alone lifelong existence in the closest of human relations is tolerable, are well set forth in this sentiment from the lips of I Yin, the minister of King Thang, which is found in the "Shu King": "To evoke love, you must love; to call forth respect, you must show respect." (Pt. iv., bk. iv., 2.)

For the purposes of discipline within the family, as well as for material support and protection, the woman was counselled to subject herself to the man. In the "Li Ki" it was ordered thus: "The woman follows the man. In her youth she follows her father and elder brother; when married, she follows her husband; when her husband is dead, she follows her son." (Bk. ix., 10.)

About the worst that, in the opinion of Confucius, could be said of any man, was this remark of Yu, in the "Shu King," speaking of Ku of Tan, son of Yao: "He introduced licentious associates into his family." (Pt. ii., bk. iv., 1.)

The delights of a well-ordered household, where love and harmony hold sway, are pictured by the sage as follows: "It is said in the Book of Poetry: 'A happy union with wife and children is like the music of lutes and harps! When there is concord among brethren, the harmony is delightful and enduring. Thus may you regulate your family and enjoy the delights of wife and children!' The Master said, 'In such a condition parents find perfect contentment.'" (Doctrine of the Mean, C. xv., v. 2, 3.)

Wedlock. "The observance of propriety commences with careful attention to the relations between husband and wife." (Li Ki, bk. x., sect. ii., 13.)

In these words, the "Li Ki," the book of the rules of propriety, celebrates the prime importance of the marriage relation and of the useful principles for the regulation of human conduct which spring out of it. This was a favourite and familiar idea of Confucius and will be adverted to frequently in the development of his theories of the regulation of the family and of the government.

In his days, as in these days, there were not wanting those who saw in marriage a mere ceremony, conformity with which added no element of sacredness to a natural and necessary relation. These were rebuked in the "Li Ki" in these terms: "He who thinks the old embankments useless and destroys them, is sure to suffer from the desolation caused by overflowing water; and he who should consider the old rules of propriety useless and abolish them, would be sure to suffer from the calamities of disorder. Thus if the ceremonies of marriage were discontinued, the path of husband and wife would be embittered and there would be many offences of licentiousness and depravity." (Bk. xxiii., 7, 8.)

Again in the same book this is put tersely and pointedly, thus: "This ceremony [*i.e.*, marriage] lies at the foundation of government." (Bk. xxiv., 11.) In the "Doctrine of the Mean," the "duties of universal obligation" are given as follows: "The duties are between sovereign and minister, father and son, husband and wife, elder and younger brother, friend and friend." (C. xx., v. 8.)

In the "Elder Tai's Book of Rites" (bk. lxxx.), are certain advisory regulations as to the choice of a wife, chiefly that she shall be of a family of a high standard of moral conduct and shall not be a daughter of a disloyal house, of a disorderly house, of a house with more than one generation of criminals or of a leprous house, nor be taken if the mother is dead and the daughter is old.

The one inexorable rule as regards marriage was this: "The Master said: 'A man in taking a wife does not choose one of the same surname as himself.'" (Li Ki, bk. xxvii., 34.)

This, rather than any other rule based upon kinship, was enforced because the wife was considered to merge herself in her husband's family, to join in sacrifices to his ancestors and to give her life over to bearing and rearing sons to continue his race and to preserve his ancestral temples. She thus lost her relationship to her own kindred, during the continuance of the marriage relation, and permanently unless it were dissolved by divorce; and therefore relatives on the mothers' side, however near, were not considered to be within the prohibited degrees of consanguinity, while relatives on the father's side, however remote, were so esteemed.

In the "Tso Chuan" or "Tso's Commentary" the following reason for this rule is given: "When husband and wife are of the same surname, their children do not do well and multiply."

This observation, applied, however, to relatives on either side, is in harmony with the most modern discoveries concerning the effect of persistent inbreeding as well as modern views of propriety. In "Spring and Autumn" and later in the "Code of the Ts'ing Dynasty" (c. x.), this was extended to proscribe marriages within certain degrees of relationship on the mother's side. The wife became, by her marriage, of the same rank as her husband, thus being identified closely with his family. In the "Li Ki" it is said of this: "Though the wife had no rank, she was held to be of the rank of her husband and she took her seat according to the position belonging to him." (Bk. ix., sect. iii., 11.)

The demoralizing "morganatic" marriage, indulged by certain royalties of Europe, is accordingly unknown in China.

As a part of the ceremony of marriage, the bridegroom went in person to bring his bride home to his father's house, where she became a member of his father's family and a daughter to his mother. This is referred to in the "Li Ki" as follows: "The bridegroom went in person to meet the bride, the man taking the initiative and not the woman—according to the idea that regulates the relation between the strong and the weak." (Bk. ix., sect. iii., 8.)

In the same book there is recorded an argument upon the propriety of this custom, in which Confucius is represented as taking part. The record runs as follows: "The duke said, '. . . For the bridegroom in his square-topped cap to go in person to meet his bride, is it not making too much of it?' Confucius looked surprised, became very serious and said, 'It is the union of two sur-names in friendship and love, to continue the posterity of the sages of old, to supply those who shall preside at the sacrifices to Heaven and Earth, at sacri-fices to ancestors, at sacrifices to the spirits of the land and grain; how can you, then, call the ceremony too great?'" (Bk. xxiv., 10.)

Mencius thus quotes from the Ritual the instructions which the bride's mother gives her in view of the approaching nuptials: "At the marriage of a young woman, her mother admonishes her, accompanying her to the door on her leaving and cautioning her with these words, 'You are going to your home. You must be respectful. You must be careful. Do not disobey your husband!'" (Bk. iii., pt. ii., c. ii., v. 2.)

Though the Chinese girl was brought up, then as now, with matrimony in view as her goal, and though she was trained with an eye to subjection to her husband in the regulation of the family and to obedience to her husband's mother in the home, it does not appear that she was trained in respect to rearing of children; for of this it is said in "The Great Learning" (c. ix., v. 2): "If a mother is really anxious to do so, though she may not hit precisely the wants of her child, she will not be far from it. There has never been a girl who learned to bring up a child, that she might afterwards marry."

Concubinage was then and theretofore, as now, also an institution in China and is recognized by Confucius and rules laid down also for its regulation. The relationship was treated as not less regular than that of marriage but it in-volved lower standing for the concubine and her offspring; notwithstanding which frequently the wife's younger sister became the concubine, not without the active connivance of the wife, lonely amid unfamiliar surroundings and longing for the companionship of her own kin. The wife had dominion in the home over concubines and their children.

The double standard was therefore known and its consequences openly accepted, though in the majority of homes one wife reigned supreme and, as has been seen, it was such a home the felicity of which Confucius portrayed in his tribute to the marriage relation, quoted at the close of the next preceding subdivision.

Concubinage was deemed not merely permissible but commendable when the wife remained barren or even when there were daughters but no son to perpetuate the name of the husband and maintain the altars of devotion of his ancestors. Had it been otherwise, undoubtedly divorces, with their hardships, would have been more common and would have extended to most cases of infertility, even though no personal incompatibility accompanied it.

The institution of concubinage cast no doubt upon the parentage of any child; no other woman could claim the maternity nor was the paternity of the child of the wife or of the concubine rendered dubious thereby. To this circumstance, perhaps, is attributable the countenance given to this form of the double standard. The contrary condition, i.e., that want of fidelity on the part of the woman exposes her progeny to question as to their paternity, doubtless accounts for the great stress then and ever placed upon fidelity on the part of woman. This applies, of course, to concubine as to wife and for the same reason; but constancy is, notwithstanding, deemed pre-eminently the virtue of a wife.

The dignity of marriage and of procreation is thought by Confucius and his followers to be such that the husband and wife, together with Heaven, form a "ternion," co-operating to people the earth, in that wherever there is true marriage, there also God is to give the increase. It is thus put in Ku-liang's Commentary: "The female alone cannot procreate; the male alone cannot propagate; and Heaven alone cannot produce a man. The three collaborating, man is born. Hence any one may be called the son of his mother or the son of Heaven."

And in "Many Dewdrops of the Spring and Autumn" (bk. lxx.), this passage strongly emphasizes the function of the divine forces in the reproduction of men: "There has never been a birth without the collaboration of Heaven. God is the creator of all men."

In the "Li Ki," the sacredness and permanence of marriage are thus inculcated: "Faithfulness is requisite in all service of others and faithfulness is especially the virtue of a wife. Once mated with her husband, all her life she will not change her feeling of duty to him; hence, when the husband dies, she will not marry again." (Bk. ix., sect. iii., 7.)

Divorce. In the Confucian conception of marriage, based upon the ancient Chinese customs, there seems to be more constraint about entering into wedlock than about continuing in it.

Thus a father might choose the bride for his son, though of course conceivably the son might—but under the Chinese rules of family discipline, seldom would—refuse to accept the choice. The father of the bride was then approached by the father of the prospective bridegroom; his consent was the consent of his daughter. Of course, again, she could refuse to acquiesce and a considerate father would not coerce her choice; but filial obedience and confidence were often the only elements operative in determining that choice.

It was thus, indeed, that the marriage which resulted in the birth of Confucius came about. It was between a widower of seventy years, already the father of nine daughters but of only one son, a hopeless cripple, on the one hand, and a maiden of seventeen years on the other, both of whose older sisters had declined the offer while she followed her father's counsel.

Once wedded, however, the husband and the wife were free to separate at will and without constraint, save as the authority of the husband's parents over him—not relaxed upon his marriage—might restrain him. Marriage, therefore, was treated as a contract which was at all times mutual, binding only as the parties continued to consent that it should bind. Either party could with a word dissolve it.

In the "Li Ki" the following account is given of the proper forms to be observed in divorcement: "When a feudal lord sent his wife away, she proceeded on her journey to her own state, and was received there with the observances due a lord's wife. The messenger accompanying her then discharged his commission, saying: 'My poor master, from his want of ability, was not able to follow her and to take part in the services at your altars and in your ancestral temple. He has, therefore, sent me, so-and-so; and I venture to inform your officer, appointed for the purpose, of what he has done.' The officer presiding on this occasion replied: 'My poor master in his former communication to you did not inform you about her and he does not presume to do anything but to receive your master's message, respectfully.' The officers in attendance on the commissioner then set forth the various articles sent with the lady on her marriage and those on the other side received them.

"When the wife went away from her husband, she sent a messenger and took leave of him, saying: 'So-and-so, through her want of ability, is not able to keep on supplying the vessels of grain for your sacrifices; and has sent me, so-and-so, to presume to announce this to your attendants.' The principal party on the other side replied: 'My son, in his inferiority, does not presume to avoid your punishing him, and dares not but respectfully receive your orders.' The messenger then retired, the principal party bowing to him and escorting him. If the husband's father were living, he named himself as principal party; if he were dead, an elder brother of the husband acted for him and the message was given as from him; if there were no elder brother, it ran as from the husband, himself." (Bk. xviii., sect. ii., pt. ii., 34, 35.)

Though this was given in the "Li Ki" or book of the rules of propriety as a description of the customs of the ancients of high rank, it was intended, with such modifications in the matter of greater directness and simplicity as the lowliness and poverty of the parties might require, to supply rules of ceremony for the divorce of all mismated husbands and wives.

The utter absence of recrimination and abuse, due of course to the circumstance that charges of evil conduct were not required as a condition to the divorce being allowed and that, instead, the mere will of either party was enough, contrasts—to the advantage of which need not be said—sharply and strongly with the invasion of family privacy, the exposure of family shame, and the defamation of character which accompany divorce proceedings under the laws of the advanced civilization of Occidental countries; and the contrast evokes the query: Do we thus assure the indissolubility of the marriage tie in a degree that more than offsets the mischief which divorce actions inflict upon society?

There was, and is, even under such a system, much moral restraint upon the wife to continue such, even though not satisfied with her lot. Her prospects of a second and happier marriage are often not alluring. The reception at her own home which she may expect, is not likely to be a warm welcome and it may be cold or even harsh. And if she has children, her lot is even more deplorable for, after very early infancy, they become members of her husband's family and are lost to her, forever. There is also the prosaic bread-and-butter question in many cases and it is presented in an aggravated form in a country where by general consent a virtuous woman's place is in a home.

Not the least of the mother's hardships if she be the mother of the eldest living son, who becomes, after his father's death, the head of the family, is that after her death he may not go into mourning for her if divorced; for he is too completely identified with the service of the departed ancestors of the family of which he is the head and which she has abandoned.

The hardships inflicted upon the husband by divorce may not be so serious. He must return the dower but he retains the more precious fruits of the marriage, his children. Yet consciousness of this very inequality, coupled with the traditional protective attitude toward the women of one's own family, must act upon the husband as a powerful deterrent, especially in view of the fact that he may seek through concubinage a more acceptable consort and mother for his children, without thus entirely displacing, humiliating, and perhaps greatly injuring his spouse.

In the Elder Tai's Record of Rites (bk. lxxx.), recognized causes for divorcing a wife are set forth as follows: "Disobedience to parents-in-law, failure to bear a son, adultery, jealousy of her husband, leprosy, garrulity, theft"; but the husband should not divorce her if she has no home to return to, if she has with him mourned three years for his parents, or if his condition was formerly poor and mean and is now rich and honourable. These rules are found in the code of the Manchu dynasty, also.

But in practice the only restraints upon the husband, other than the requirement that he must return the dower, are, first, that he must obtain the approval of his father, if living, or his elder brother, if the father is dead, and, second, that his wife may, through her ranking male relative, appeal to the court if one of the three conditions under which divorce is not permissible is alleged to exist. The husband and his father or elder brother are sole and final judges whether or not one of the seven causes is present. The wife may divorce her husband with his consent, which means, again, with the consent of his father or elder brother, also; and, since she must return to her father or elder brother, she must of course first obtain their consent and approval. Divorce, then, is by the parties, themselves, and not by a court, though under certain circumstances subject to judicial review. It is not especially common in China; and monogamy is also there the rule. In other words the admonition with which the last chapter closed, is there well heeded, both as to union with but one wife and as to permanence of marriage, though both marriage and divorce are so little limited by law; as is also well said in the "Yi King" (appendix vi., sect. ii., 32): "The rule for the relation of husband and wife is that it should be enduring."

Parenthood. "Here now is the affection of a father for his sons: He is proud of the meritorious among them and ranks those lower who are not so able. But that of a mother is such that, while she is proud of the meritorious, she cherishes those who are not so able. The mother deals with them on grounds of affection rather than of pride; the father on grounds of pride rather than affection." (Li Ki, bk. xxix., 29.)

The justice and discrimination which the superior man displays as a father, and without which he would act as an unreasoning animal rather than as a superior man, are tempered, however, by his natural affection for his progeny. Their relations are reciprocal, thus: "As a son he rested in filial piety. As a father he rested in kindness." (Great Learning, c. iii., v. 3.)

This mutual fondness is given apt expression in this saying: "Everyone calls his son, his son, whether he has talents or has not talents." (Analects, bk. xi., c. vii., v. 2.)

But its propriety and the extent of its application are better illustrated by this narrative: "The duke of She informed Confucius, saying, 'Among us here there are those who may be styled upright in conduct. If their father have stolen a sheep, they will bear witness to the fact.' Confucius said, 'Among us, in our part of the country, those who are upright are different from this. The father conceals the misconduct of his son and the son conceals the misconduct of the father. Uprightness is to be found in this.'" (Analects, bk. xiii., c. xviii.)

In the "Analects," Confucius says: "A youth, when at home, should be filial, and, abroad, respectful to his elders. He should be earnest and truthful. He should overflow in love to all and cultivate the friendship of the good. When he has time and opportunity, after the performance of these things, he should employ them in polite studies." (Bk. i., c. vi.)

The cultivation of these qualities is necessary in order that he may be regarded as filial; for while, as will be seen, much stress is placed upon filial observances, the most important thing is to be a worthy son. Thus in the "Li Ki" it runs: "He whom the superior man pronounces filial is he whom the people of the state praise, saying with admiration, 'Happy are the parents who have such a son as this!'" (Bk. xxi., sect. ii., 11.)

The opposite picture is unflinchingly and unsparingly presented in these texts of the "Analects," already quoted: "In youth, not humble as befits a junior; in manhood, doing nothing worthy of being handed down; and living on to old age: this is to be a pest." (Bk. xiv., c. xlvi.) "I observe that he is fond of occupying the seat of a full-grown man; I observe that he walks shoulder to shoulder with his elders. He is not one who is seeking to make progress in learning. He wishes quickly to become a man." (Bk. xiv., c. xlvii., v. 3.)

Yet the mere shortcomings of youth are to be viewed charitably and judgment is to be suspended until time shall tell. This Confucius puts as follows: "A youth is to be regarded with respect. How do we know that his future will not be equal to our present? If he reach the age of forty or fifty, and has not made himself heard of, then indeed he will not be worth being regarded with respect." (Analects, bk. ix., c. xxii.)

And one of the three things which he especially enjoins in relations to others is that all deal considerately with the young; he says in the "Analects" that his wishes are: "In regard to the aged, to give them repose; in regard to friends, to show them sincerity; in regard to the young, to treat them tenderly." (Bk. v., e. xxv., v. 4.)

The responsibilities of the father are of course more serious and grave. They extend even to the avoidance of such comradeship with his son as might be misunderstood and so tend to impair the son's veneration. Thus, as has already been quoted, it is said: "I have also heard that the superior man maintains a distant reserve towards his son." (Analects, bk. xvi., c. xiii., v. 5.)

He must keep himself a veritable hero in his son's eyes, in order that he may command, and may be worthy to command, his admiration and reverence. This also he must achieve in very truth and not by deception; for in the "Li Ki" it is said: "A boy should never be permitted to see an instance of deceit." (Bk. i., sect. i., pt. ii., c. v., 17.)

Lest the son should thereby come to regard the. father otherwise than as an ever-watchful and loving guardian, happy in his son's well-doing and grieved, rather than wroth, at his misdoings, it was enjoined by Mencius that the father should not be his son's tutor, for fear the necessary discipline estrange them, thus:

"Kung-sun Chow said, 'Why is it that the superior man does not himself teach his son?'

"Mencius replied, 'The circumstances of the case forbid its being done. The teacher must inculcate what is correct. When he inculcates what is correct and his lessons are not practised, he follows them up with being angry. When he follows them up with being angry, then contrary to what should be, he is offended with his son. At the same time the pupil says, "My master inculcates in me what is correct and he himself does not proceed in a correct path." The result of this is, that father and son are offended with each other. When father and son come to be offended with each other, the case is evil.

"'The ancients exchanged sons, and one taught the son of another.

"'Between father and son, there should be no reproving admonitions to what is good. Such reproofs lead to alienation, and than alienation there is nothing more inauspicious.'" (Bk. iv., pt. i., c. xviii.)

And in book v. of Pan Ku, a Confucian writer of the first century, the power of the father over the son was distinctly limited, as a matter of law, on the ground of the universal fatherhood of God, thus: "'Among all the lives given by

Heaven and Earth, man is the noblest.' All men are children of God and are merely made flesh through the spirits of father and mother...Therefore, the father has not absolute power over the son."

Essentials of Filial Piety. "Our bodies, to every hair and shred of skin, are received from our parents. We must not presume to injure or to wound them. This is the beginning of filial piety. When we have established our character by the practice of this filial course, so as to make our name famous in future ages and thereby glorify our parents, this is the end of filial piety." (Hsiâo King, "Book of Filial Piety," c. i.)

It is remarkable and significant that it should in these modern days be necessary to say "filial piety." "Pietas" originally signified reverent devotion to parents and unflagging service of them. Through this the meaning, "service of the Heavenly Father," has been derived. Meanwhile the original meaning of the word has been lost—indeed, as a serious duty, the very thing itself is near to have been lost—and it is now requisite to use the tautology, "filial piety," to express the idea for which "piety" alone once stood.

The Romans and the Greeks, however, scarcely at any time knew filial piety of the same type as this institution of the Chinese; for, though they possessed their "Lares and Penates," or household divinities, making sacrifices to departed ancestors was probably never erected into a well-established, long-cherished, everywhere honoured practice.

The piety of the ancient Chinese, nevertheless, did not solely or even primarily consist in sacrifices to the spirits of the dead. It called for the greatest reverence and devotion while the parent is yet living. Its most important phase, indeed, was the obligation it imposed to live an honourable and creditable life, that the parents might not have occasion to blush for their offspring.

This feature cannot be overemphasized; for it is the chief sanction for ethical conduct, according to the morals of Confucius, aside from the ambition to become a superior human being as an end in, and of, itself. In the "Li Ki" this view is ascribed directly to Confucius, thus: "I heard from Tsang-Tsze that he had heard the Master say that of all that Heaven produces and Earth nourishes there is none so great as man. His parents give birth to his person all complete and to return it to them complete may be called filial duty." (Bk. xxi., sec. ii., 14.)

This is enjoined again and again in this book of the rules of propriety, as in the following: "The superior man's respect extends to all. It is at its greatest when he respects himself. He is but an outgrowth from his parents; dare he do otherwise than preserve his self-respect? If he cannot respect himself, he injures them." (Bk. xxiv., 12.)

The following more detailed statement from the same book is ascribed to Tsang-Tsze, himself: "The body is that which has been transmitted to us by our parents; dare any one allow himself to be irreverent in the employment of their legacy? If a man in his own house and privacy be not grave, he is not filial; if in serving his ruler he be not loyal, he is not filial; if in discharging the

81

duties of office he be not reverent, he is not filial; if with friends he be not sincere, he is not filial; if on the field of battle he be not brave, he is not filial. If he fail in these five things, the evil will reach his parents; dare he then do otherwise than reverently attend to them?" (Bk. xxi., sect. ii., 11.)

The reverential service, due to parents as an act of filial piety, is not confined to service of the father, though he is the more frequently mentioned; the mother is equally the object of the devotion and love of their offspring. Thus in the "Hsiâo King," or Book of Filial Piety (c. v.), it is said: "As they serve their fathers, so they serve their mothers, and they love them equally. As they serve their fathers, so they serve their rulers and they reverence them equally. Hence love is what is chiefly rendered to the mother and reverence is what is chiefly rendered to the ruler, while both of these things are given to the father."

The same book contains also the following statement of the reciprocal and mutual duties of parent and child: "The son derives his life from his parents and no greater gift could possibly be transmitted; his ruler and parent, his father, deals with him accordingly and no generosity could be greater than his." (C. ix.)

The effectiveness of filial piety as a motive of well-doing and the inspiration which it supplies are well set forth in this passage from the "Li Ki" "The superior man, going back to his ancient fathers and returning to the authors of his being, does not forget those to whom he owes his life; and therefore he calls forth all his reverence, gives full vent to his feelings, and exhausts his strength in discharging this service—as a tribute of gratitude to his parents he dares not but do his utmost." (Bk. xxi., sect. ii., 4.)

The following panegyrics of filial piety from the "Hsiâo King" show the exalted regard in which Confucius and his predecessors held this virtue, which indeed they made the foundation for all other virtues:

"There are three thousand offences against which the five punishments are directed; there is none of them greater than to be unfilial." (C. xi.)

"The disciple Tsang said, 'Immense, indeed, is the greatness of filial piety!' The Master replied, 'Yes, filial piety is the constant requirement of Heaven, the righteousness of earth, and the practical duty of man.'" (C. vii.)

"The disciple Tsang said, 'I venture to ask whether in the virtue of the sages there was not something greater than filial piety?' The Master replied, 'Of all creatures produced by Heaven and Earth, man is the noblest. Of all man's actions there is none greater than filial piety.'" (C. ix.)

Pious Regard for Living Parents. "Tsang-Tsze said, 'There are three degrees of filial piety. The highest is being a credit to our parents; the next is not disgracing them; and the lowest is merely being able to support them.'" (Li Ki, bk. xxi., sect. ii., 9.)

Thus in the "Li Ki" the nature of filial piety toward living parents is indicated. Much the same is yet more urgently inculcated in another passage from the same book: "He should not forget his parents in the utterance of a single word and therefore an evil word will not issue from his mouth and an angry word will not react upon himself. Not to disgrace himself and not to cause shame to his parents may be called filial duty." (Bk. xxi., sect. ii., 14.)

The duty to support parents is in the "Li Ki" enjoined in these sweeping terms: "While his parents are alive, a son should not dare to consider his wealth his own nor hold it for his own use only." (Bk. xxvii., 30.)

Mencius has it: "I have heard that the superior man will not for all the world be niggardly toward his parents." (Bk. ii., pt. ii., c. vii., v. 5.)

In the "Hsiâo King" the sacrifice of personal comforts is commanded as necessary for even the lowest order of filial piety: "They are careful in their conduct and economical in their expenditures, in order to nourish their parents. This is the filial piety of the common people." (C. vi.)

Confucius was not wholly satisfied with this even as a statement of the duty of ordinary people. He deemed reverence, love, and obedience equally necessary in order that there might truly be a sentiment of pious regard and not a mere counterfeit of it. This colloquy taken from the "Analects" illustrates his position: "Tsze-hea asked what filial piety is. The Master said, 'If, when their elders have burdensome duties, the young take the toil off them, and if, when the young have wine and food, they set them before their elders, is this to be deemed filial piety?'" (Analects, bk. ii., c. viii.)

Again, in replying to the inquiry of another disciple, he refers to this as follows: "Tsze-yew asked what filial piety is. The Master said, 'The filial piety of nowadays means the support of one's parents. But dogs and horses likewise are able to do something in the way of support; without reverence, what is there to distinguish the one support from the other?'" (Analects, bk. ii., c. vii.)

And to the query of yet another disciple he responded: "It is not being disobedient." (Analects, bk. ii., c. v., v. 1.)

In the "Li Ki" the same idea is put thus, involving both instant obedience and sincere respect: "When his father or his teacher calls, he should not merely say 'Yes' but also rise." (Bk. i., pt. iii., c. iii., v. 14.)

Yet mere obedience is not enough and there are not failing instances when neither obedience nor respect should restrain the son from remonstrating; as it is said in the "Hsiâo King": "When unrighteous conduct is concerned, a son must by no means refrain from remonstrating with his father nor a minister from remonstrating with his ruler. Since, then, remonstrance is required in the case of unrighteous conduct, how can mere obedience to a father be accounted filial piety?" (C. xv.)

And in the "Analects," Confucius lays down the true rule of action in the following: "In serving his parents, a son may remonstrate with them, but gently; when he sees that they are not disposed to acquiesce, he should show increased reverence but not give up; and, should they punish him, he ought not to murmur." (Bk. iv., c. xviii.)

Remonstrance may not, however, be carried to excess and certainly not to such excess as is involved in exposing a father's shortcomings to the eyes of others or crying aloud his shame; for the "Li Ki" represents Confucius to declare, in conformity also with other sayings elsewhere: "The Master said, 'The superior man will overlook and not magnify the errors of his father and will show his veneration for his excellences.'" (Bk. xxvii., v. 17.)

Mencius, apparently, would yet further limit the right of the son to reprove; indeed, he would all but destroy it for he says: "To urge one another to what is good by reproof is the way of friends. But between father and son reproof is the greatest offence against that tenderness which should subsist." (Bk. iv., pt. ii., c. xxx., v. 4.)

In the same connexion, Mencius says: "There are five things which are commonly recognized to be unfilial. The first is laziness about employing legs and arms, resulting in failure to support parents. The second, gambling and chess-playing and fondness for wine, with the same result. The third, prizing goods and money and selfish devotion to wife and children, with the same result. The fourth, giving way to the temptations that assail one's eyes and ears, thus bringing his parents to shame. The fifth, reckless bravery, fighting and quarrelling, endangering thereby the happiness and the support of one's parents." (Bk. iv., pt. ii., c. xxx., v. 2.)

Mencius also relates an extravagant but obviously apocryphal story of the filial piety of Shun, who however married without notifying his unforgiving parents, which act Mencius thus defends: "If he had informed them, he would not have been permitted to marry. That male and female should dwell together is the greatest of all human relations. Had he informed his parents, he must have missed this greatest of human relations and thereby have incurred their just resentment. Therefore was it that he did not inform them." (Bk. v., pt. i., c. ii., v. 1.)

This is also quite in keeping with another clever saying of Mencius, which likewise embodies an ethical principle much insisted upon in China: "There are three things which are unfilial and to have no posterity is the greatest of them." (Bk. iv., pt. i., c. xxvi., v. 1.)

Even in filial piety, more is not required of any man than he is able to do. Thus in the "Analects" it is related: "Tsze-hea said, 'If a man . . . in serving his parents exert his utmost strength . . . although men say that he has not learned, I shall certainly say that he has." (Bk. i., c. vii.)

In another place the test is made this: Does the general judgment of the son's treatment of his parents coincide with their report—always sure to be favourable, no matter how he wrongs them? It runs thus: "Filial indeed is Min Tsze-K'een! Other people say nothing of him different from the report of his parents and brothers." (Analects, bk. xi., c. iii.)

King Wu is quoted in the "Shu King" as condemning unfilial and unfraternal behaviour in no uncertain terms as follows: "Oh Fang, such great criminals are greatly abhorred, and how much more the unfilial and unbrotherly! As the son who does not reverently discharge his duty to his father but greatly wounds his father's heart; and the father who cannot love his son but hates him; as the younger brother who does not regard the manifest will of Heaven and refuses to respect his elder brother and the elder brother who does not think of the toil of their parents in bringing up their children and hates his younger brother." (Pt. v., bk. ix., 3.)

In the "Analects," the disciple, Yu Tze, with feeling declares that all generous conduct flows from filial and fraternal sentiments, saying: "Filial piety and fraternal submission, are they not the root of all benevolent actions?" (Bk. i., c. ii., v. 2.)

In the "Hsiâo King" the following encomiums for good and useful traits, flowing plainly out of early training in filial piety, are heaped upon him who has been truly filial: "He who serves his parents, in a high situation will be free from pride; in a low situation, will be free from insubordination; and, among his equals, will not be quarrelsome." (C. x.)

Mencius bluntly declares that filial piety necessarily results from a benevolent spirit and that one cannot exist without the other: "There never has been a man trained to benevolence who neglected his parents." (Bk. i., pt. i., c. i., v. 5.)

The assiduous, brooding care, resembling that of a mother for her infant child, which the son is expected to cultivate as regards his aging parents, is nowhere better illustrated than in this saying of Confucius: "The ages of parents may by no means not be kept in the memory, as an occasion at once for joy and for fear." (Analects, bk. iv., c. xxi.)

It is for this reason, also, *i.e.*, that in the hour of need he may be within call, that this is enjoined by the sage: "While his parents are living, a son must not go abroad to a distance; or, if he should do so, he must have a fixed place to which he goes." (Analects, bk. iv., c. xix.)

Pious Observances after the Death of Parents. "Filial piety is seen in the skilful carrying out of the wishes of our forefathers and the skilful carrying forward of their undertakings." (Doctrine of the Mean, c. xix., v. 2.) "While a man's father is alive, look at the bent of his will; when his father is dead, look at his conduct. If for three years he does not alter from the way of his father, he may be called filial." (Analects, bk. i., c. xi.)

These passages from the "Doctrine of the Mean" and the "Analects" enjoin the continuance of filial piety, unabated, after the demise of parents.

The filial piety of the poor may not be more than decent burial, with genuine grief and reverence; for it is not the expenditure or even the wealth of ceremony which constitutes the tribute—though the absence of either, if it can be afforded, is unpardonable—but rather the spirit of real veneration and sorrow. Confucius says of this: "In the ceremonies of mourning it is better that there be deep sorrow than a minute attention to observances." (Analects, bk. iii., c. iv., v. 3.)

Mencius gives an interesting and reasonable, though scarcely verifiable, account of the origin of burial, in this abiding tenderness for the authors of one's being: "In the most ancient times there were some who did not inter their parents. When their parents died, they took the bodies up and cast them into some water-channel. Afterwards, when passing by, they saw foxes and wildcats devouring the bodies and flies and insects covering them. The sweat burst forth upon their brows; they looked away, unable to bear the sight. For other people such perspiration did not burst out; but now their hearts' emotions affected their faces and their eyes. Instantly they hurried home, returned with spades and baskets, and covered the bodies. If this indeed was right, it is obvious that the filial son and virtuous man, in burying his parents, will behave according to propriety." (Bk. iii., pt. i., c. v., v. 4.)

This was advanced by Mencius in reply to an argument by the philosopher Mih, that there should be economical simplicity in funerals and burials—an argument often renewed to this day, the constant occasion for which shows how universal and deeply seated is the sentiment which provokes expenditure sufficient to afford what is deemed a suitable tribute of affection to the dead.

A stern duty, never to be shirked by a son, is to avenge his father if slain by the hand of an enemy. If the execution of the criminal law does this, well and good; but if not, the responsibility is on the son. In the "Li Ki" it is put thus: "With him who has slain his father, a son should not live under the same sky." (Bk. i., sect. i., pt. v., c. ii., v. 10.)

Otherwise, however, the immediate duty of the son is fully performed by his grief, by proper burial, and the prescribed period of retirement and mourning; as it is said in the "Hsiâo King": "The services of love and reverence to parents when alive, and those of grief and sorrow for them when dead—these completely discharge the duty of living men." (C. xviii.)

This mourning, however, must be the genuine expression of grief, deep and unassuageable; else the slight and feeble character of the son's piety is apparent. Confucius deems this the severest and most reliable test of the earnestness and depth of filial devotion, saying: "Men may not have shown what is in them to the full extent, and yet they will be found to do so on occasion of mourning for their parents." (Analects, bk. xix., c. xvii.)

And he comments upon the mere show of it as comparable with two other destructive hypocrisies, as follows: "High station filled without indulgent generosity; ceremonies performed without reverence; mourning conducted without sorrow—wherewith should I contemplate such ways?" (Analects, bk. iii., c. xxvi.)

The period of mourning for a father had been fixed at three years—interpreted as twenty-seven months—before the time of Confucius. The following is his statement about it and the reason for it: "It is not till a child is three years old that it is allowed to leave the arms of its parents. And three years' mourning is universally observed throughout the empire." (Analects, bk. xvii., c. xxi., v. 6.)

During this period of mourning the son, if he can afford it, lives retired from the world, leaving the management of his affairs to others and abandoning himself to meditation, spiritual communion with the departed, and grief. He utterly eschews meanwhile every alleviation of his sorrow, including very particularly the solace of music.

But, with the expiration of this long period of retirement, his mourning is by no means at an end. On the contrary it ends only with life itself. His father's name must not be spoken in his presence, except at the sacrifices upon the anniversary of his death; and never without tears. Thus in the "Li Ki" it is said: "The saying that the superior man mourns all his life for his parents has reference to the recurrence of the day of their death. That he does not do his ordinary work on that day, does not mean that it would be unpropitious to do so; it means that on that day his thoughts are occupied with them and he does not dare occupy himself, as on other days, with his private and personal affairs." (Bk. xxi., sect. i., 5.)

The greatest of all filial obligations to deceased parents, however, is creditable conduct; for by that only can that which they have created, their son, worthily represent what they have sought to accomplish in the world through him. The consideration of this phase of the Confucian conception of filial piety is most important since it is the sanction most relied upon to enforce all the injunctions, whether directly regarding self-development or its concomitant essential, propriety in relations with other human beings. This devotion both to living and to departed parents—the so-called "ancestor worship" of the Chinese; it scarcely extends beyond three generations in any case, and as regards the lowly, not beyond one—is the chief incentive, other than self-respect and the innate desire to grow and to become and be a superior human being, to which Confucius appeals.

In the "Li Ki" the nature of this appeal is thus revealed: "Although his parents be dead, when a son is inclined to do what is good, he should think that he will thereby transmit the good name of his parents and so carry his wish into effect. When he is inclined to do what is not good, he should think that he will thereby bring disgrace on the name of his parents and in no wise carry his wish into effect." (Bk. x., sect. i., 17.)

And in yet simpler and stronger terms in this passage: "When his parents are dead and the son carefully watches over his actions so that a bad name involving his parents may not be handed down, he may be said to be able to maintain his piety to the end." (Li Ki, bk. xxi., sect. ii., 12.)

This union of all the sentiments which compose the piety of a son toward his parents, both while they are living and after their death, is set forth in these words in the same book: "The superior man while his parents are alive, reverently nourishes them; and when they are dead, reverently sacrifices to them. His chief thought is how, to the end of life, not to disgrace them." (Bk. xxi., sect. i., 5.)

And in the "Shi King," the Book of Odes, it is thus beautifully phrased:

"When early dawn unseals my eyes,
　Before my mind my parents rise."

—(Minor Odes, Decade v., Ode 2, quoted also in the Li Ki, bk. xxi., sect. i., 7.)

Chapter Five - The State

IN logical progression Confucius rises from a discussion of duties toward the family to those toward the state, which social organization he regards as only a larger household, having all its ethical principles founded on those of the primary unit.

The Foundation of Government. "This is meant by 'To rightly govern the state, it is necessary first to regulate one's own family.' One cannot instruct others who cannot instruct his own children. Without going beyond the family, the prince may learn all the lessons of statecraft, filial piety by which the sovereign is also served, fraternal submission by which older men and superiors are also served, kindness by which also the common people should be ministered unto." (Great Learning, c. ix., v. 1.)

"From the loving example of one family, love extends throughout the state; from its courtesy, courtesy extends throughout the state; while the ambition and perverse recklessness of one man may plunge the entire state into rebellion and disorder." (Great Learning, c. ix., v. 3.)

By these words in "The Great Learning" the position of the family as the foundation of society and of its proper regulation as the basis for government is dwelt upon. The significance of this is perhaps obvious though not too familiar in these days when family ties and family discipline both tend to loosen. In the "Hsiâo King," the application of these principles is adroitly indicated as follows: "The filial piety with which the superior man serves his parents may be transferred as loyalty to the ruler; the fraternal duty with which he serves his elder brother may be transferred as deference to elders; his regulation of his family may be transferred as good government in any official position." (C. xiv.)

In the "Li Ki" the same results are deduced from the three primary human functions and duties as there set forth: "Husband and wife have their separate functions; between father and son there should be affection; between ruler and minister there should be strict application to their respective duties. If these three relations be rightly discharged, all other things will follow." (Bk. xxiv., 8.)

The strictly practical character also of this application is revealed by this saying of Yu Tze concerning the fount of orderly behaviour on the part of the citizen: "They are few who, being filial and fraternal, are fond of offending against their superiors. There have been none who, not liking to offend against their superiors, have been fond of stirring up confusion." (Analects, bk. i., c. ii., v. i.)

To support and elucidate this view, also, Confucius cites the Book of Odes saying: "From them you learn the more immediate duty of serving one's father and the remoter one of serving one's prince." (Analects, bk. xvii., c. ix., v. 6.)

And again he cites and even quotes the "Shu King" to show the immediate and causal relation between the exercise of filial and fraternal piety and the establishment of government upon a sound and secure foundation: "What does the 'Shu King' say of filial piety? 'You are filial, you discharge your fraternal duties. These qualities are displayed in government. This, then, also constitutes the exercise of government.'" (Analects, bk. ii., c. xxi., v. 2.)

The Function of Government. "To govern means to rectify." (Analects, bk. xii., c. xvii.)

This from the "Analects" is repeated with greater particularity in the "Li Ki," accompanied by a lesson which the Chinese sages, who were almost invariably the instructors of princes, never wearied of insisting upon, thus: "Government is rectification. When the ruler does right, all men will imitate his self-control. What the ruler does, the people will follow. How should they follow him in what he does not do?" (Bk. xxiv., 7.)

This also, in the passage from the "Analects" just now quoted from, is similarly explained by Confucius, thus: "Ke K'ang Tze asked Confucius about government. Confucius replied, 'To govern means to rectify. If you lead with correctness, who will dare not to be correct?'" (Bk. xii., c. xvii.)

In the "Li Ki" the sentiment is expressed: "As men are constituted, the thing most important to them is government." (Bk. xxiv., 6.)

This refers, of course, to its indispensable office of rectification; and its importance is vividly illustrated by Mencius in the following passage, which also points out the normal play of cause and effect in the operation of government upon men's characters: "When right government prevails in the empire, men of little virtue submit to those of great virtue and men of little worth to those of great worth. When bad government prevails in the empire, men of little power submit to those of great power and the weak to the strong. Both are in accord with divine law." (Bk. iv., pt. i., c. vii., v. 1.)

The mode—or, rather, one of the simpler and more obvious modes—by which this may be accomplished, Confucius indicates in this saying: "Employ the upright and put aside the crooked; in this way, the crooked may be made to be upright." (Analects, bk. xii., c. xxii., v. 3.)

And that, in order that government may be stable, not to say benign, this course must perforce be followed, he inculcates in this colloquy: "The duke Gae asked, saying: 'What should be done in order to secure the submission of the people?' Confucius replied, 'Advance the upright and set aside the crooked, then the people will submit. Advance the crooked and set aside the upright, then the people will not submit.'" (Analects, bk. ii., c. xix.)

Government Exists for the Benefit of the Governed. "The duke of She asked about government. The Master said, 'Good government obtains when those who are near are made happy, and those who are far are attracted.'" (Analects, bk. xiii., c. xvi.)

This Mencius reiterated in this direct fashion: "The people are the most important element; ... the sovereign, least important." (Bk. vii., pt. ii., c. xiv., v. 1.)

The "Li Ki" quotes the "Book of Poetry" as saying that government is fraternal and parental—rather than paternal, in the offensive sense usually attached to that word when applied to government—thus:

"The happy and gracious sovereign
  Is the father and mother of the people."
                    (Bk. xxvi., i.)

And perhaps even more strikingly:

"When among any of the people there was a death,
  I crawled upon my knees to help them."
                    (Bk. xxvi., 3.)

This, moreover, is not wholly sentimentalism; for with much practical force Confucius says:

"Therefore, if remoter people are not submissive, all the influences of civil culture and virtue are to be cultivated to attract them to be so; and when they have been so attracted, they must be made contented and tranquil.

"'Now here are you, Yew and Kew, assisting your chief. Remoter people are not submissive and, with your help, he cannot attract them to him. In his own territory, there are divisions and downfalls, leavings and separations, and, with your help, he cannot preserve it. And yet he is planning these hostile movements within our state.'" (Analects, bk. xvi., c. i., v. 11, 12, 13.)

The hard-headed, severely practical Mencius, who about a century later exemplified in governmental theories so many of the most valuable of the principles laid down by Confucius, gives this yet more concrete form in these words: "If the seasons of husbandry be not interfered with, the grain will be more than can be eaten. If close nets are not allowed to enter the pools and ponds, the fishes and turtles will be more than can be consumed. If the axes and bills enter the hills and forests only at the proper time, the wood will be more than can be used. When the grain and fish and turtles are more than can be eaten and there is more wood than can be used, this enables the people to nourish their living and bury their dead, without any feeling against any. This condition, in which the people nourish their living and bury their dead, is the first step in kingly government." (Bk. i., pt. i., v. 3.)

The foregoing precedent, more than two thousand years old, for modern agricultural departments and experiment stations and yet more recently instituted and still suspiciously regarded conservation movements is sufficiently startling; but Mencius goes far beyond that, as, for instance, when he says to King Seuen of Ts'e: "Therefore an intelligent ruler will regulate the livelihood of the people, so as to make sure that they shall have sufficient wherewith to serve their parents and also sufficient wherewith to support their wives and children." (Bk. i., pt. i., c. vii., v. 21.)

This picture of the blessings of a truly beneficent government and of its attractions, when accompanied by widespread prosperity of families, has been so recently presented in the United States of America, to which within three or four generations the needy and oppressed have thronged to make it one of the greatest of the nations, that it is surely worth while farther to exhibit the views of this later Chinese sage upon this subject: "Now if Your Majesty will institute a government whose action will all be benevolent, this will cause all the officers in the empire to wish to stand in Your Majesty's court, and the farmers all to wish to plough in Your Majesty's fields, and the merchants, both travelling and stationary, all to wish to have their goods in Your Majesty's market-places, and travelling strangers all to wish to make their tours on Your Majesty's roads, and all throughout the empire who feel aggrieved by their rulers, to wish to come and complain to Your Majesty. And when they are so bent, who can hold them back?" (Bk. i., pt. i., c. vii., v. 18.)

The folly of the contrary policy and the office which it has performed in causing immigration into countries which are well-governed, that is, governed in the interests of the people, Mencius expatiates upon as follows: "Now among the shepherds of men throughout the empire, there is not one who does not find pleasure in killing men. If there were one who did not find pleasure in killing men, all the people in the empire would look towards him with outstretched necks. Such being indeed the case, the people would flock to him, as water flows downward with a rush, which no one can repress." (Bk. i., pt. i., c. vi., v. 6.)

In "The Great Learning" it is put thus, sententiously: "To centralize wealth is to disperse the people; to distribute wealth is to collect the people." (C. x., v. 9.)

And in the "Li Ki" Confucius is reported as saying: "With the ancients, in their government the love of men was the great point." (Bk. xxiv., 9.)

Mencius erected his advanced and detailed propositions concerning good government upon benevolence or the love of men, in an age when discussions concerning first principles, like " Love thine enemies!" over against "Be just to thine enemies and reserve love for friends!" had given way to discussions of applied principles, like Tolstoian individualism or communism. Accordingly Mencius, addressing princes as their tutor, admonished them, saying: "Let benevolent government be put in practice and the people will be delighted with it, as if they were relieved from hanging by their heels." (Bk. ii., pt. i., c. i., v. 13.)

And with this in another place he coupled an inducement and a promise, thus: "If you will put benevolence in practice in your government, your people will love you and all in authority, and will be ready to die for them." (Bk. i., pt. ii., c. xii., v. 3.)

This has been said in the "Analects" in another way and with a warning as well as a promise, in these words: "If the people have plenty, their prince will not be left to want alone. If the people are in want, their prince will not be able to enjoy plenty alone." (Analects, bk. xii., c. ix., v. 4.)

The responsibility for evil conditions, also, Confucius fastens unescapably upon the corrupt or incompetent administrator who seeks to profit and enjoy, not as a reward for genuine service of his people, but because, in effect if not by design, he has despoiled them. This is his scathing denunciation of such rulers: "How can he be used as a guide to a blind man who does not support him when tottering or raise him up when fallen? And further, you speak wrongly. When a tiger or a wild bull escapes from his cage, when a tortoise or gem is injured in its repository—whose is the fault?" (Analects, bk. xvi., c. i., v. 6, 7.)

The heartless suggestions regarding the unfortunate of earth's children, which are often brought forward on pseudo-scientific grounds, find no welcome in the breast of the sage, as this will show: "Ke K'ang Tse asked Confucius about government, saying, 'What do you say to killing the unprincipled for the good of the principled?' Confucius replied, 'Sir, in carrying on your government, why should you use killing at all? Let your desires be shown to be for what is good, and the people will be good. The relation between superiors and inferiors is like that between the wind and the grass; the grass must bend when the wind blows across it.'" (Analects, bk. xii., c. xix.)

The "Analects" enjoin, instead, infinite mercy and commiseration for the human wrecks into which evil government distorts our common human nature, as in this passage, quoting the philosopher Tsang, with manifest approval: "The chief of the Mang family having appointed Yang Foo to be chief criminal judge, the latter consulted the philosopher Tsang. Tsang said, 'The rulers have failed in their duties and the people consequently have been disorganized for a long time. When you have found out the truth about any accusation, be grieved over it, pity the malefactor, and take no pride in your superior discernment.'" (Analects, bk. xix., c. xix.)

And in the "Shu King," the ancient worthy, Pan-Kang, is represented to have said: "Do not despise the old and experienced and do not make little of the helpless and young." (Pt. iv., bk. vii., 2.)

It is to fidelity to this fundamental principle of correct government, i.e., that it was instituted and maintained for the benefit of the governed, and to the correlate principles by which it may be so applied, that Confucius refers when he says: "When right principles prevail in the empire, there will be no controversies among the common people." (Analects, bk. xvi., c. ii., v. 3.)

The true requisite for the attainment of antipoverty aspirations, namely, that the poor be not despoiled, and thus all things be turned topsy-turvy in the state, Confucius sets forth in the "Analects": "When the people keep their respective places, there will be no poverty; when harmony prevails, there will be no scarcity of people; when there is repose, there will be no rebellions." (Analects, bk. xvi., c. L, v. 10.)

The view of the immediate disciples of Confucius as to what a well-governed country would look like, as well as their confidence that their great teacher could have realized it, had he been invested with the sovereignty, are announced in these burning sentences: "Were our Master in the position of the prince of a state or the chief of a family, we should find this description verified: He would plant the people and forthwith they would be established; he would lead them and forthwith they would follow him; he would make them happy and forthwith multitudes would resort to his dominions; he would cheer them and forthwith they would become harmonious. While he lived, he would be glorious. When he died, he would be bitterly lamented." (Analects, bk. xix., c. xxv., v. 4.)

The Essentials of Good Government. "Tsze-kung asked about government. The Master said, 'The requisites of government are that there be sufficiency of food, sufficiency of military equipment, and the confidence of the people in their ruler.'

"Tsze-kung said, 'If it cannot be helped and one of these must be dispensed with, which of the three should be forgone first?' 'The military equipment,' said the Master.

"Tsze-kung again asked, 'If it cannot be helped and one of the remaining two must be dispensed with, which of them should be forgone?' The Master answered, 'Part with the food. From of old death has been the lot of all men; but if the people have not confidence in their rulers, there is no stability for the state.'" (Analects, bk. xii., c. vii.)

The manner in which the confidence so discussed in the "Analects" may be gained and held is variously described but perhaps never more aptly than in this passage from "The Great Learning":

"On this account, the ruler will first take pains about his own virtue. Possessing virtue, he will win the people. Possessing the people, he will win the realm. Possessing the realm, he will command revenue. Possessing revenue, he will have resources for all demands.

"Virtue is the root; ample revenue the fruit.

"If he make the root secondary and the fruit the prime object, he will but wrangle with his people and teach them rapine." (C. x., v. 6, 7, 8.)

In the "Analects," also, it is remarked: "The superior man, having obtained their confidence, may impose tasks upon the people. If he have not gained their confidence, they will deem his acts oppressive." (Bk. xix., c. x.)

Mencius, however, much more circumstantially describes the essentials of a worthy government in a tribute to the glorious rule of King Wan, in these words:

"The king said, 'May I hear from you what the truly kingly government is?'

"'Formerly,' was the reply, 'King Wan's government of K'e was as follows: Farmers cultivated one ninth of the land for the government; descendants of government servants were pensioned; at the passes and in the markets, strangers were inspected, but goods were not taxed; there were no prohibitions respecting the ponds and weirs; the wives and children of criminals were not involved in their guilt. There were old widowers, old widows, old bachelors and maidens, fatherless or orphan children;—these four classes are the most destitute of the people and have none to whom they can tell their wants; and King Wan, in the institution of his government with its benevolent influence, made them the first objects of his regard.'" (Bk. i., pt. ii., c. v., v. 3.)

The benign consequences of beneficent rule and the confidence and willing obedience of the people when the ruler is worthy of it, Mencius sets forth thus: "It is said in the Book of History, that as soon as Tang began his work of executing justice, he commenced with Ko. The whole empire had confidence in him. When he pursued his work in the east, the rude tribes on the west murmured. So did those on the north when he was engaged in the south. The cry was,—'Why does he leave us until the last?' The people looked unto him as when looking in time of severe drought to clouds and rainbows. The men of the markets stopped not, the husbandmen did not turn from their labours. He blessed the people as he punished their rulers. It was like an opportune shower and the people rejoiced." (Bk. i., pt. ii., c. xi., v. 2.)

How he responded to King Seuen of Ts'e about the means of securing this limitless confidence of the people is thus recorded: "The King said, 'What virtue must there be in order to the attainment of imperial sway?' Mencius replied, 'The love and protection of the people; with this, there is no power which can prevent a ruler from attaining it.'" (Bk. i., pt. i., c. vii., v. 3.)

In "Shuo Yuan" (bk. xi.), Yen Yuan says: "I wish to have a wise king or a sage ruler and to become his minister. I should cause there to be no reason to repair the city walls, the moats and ditches to be crossed by no foeman, and the swords and spears to be melted into tools of agriculture. I should cause the whole world to have no calamity of warfare anywhere for thousands of years," and Confucius is reported to have said, "What I wish is the plan of the son of Yen."

In the "Great Model," however, Confucius yet more clearly sets forth the utilitarian basis of all government, asserting that it is instituted among men to secure for them the five blessings and secure them against the six calamities. The five blessings are: Ample means, long life, health, virtuous character, and an agreeable personal appearance; the six calamities, early death, sickness, misery, poverty, a repulsive appearance, and weakness.

Certainly these, as objects to be attained by civil government, embrace all that even the most enlightened peoples of modern times aim at, hope for, and struggle to achieve.

In the "History of Han" (chap. xci.), Pan Ku gives the following account, strangely applicable to our own day, of the consequences of the perversion of government to the enrichment of the few and the impoverishment of the many: "Under the influence of luxury and extravagance, the students and the common people all disregarded the regulations and neglected the primary occupation. The number of farmers decreased, and that of merchants increased. Grain was insufficient, but luxurious goods were plenty. After the age of Duke Huan of Ch'i and Duke Wên and Tsin, moral character was greatly corrupted, and social order was confused. Each state had a different political system, and each family had different customs. The physical desires were uncontrolled, and extravagant consumption and social usurpation had no end. Therefore, the merchant transported goods which were difficult to obtain; the artisans produced articles which had no practical use; and the student practised ways which were contrary to orthodoxy; all of them pursued the temporary fashion for the getting of money. The hypocritical people turned away from truth in order to make fame, and guilty men ran risks in order to secure profit. While those who took the states by the deed of usurpation or regicide became kings or dukes, the men who founded their rich families by robbery became heroes. Morality could not control the gentlemen, and punishment could not make the common people afraid. Among the rich, the wood and earth wore embroidery, and the dog and horse had a superabundance of meat and grain. But, among the poor, even the coarsest clothes could not be completed; beans made their food and water was their drink. Although they were all in the same rank of common people, the rich, by the power of wealth, raised themselves to kings, while the others, although their actual condition was slavery and imprisonment, had no angry appearance. Therefore, those who were deceitful and criminal were comfortable and proud in the world, but those who held principles and followed reason could not escape hunger and cold. Such an influence came from the government, because there was no regulation to control the economic life."

In the "Li Ki" Confucius lays bare the cause which creates such consequences, thus: "The small man, when poor, feels the pinch of his straitened circumstances; and when rich, is liable to become proud. Under the pinch of that poverty, he may proceed to steal; and when proud, he may proceed to deeds of disorder. The social rules recognize these feelings of men, and lay down definite regulations for them, to serve as preventions for the people. Hence, when the sages distributed riches and honours, they made the rich not have power enough to be proud; and kept the poor from being pinched and the honourable men not be intractable to those above them. In this way the causes of disorder would more and more disappear." (Bk. xxvii., 2.)

And Tung Chung-Shu says of these conditions: "It is said by Confucius, 'We are not troubled with fears of poverty, but are troubled with fears of a lack of equality of wealth.' Therefore, when there is here a concentration of wealth, there must be an emptiness there. Great riches make the people proud; and great poverty makes them wretched. When they are wretched, they would become robbers; when they are proud, they would become oppressors; it is human nature. From the nature of the average man, the sages discovered the origin of disorder. Therefore, when they established social laws and divided up the social orders, they made the rich able to show their distinction without being proud, and the poor able to make their living without misery; this was the standard for the equalization of society. In this way, wealth was sufficient, and the high and low classes were peaceful. Hence, society was easily governed well. In the present day, the regulations are abandoned, so that everyone pursues what he wants. As human wants have no limit, the whole society becomes indulgent without end. The great men of the high class, notwithstanding they have great fortune, lament the insufficiency of their wealth; while the small people of the lower classes are depressed. Therefore, the rich increase in eagerness for money, and do not wish to do good with it; while the poor violate the laws every day, and nothing can stop them. Hence, society is difficult to govern well." (Many Dewdrops of the Spring and Autumn, bk. xxvii.)

The Nourishment of the People. "When a country is well governed, poverty and a mean condition are things to be ashamed of. When a country is ill governed, riches and honours are things to be ashamed of." (Analects, bk. viii., c. xiii., v. 3.)

The meaning of this passage from the "Analects" is, that the most important function of government is to secure the equitable distribution of the products of human labour to the end that no deserving person shall suffer want. Obviously, also, if the mere acquisition of wealth were, by reason of just conditions, truly a test of desert, the most important step would have been taken toward the rectification of men; for if virtue were the only road to affluence, many are they who would walk therein.

Mencius put this convincingly, thus: "When a sage governs the world, he will cause pulse and grain to be as abundant as water and fire. If pulse and grain were as abundant as water and fire, should the people be otherwise than virtuous?" (Bk. vii., pt. i., c. xxiii., v. 3.)

The first office of the government in this regard is, of course, instruction; and it is interesting to find the most modern of governmental inventions, an agricultural department and its stations, thus forestalled by Mencius: "Let mulberry trees be planted about the homesteads with their five mow and persons of fifty years may be clothed with silk. In keeping fowls, pigs, dogs, and swine, let not their breeding time be neglected and persons of seventy years may eat flesh." (Bk. i., pt. i., c. iii., v. 4.)

And the yet more recent innovation, conservation, was pronounced a duty in the "Li Ki" in these words: "Where the wide and open country is greatly neglected and uncultivated, it speaks ill for those in authority." (Bk. i., sect. i., pt. v., c. iii., v. 11.)

Both in its external relations with other states and peoples, and in its internal affairs, Confucius held that the government must frown upon conduct which proceeds from sordid motives. It is put, briefly and pointedly, in this saying: "In a state, gain is not to be considered prosperity, but its prosperity will be found in righteousness." (Great Learning, c. x., v. 23.)

Mencius dwells upon one phase of the significance of this text, in answering a king who sought gain for his kingdom to the disadvantage of others, in this fashion: "If Your Majesty say, 'What is to be done to profit my kingdom?' the great officers will say, 'What is to be done to profit our families?' and the inferior officers and the common people will say, 'What is to be done to profit us?' Superiors and inferiors will try to snatch this profit the one from the other and the kingdom will be endangered." (Bk. i., c. i., v. 4.)

The "Li Ki" supplies this picture of the demoralization which reigns when the government does not restrain the powerful and the unscrupulous: "The strong press upon the weak, the many are cruel to the few, the knowing impose upon the dull, the bold make it bitter for the timid, the sick are not nursed, the old and young, the orphans and solitaries are neglected; such is the great disorder that ensues!" (Bk. xvii., sect. i., 12.)

Mencius makes a most pertinent inquiry, the answer to which may well stagger the advocates of unrestricted *laissez-faire*, in the following colloquy with King Hwuy of Leang:

"'Is there any difference between killing a man with a stick and with a sword?' The king said, 'There is no difference.'

"'Is there any difference between doing it with a sword and with the government?' The reply was, 'There is no difference.'

"'In your kitchen there is fat meat; in your stables there are fat horses. Your people have the look of hunger, and on the wilds lie those who have died of famine. This is leading on beasts to devour men.'" (Bk. i., pt. i., c. iv., v. 2, 3, 4.)

Mencius, however, by no means approved of applying undeservedly harsh epithets even to those who despoil the people, or of intemperately denouncing, by means of false similes, their conduct, however reprehensible: "Wan Chang said, 'The princes of the present day take from their people just as a robber despoils his victim. Yet if they put a good face of propriety on their gifts, the superior man receives them. I venture to ask how you explain this.'

"Mencius answered: 'Do you think that if there should arise a truly Imperial sovereign, he would collect the princes of the present day and put them to death? Or would he admonish them and, on their not changing their ways, put them to death? Indeed, to call everyone who takes what does not properly belong to him, a robber, is pushing a point of resemblance to the utmost and insisting on the most refined idea of righteousness.'" (Bk. v., pt. ii., c. iv., v. 5.)

The idea of Utopia, where everybody's desires, however extensive, will be sated, is thus entirely foreign to the conception of Confucius and his followers. It is also said in the "Many Dewdrops of the Spring and Autumn": "The objects of wants are limitless; the supply can never be adequate. Therefore is there the keen sense of deprivation." (Bk. xxvii.)

But fair and equitable distribution is necessary, both for the material and the ethical well-being of the community. And in the Commentary of Kung-Yang on "The Spring and Autumn," Ho Hsiu is represented as saying concerning the deadly destruction of the poor by the competition of the rich and powerful, these words which are so applicable to these modern days of trusts and combinations: "When the rich compete with the poor, even though the law were made by Kau Yau, nothing can prevent the strong from pressing on the weak."

Confucius warns of the consequences of driving the people to desperation, thus: "The man who is fond of daring and is discontented with his poverty, will proceed to insubordination." (Analects, bk. viii., c. x.)

Mencius gave much attention to the duty of the ruler to provide for the certain support, comfort, and even pleasure and entertainment of the people,— not the enervating, brutal, degrading, pauperizing largess of ancient Rome, but protection against force, fraud, and fortune, the triad of enemies of the just distribution of the products of labour. These are a few of his aptest statements:

"If Your Majesty loves wealth, let the people be able to gratify the same feeling and what difficulty will there be about your attaining the Imperial sway?" (Bk. i., pt. ii., c. iv., v. 4.)

"If Your Majesty now will make pleasure a thing common to the people and yourself, the Imperial sway awaits you." (Bk. i., pt. i., c. i., v. 8.)

"The ancients caused the people to have pleasure as well as themselves, and therefore they could enjoy it." (Bk. i., pt. i., c. i., v. 3.)

"When a ruler rejoices in the joy of his people, they also rejoice in his joy; when he grieves at the sorrow of his people, they also grieve at his sorrow. A common feeling of joy will pervade the empire, a common feeling of sorrow the same. In such a condition, it cannot be but that the ruler will attain to the Imperial dignity." (Bk. i., pt. ii., c. iv., v. 3.)

The reverse side of the picture this reverent follower of Confucius thus presents: "Their feeling thus (*i.e.*, disaffected and disloyal) is for no other reason than that you do not permit the people to have pleasure as well as yourself." (Bk. i., pt. ii., c. i., v. 6.)

The establishment of public holidays is also enjoined, in which all classes of the people partake under the guidance of public officials. At these there was the "Rite of District Drinking," *i.e.*, the custom of liberal alcoholic potations in celebration of the occasion and as a part of the good-fellowship. Wines, brewed and distilled liquors appear to have been known to the ancient Chinese; and Confucius favoured festivals at which, under proper ceremonial restrictions, jollity and merriment were given full rein. The manner of drinking but not the amount was strictly regulated.

Most vividly and in sharp contrast with these days of high prices and dear living, with the growth of luxury, the diminution of the marriage rate, and the yet greater fall of the birth rate, Mencius presents this view of what good government should provide for the citizens and through them for mankind: "At that time, in the seclusion of home there were no pining women, and outside of it no unmarried men." (Bk. i., pt. ii., c. v., v. 5.)

And here he affirms the consequences of evil government consequences so alarmingly like those over which the great nations are now lamenting as to awaken wonder whether the same causes may not always be at work when such results are again found: "In years of calamity and famine, the weak and old, lying in the ditches and water-courses, and the able-bodied, scattered to the four quarters, have been myriads in number." (Mencius, bk. i., pt. ii., c. xii., v. 2.)

It has not required physical calamity or famine, also, to bring these demoralizing conditions to the peoples of the most modern and civilized nations!

This worthy apostle of the doctrine of Confucius, however, has yet clearer insight into the causes of the utter demoralization of the despairing and destitute. What a sermon upon the text, "The destruction of the poor is their poverty!" is spoken in these two sentences: "In such circumstances they only try to save themselves from death and are afraid they will not succeed. What opportunity have such to cultivate propriety and righteousness?" (Bk. i., pt. i., c. vii., v. 22.)

Or, indeed, opportunity or inducement to cultivate efficiency as men and workmen?

This involves the germ of the newest truths conceived by modern states-men, namely: That absolute assurance of freedom from want, for self and de-pendents, this to be obtainable only by efficient labour but as its sure reward, is the most powerful incentive to efficiency and industry; and that, whenever the conditions created by the government fall short of this, their influence is to this extent demoralizing and destructive to the men, women, and children who form the nation.

Upon this Mencius said to King Seuen of Ts'e, in a memorable conversation upon the duties of a ruler: "Only men of training can, without a certain liveli-hood, maintain a fixed heart. As to the people, if they have not a certain liveli-hood, it follows that they will not have a fixed heart. If they do not have a fixed heart, there is nothing which they will not do in self-abandonment, moral de-flection, depravity, and wild license. When they have thus been involved in crime, to pursue them and punish them is to entrap the people." (Bk. i., pt. i., c. vii., v. 20.)

This light is even now just dawning upon the minds of the pioneers in pro-gress in the most advanced nations. Fortunate that people which first realizes it in its national life and practice, and lamentable the case of that nation and its people who longest sin against that light!

Mencius, following out the Confucian concept of the state as founded upon the family, boldly asserts that good government must be parental. The word "paternal" would have had no terrors, surely, in a land where the most sacred name, next to that of God himself, is father. And if the people, as in a republic, choose them who are to rule over them, this would seem but to increase the obligation to deal in a fatherly and not an unfatherly manner, toward the peo-ple who have so displayed their trust.

Accordingly Mencius could find nothing worse to say of a delinquent ruler than this, quoted from Lung Tze: "When the parent of the people causes them to look distressed and, after toiling the entire year, not to be able to support their parents, so that they must borrow to increase their income and so that the old and the little children are found lying in the ditches and streams— where, then, is there anything parental in his relation to the people?" (Bk. iii., pt. i., c. iii., v. 7.)

Confucius fully shared this view as clearly appears from all that he has spo-ken concerning the character and duties of the great and worthy ruler of his fellow-men. These sayings are scattered throughout this book; but this reply to one of his disciples discloses in few words his conception of the highest qualities attainable by a true servant of the people: "Tsze-kung said: 'Suppose the case of a man extensively conferring benefits on the people, and able to assist all, what would you say of him? Might he be called perfectly virtuous?'

99

The Master said: 'Why speak only of virtue in connection with him? Must he not have the qualities of the sage?'" (Analects, bk. vi., c. xxviii., v. 1.)

In the "Li Ki" this parable is told to illustrate the people's well-grounded terror of misrule: "In passing by the side of Mount Thai, Confucius came upon a woman who was wailing bitterly by a grave. The Master bowed forward to the crossbar, and hastened to her; and then sent Tsze-loo to question her. 'Your wailing,' said he, 'is altogether like that of one who has suffered sorrow on sorrow.' She replied, 'It is so. Formerly my husband's father was killed here by a tiger. My husband was also killed by one, and now my son has died in the same way.' The Master said, 'Why do you not leave this place?' The answer was, 'There is no oppressive government here.' The Master then said to his disciples: 'Remember this, my little children. Oppressive government is more terrible than tigers.'" (Bk. ii., sect. ii., pt. iii., 10.)

The Middle Path in Political Economy. "Hence there is this saying: 'Some labour with their minds and some with their muscles. They who labour with their minds, govern others; they who labour with their muscles are governed by others. They who are governed by others, support them; they who govern others, are supported by them.' This is a principle universally recognized." (Mencius, bk. iii., pt. i., c. iv., v. 6.)

In the time of Confucius, it does not appear that either extreme, anarchism or communism, was so urged upon men's notice as to compel his attention; but Mencius, from whose sayings this passage is taken and who lived over a century later, was frequently confronted with their specious arguments.

This deliverance was in reply to the following argument in favour of Tolstoian individualism, presented to Mencius by Ch'in Seang: "Now wise and able princes should cultivate the ground equally and along with their people and eat the fruit of their labours. They should prepare their own meals, morning and evening, while at the same time they carry on the government." (Mencius, bk. iii., pt. i., c. iv., v. 3.)

The doctrine of the division of labour and of the interchange of services and of the products of labour, Mencius again supported in this passage: "If you do not have an exchange of the products of labour and an interchange of service, so that too much there will make good too little here, then farmers will have a surplus of grain and women of cloth. If you have such an interchange, carpenters and wagon-makers may earn and receive their sustenance." (Bk. iii., pt. ii., c. iv., v. 3.)

The doctrine of extreme individualism, when presented in another guise, is thus characterized by the Duke King of Ts'e, as reported by Mencius: "Not to be able to command others and at the same time to refuse to receive their commands, is to cut one's self off from all intercourse with men." (Bk. iv., pt. i., c. vii., v. 2.)

At another time he thus showed the destructive and anarchical effects, now only too well known by experience, of the full adoption of either the extreme individualistic or the extreme communistic view: "Yang's principle is: 'Every man for himself,' which does not recognize the superior claim of the sovereign. Mih's principle is: 'Equal favour for all,' which does not acknowledge the superior claim of a father. But to acknowledge neither sovereign nor father is to lapse into barbarism...If the principles of Yang or of Mih were urged and the principles of Confucius were not urged, these perverse reasonings would delude the people and check the course of benevolence and righteousness. When such are checked, beasts will be led forth to devour men and men will devour one another." (Bk. iii., pt. ii., c. ix., v. 9.)

Provision for the Aged, Widows, Orphans, and Other Unfortunates. "A competent provision was secured for the aged till their death, employment for the able-bodied, and the means of growing up to the young. They showed kindness and compassion to widows, orphans, childless men, and those who were disabled by disease; so that they were all sufficiently maintained. Men had their proper work and women their homes." (Li Ki, bk. vii., sect. i., 2.)

The foregoing is the description of the blissful consequences of good government, contained in "The Grand Course" as set forth in the "Li Ki."

Mencius made the support of the old, with reverence and honour, the first care of the state, saying: "If there were a prince in the empire who knew well how to nourish the old, all good men would feel that he was the right one for them to rally around." (Bk. vii., pt. i., c. xxii., v. i.)

It is by no means sufficient that the old be supported; they must be supported respectably and, what is more to the point, respectfully. The doctrines of Confucius did not tolerate want of homage to the old. This the following passages from the "Li Ki" abundantly illustrate: "Yü, Hsiâ, Yin, and Kâu produced the greatest kings that have appeared under heaven and there was not one of them who neglected age. Long under heaven has honour been paid to length of years! To do so is next to service of one's parents." (Bk. xxi., sect. ii., 15.) "There were five things by means of which the ancient kings secured the good government of the whole kingdom: the honour which they paid to the virtuous, to the noble, and to the old, the reverence which they showed the aged, and their kindness to the young. By these five things they maintained the stability of their kingdom." (Bk. xxi., sect. i., 13.)

Confucius is quoted in the same book as saying: "When those in authority at their courts show respect for the aged, the people will be filial." (Bk. xxvii., 24.)

And in another place in the "Li Ki" he supplies this apt test of a good government of a good people: "When they saw an old man, people driving or walking gave him the road. Men who had white hairs mingling with the black did not carry burdens along the highways." (Bk. xxi., 17.)

But it is not alone the aged who are by the authorities of a well-governed state made the objects of affectionate, prudent care, not as a matter of charity but as a right. Mencius in these words of practical wisdom offered mutual insurance as a solution for this, effectual so far as anything human can equalize inequalities, to ward off disasters that overwhelm a man when standing utterly alone. The following expression of his views has a decidedly twentieth-century, even Bismarckian tang: "In the fields of a district, those who belong

101

to the same nine squares, render all friendly offices to one another in their going out and coming in [*i.e.*, death and birth], aid one another to safeguard life and property, and support one another in sickness." (Bk. iii., pt. i., c. iii., v. 18.)

Mencius also thus describes another sort of social insurance, already prevalent in those days: "In the spring they examined the ploughing and supplied any deficiency of seed; in the fall they examined the reaping and supplied any deficiency of yield." (Bk. i., pt. ii., c. iv., v. 5.)

Surely if such a system were now in vogue in China, effective and nation-wide, a famine would be unknown and indeed unthinkable!

Taxation, Innocent and Destructive. "If in the market-place, he levy a ground rent on the shops but do not tax the goods, or enforce proper regulations without levying a ground rent,—then all the merchants of the empire will be pleased and will wish to have their goods in his marketplace. If at his frontier there be an inspection of persons but no import duties, all travellers throughout the empire will be pleased, and wish to make their tours on his roads." (Mencius, bk. ii., pt. i., c. v., v. 2, 3.)

Mencius, as in the foregoing, considered the question of the proper modes of levying taxes, taking into account their effect upon those who are engaged in agriculture, in commerce, and in the trades. In his day, the question of the proper methods of taxation was evidently a live one, as in these days; and about the same issues arose in all essential particulars. The foregoing quotation from the Book of Mencius favours "ground rent," *i.e.*, a tax upon the ground, itself, now known as the "single tax" as proposed by Henry George,— or "proper regulations," by which is doubtless meant licenses for use—but not a tax on goods, *i.e.*, upon personal property. Still less does he favour import duties.

The reasons which he gives for opposition to import duties were undoubtedly valid in China and as between the various states which compose the Chinese empire, as they would be against import duties of one state of the United States against other states. Especially in this day when, by reason of the marvellous improvement of means of communication and transportation, the world has grown so small, they may also seem valid, save in very exceptional circumstances, as regards the entire sisterhood of nations.

Mencius thus describes, in quite a "single tax" fashion, the origin of "ground rents" levied in order to appropriate to the community the value of a superior location: "In olden times in the market men exchanged their wares for the wares of others and merely had certain officers to keep order. It chanced there was a mean fellow who made it a point to find a conspicuous mound and get upon it. Thence he commanded the right and the left, so as to draw into his net all the bargains of the market. All considered his conduct contemptible and so they proceeded to levy a tax upon his wares. The tax upon merchants thus sprang from this fellow's sordidness." (Bk. ii., pt. ii., c. x., v. 7.)

Mencius could find no excuse, however, for duties, whether internal or import, as the following conversation shows:

"Tae Ying-che said, 'I am not able at present to get along at once with the tithes only and so to abolish the duties imposed at the ports of entry and in the markets. With your leave, however, I will reduce both these duties until next year and then will abolish them altogether. What do you think of such a course?'

"Mencius said, 'Here is a man who every day appropriates some of his neighbour's strayed fowls. Someone says to him: "Such is not the way of a good man." He replies: "With your leave, I will diminish my appropriations, and will take but one fowl per month until next year when I will make an end of the practice." If you know the thing to be wrong, hasten to get rid of it! Why wait until next year?'" (Bk. iii., pt. ii., c. viii.)

The system of levies upon the holders of cultivable land, which anciently obtained, is thus described by Mencius: "A square le covers nine squares of land which nine squares contain nine hundred mow. The central square is the public field; and eight families, each having its private hundred mow, cultivate the public field in common; and not until this public work is done, dare they attend to tilling their own fields." (Bk. iii., pt. i., c. iii., v. 19.)

The change from this to a tithing or income tax system in the more populous districts is thus indicated: "I would ask you, in the remoter districts, observing the nine Squares division, to reserve one division to be cultivated on the system of mutual aid, and in the more central parts of the kingdom, to require the people to pay a tenth part of their produce." (Bk. iii., pt. i., c. iii., v. is.)

As has already been quoted in the section on "Nourishment of the People," Mencius regarded any system of taxation, based upon values, as of land or goods or both, regardless of the product, as destructive and in bad seasons even ruinous, resulting accordingly in the demoralization and pauperization of the people, while the tithe or income tax falls or rises with the ability to respond. This is also enforced by the following from the Book of Mencius: "Lung said, 'For regulating farms, there is no better system than that of mutual aid and none which is worse than that of taxing. By taxing, the amount to be paid regularly is fixed by taking the average of several years. In good years, when there is grain in abundance, much might be taken without its being oppressive, and the actual detriment would be small; but in bad years, the produce not being sufficient to repay manuring the fields, the tax system requires taking the full amount.'" (Bk. iii., pt. i., c. iii., v. 7.)

Military Equipment. "To lead an uninstructed people to war, is to throw them away." (Analects, bk. xiii., c. xxx.)

Confucius scarcely referred to the subject of war, except in the matter of indicating methods by which both misunderstandings with the peoples of neighbouring states and revolts on the part of classes of the citizens may be avoided. This indicates the relatively peaceful conditions already obtaining there.

Yet the saying quoted above from the "Analects" seems full of insight and of prescience, when applied to the fate of the soldiers and marines of China and of Russia when at different times of late pitted against the trained and disciplined naval and military forces of Japan. May it not also be of some importance to another great people of a hundred million souls which leaves its free citizens without military training? Are the Russians and the Chinese the only fatuous people in the world?

It is also enforced by the sage as follows: "Let a good man teach the people seven years, and they may then be led to war." (Analects, bk. xiii., c. xxix.)

These texts must have been often in the minds of the people, since the catastrophes of the two Japanese wars; and the long belated seven years' preparation may now be fairly under way.

Confucius gave some notion of what he deemed the requisites of a great military leader in the following: "Tsze-loo said, 'If you had the conduct of the armies of a great state, whom would you have to act with you?' The Master said, 'I would not have him to act with me, who will unarmed attack a tiger or cross a river without a boat, dying without regret. My associate must be a man who proceeds to action full of solicitude, who is fond of adjusting his plans and then carries them into execution!' (Analects, bk. vii., c. x., v. 2, 3.)

Yet this people, whose great teacher gave so little attention to military subjects, notwithstanding that he ranked it as one of the three essentials of good government, is the only one among the great nations which has maintained real continuity for itself through thousands of years; and the great wall which it constructed to ward off northern invasions is quite the most remarkable line of defences ever constructed.

Mencius also advises this course, duly emphasizing the necessity for the spirit of patriotic devotion among the people, in these words: "If you will have me counsel you, there is one thing I can suggest. Dig deeper your moats; build higher your walls; guard them, you and your people. Be prepared to die if need be, and have the people so attached that they will not desert you!" (Bk. ii., pt. ii., c. xiii., v. 2.)

The great impropriety of maintaining military forces in order to overawe the people, as well as the utter want of need for such under a benevolent government, is plainly indicated by all of the teachings of the sage concerning government, yet quoted or to be quoted. Only the following need be cited: "Duke Hwan assembled all the princes together nine times and did not use weapons of war and chariots. This was through the influence of Kwan Chung. Whose beneficence was like his?" (Analects, bk. xiv., c. xvii., v. 2.)

The manner in which benevolent government knits all citizens into a united band of patriots, against whom no force, from within or without, can prevail, is thus described by Mencius: "With a territory which is only a hundred le square, it is possible to attain the Imperial dignity. If Your Majesty will give a benevolent government to your people, be sparing in punishments and fines and make the taxes and levies light, so causing fields to be ploughed deep and weeding to be carefully attended to and the strong-bodied, during their days of leisure, to cultivate filial piety, fraternal respectfulness, sincerity, truthfulness, serving thereby, at home, their fathers and elder brothers and, abroad, their elders and superiors—you will then have a people who can be employed with sticks they have prepared, to oppose the strong mail and sharp weapons of the troops of Ts'in and Ts'oo.'" (Bk. i., pt. i., c. v., v. 2, 3.)

And with yet more enthusiastic eloquence he celebrates the prowess of a united people under a leader whom all trust to the uttermost and their ability to overcome every foe and resist every assault, in this passage, condemning reliance upon mere strength of fortifications and armament: "With walls of great height, with moats of great depth, with arms, both of offence and defence, trenchant and mighty, with great stores of rice and other food, the city is surrendered and abandoned. This is because material advantages do not compensate for the absence of the spiritual union of men. Therefore is it said, 'A people is protected, not by bulwarks and ditches; a kingdom is safeguarded, not by rivers and mountains-an empire is conquered, not by the superiority of arms!'" (Bk. ii., pt. ii., c. i., v. 3, 4.)

Kingly Qualities. "What is most potent is to be a man. Its influence will be felt throughout the state." (Shi King, Sacrificial Odes of Kau, decade i., ode 4.)

Confucius makes these words of the "Shi King" more emphatic, when he says: "Let there be men and the government will flourish; but, without men, government decays and dies." (Doctrine of the Mean, c. xx., v. 2.)

And it is also remarked in "The Great Learning": "When the ruler excels as a father, a son, and a brother, then the people imitate him." (C. ix., v. 8.)

The same is put in illustrative form in this legend of China's dawn of history: "Shun, being in possession of the empire, selected from among all the people and employed Kaou-yaou, on which all who were devoid of virtue disappeared." (Analects, bk. xii., c. xxii., v. 6.)

To Shun himself Confucius attributed that perfect poise which commanded because it was commanding and showered benefits because the king with all his heart desired the welfare of his people. Of him it is said in the "Analects": "May not Shun be instanced as having governed efficiently without exertion? What did he do? He did nothing but gravely and reverently occupy the imperial seat." (Analects, bk. xv., c. iv.)

In another passage a like majesty is ascribed also to Yu: "How majestic was the manner in which Shun and Yu held possession of the empire as if it were nothing to them!" (Analects, bk. viii., c. xviii.)

In the "Yi King" a much more detailed but somewhat extravagant description of the power of character in enforcing benevolent and beneficent rules of government is given, thus: "The Master said, 'The superior man occupies his apartment and sends forth his words. If they be good, they will be responded to at a distance of more than a thousand li; how much more will they be so in the nearer circle! He occupies his apartment and sends forth his words. If they be evil they will awaken opposition at a distance of more than a thousand li; how much more will they do so in the nearer circle!'" (Appendix iii., sect. i., c. viii., v. 42.)

This subject comes abruptly out of the clouds to the level of practical, everyday life, however, when the following plain-spoken words from the lips of the sage are consulted in the "Analects":

"If a minister make his own conduct correct, what difficulty will he have about assisting in government? If he cannot rectify himself, what has he to do with rectifying others?" (Bk. xiii., c. xiii.)

Mencius paid his tribute to the power of virtue, as follows: "In the empire there are three things universally acknowledged to be honourable. Nobility is one of them, age is one of them, virtue is one of them. In courts nobility holds first place, in villages age, and for usefulness to one's generation and controlling the people, neither is equal to virtue." (Bk. ii., pt. ii., c. ii., v. 6.)

It is difficult, however, even for Confucius to avoid enthusiasm in the statement of this proposition to which he returns again and again, as thus: "He who exercises government by means of his virtue, may be compared to the north polar star which keeps its place and all the stars turn toward it." (Analects, bk. ii., c. i.)

In two other sayings, are presented different phases of this view: "When rulers love to observe the rules of propriety, the people respond readily to the calls upon them for service." (Analects, bk. xiv., c. xliv.) "The superior man does not use rewards, yet the people are stimulated to virtue. He does not show wrath, yet the people are more awed than by hatchets and battle-axes." (Doctrine of the Mean, c. xxxiii., v. 4.)

Mencius also says: "When one subdues men by force, they do not submit to him in heart but because not strong enough to resist. When one subdues men by virtue, they are pleased to the heart's core and sincerely submit." (Bk. ii., pt. i., c. iii., v. 2.)

In the "Li Ki" the consequences upon the ruler and his government, of qualities opposite to these, are indicated by this significant question: "If his heart be not observant of righteousness, self-consecration, good faith, sincerity, and guilelessness, though a ruler may try to knit the people firmly to him, will not all bonds between them be dissolved?" (Bk. ii., sect. ii., pt. iii., 11.)

This picture is given by Confucius in the "Analects," of a worthy and successful ruler: "By his generosity, he won all. By his sincerity, he made the people repose trust in him. By his earnest activity, his achievements were great. By his justice, all were delighted." (Bk. xx., c. i., v. 9.)

I Yin, as quoted in the "Shu King," thus eloquently descants upon the earnest aspirations of another ruler: "The former king, before it was light, sought to have large and clear views and then sat waiting for the dawn to put them into practice." (Pt. iv., bk. v., 2.)

The Duke of Chin, according to the same book, thus defined the qualities that characterize the great minister: "Let me have but one resolute minister, plain and sincere, without other ability but having a straightforward mind, and possessed of generosity, regarding the talents of others as if he possessed them himself, and when he finds accomplished and sage men, loving them in his heart more than his mouth expresses, really showing himself able to bear them; such a minister would be able to preserve my descendants and people and would indeed be a giver of benefits." (Pt. v., bk. xxx.)

Confucius himself, replying to the question of a disciple, gives an estimate of the most desirable qualifications for an officer of lower rank. It runs:

"Tsze-kung asked, 'What qualities must a man possess to entitle him to be called an officer?' The Master said, 'He who in his own conduct maintains a sense of shame and when sent to any quarter, will not disgrace his prince's commission, deserves to be called an officer.'

"Tsze-kung went on, 'I venture to ask who may be placed in the next lower rank,' and was told, 'He whom the circle of his relatives pronounces filial, whom his fellow-villagers and neighbours pronounce fraternal.'

"He asked once more, 'I venture to ask about the class next in order.' The Master said, 'They who are determined to be sincere in what they say and to carry out what they do. They are obstinate little men. Yet perhaps they make the next class.'" (Analects, bk. xiii., c. xx., v. 1, 2, 3.)

Some of the qualities which are most valuable in a public officer Confucius named in commending a contemporary thus: "The Master said of Tsze-ch'an that he had four of the characteristics of a superior man: 'In his own conduct, he was humble; in serving his superiors, he was respectful; in providing for the people's support, he was kind; in ordering the people, he was just.'" (Analects, bk. v., c. xv.)

The following conversation drew from Confucius a distinct statement of what quality in a ruler is most essential, *i.e.*, humility and a deep sense of responsibility, and what quality is most destructive, 1. e., a dictatorial, wrongheaded obstinacy, which brooks no advice, remonstrance, or opposition:

"The Duke Ting asked whether there was a single sentence which could make a country prosperous. Confucius replied:

"'Such an effect cannot be expected from one sentence. There is a saying, however, which people have: To be a prince is difficult, to be a minister not easy. If a ruler know this, how difficult it is to be a prince, may there not be expected from this one sentence, that the country be made prosperous?'

"The duke then asked, 'Is there a single sentence which can ruin a country?' Confucius replied:

"'Such an effect cannot be expected from one sentence. There is a saying, however, which people have: I have no pleasure in being prince, except that no one offers opposition to what I say. If a ruler's words be good, is it not also good that no one oppose them? But if not good and no one opposes them, may there not be expected from this one sentence the ruin of the country?'" (Analects, bk. xiii., c. xv.)

That to die surrounded by the splendours of absolute sway does not assure, in the face of every evidence of misrule, that one has been successful, Confucius illustrates by this reference to Chinese history: "The Duke King of Ts'e had a thousand chariots, each drawn by four horses; but on the day of his death the people did not honour him for a single virtue. P'ih-e and Shu-ts'e died of hunger at the foot of the Show-yang mountain, and yet the people honour them to this day." (Analects, bk. xvi., c. xii., v. 1.)

And this glowing and inviting prospect he discloses for the ruler of men who bases his claim upon propriety, righteousness, and good faith: "If a superior love propriety, the people will not dare not to be reverent. If he love righteousness, the people will not dare not to conform to his desires. If he love good faith, the people will not dare not to be sincere. When these things obtain, the people from all quarters will come to him, bearing their children on their backs." (Analects, bk. xiii., c. iv., v. 3.)

Power of Official Example. "The ruler must first himself be possessed of the qualities which he requires of the people; and must be free from the qualities which he requires the people to abjure." (Great Learning, c. ix., v. 4.)

Thus Confucius emphasizes the most modern principle of "noblesse oblige"; nor does he leave it doubtful that what he means is that "example speaks louder than words," especially when he whose conduct is in question stands forth in all men's sight their chief and leader, for he is quoted by Mencius as saying: "What the superior man loves, his inferiors will be found to love exceedingly. The relation between superiors and inferiors is like that between the wind and the grass. The grass must bend when the wind blows upon it." (Mencius, bk. iii., pt. i., c. ii., v. 4.)

In the "Li Ki" appears the following concerning the influence of the example set by the ruler; "The Master said, 'Inferiors, in serving those over them, do not follow what they command, but what they do. When a ruler loves a given thing, his subjects will do so, more than he. Therefore he who is in authority should be careful about what he likes and what he dislikes; for these will be examples in the eyes of the people.' (Li Ki, bk. xxx., 4.)

In the following, also from the "Li Ki," he connects it with the most powerful sanction for ethical conduct known to the Chinese, *i.e.*, filial piety: "When a man who is over others transgresses in his words, the people will fashion their speech accordingly; when he transgresses in his conduct, the people will imitate him as their model. If in his words he does not go beyond what should be said, nor in his acts beyond what should be done, then the people, without direction so to do, will revere and honour him. When this is so, he has respected himself; and having respected himself, he will have honoured his parents to the utmost." (Bk. xxiv., 13.)

"The Great Learning" thus derives both the safety and the peril of the state, in this regard, from the observation of filial and fraternal obligations within the family: "From the love within one family, the entire state may be made loving; from its courtesies, the entire state be made courteous; while from the ambition and perverseness of one man, the entire state may be led into rebellion; such is the power of example." (C. ix., v. 3.)

In the same book it is put thus: "In the Book of Poetry it is said: 'In his deportment there is nothing wrong; he rectifies all the people of the state.' When the ruler, as a father, a son, and a brother, is exemplary, the people will imitate him." (C. ix., v. 8.)

In the "Analects," Confucius has repeatedly announced this truth, as in these words: "When a prince's personal conduct is correct, his government is effective without the issuing of orders. When his personal conduct is not correct, he map issue orders but they will not be obeyed." (Bk. xiii., c. vi.)

One reason that so much greater potency inheres in what he who presides over the destiny of a people does, than in what he says or even commands, Confucius assigns in this saying: "The people may be made to follow a course of action, but they may not be made to understand it." (Analects, bk. viii., c. ix.)

And Confucius accentuates the lesson in this: "Though a man have abilities as admirable as those of the duke of Chow, yet if he be proud and niggardly, those other things are really not worth being looked at." (Analects, bk. viii., c. xi.)

Yet not too much, nor that too soon, must be expected even of the most brilliant and efficacious righteousness of the man in command, when for a long time disorder and demoralization have prevailed. In the "Analects" Confucius says of this: "If a truly royal ruler were to arrive, it would require a generation and then virtue would prevail." (Bk. xiii., c. xii.)

Yet he urged that the ruler rely upon the purity of his desire, his example, and persuasion of the people to love and practise what is good, rather than upon proscription and penalties; and he says: "If the people be led by laws and uniformity sought to be given them by punishments, they will try to avoid the punishment but have no sense of guilt. If they be led by virtue and uniformity sought to be given them by the rules of propriety, they will have the sense of guilt and moreover will become good." (Analects, bk. ii., c. iii.)

Again he inquires, most significantly: "In carrying on your government, why should you use killing at all? Let your desires be for what is good, and the people will be good." (Analects, bk. xii., c. xix.)

And in a like spirit he rebukes a prince who complained to him, thus: "Ke K'ang Tze, distressed about the prevalence of thieves, inquired of Confucius how to suppress them. Confucius replied: 'If you yourself were not covetous, they would not steal, though you should offer a reward for stealing.'" (Analects, bk. xii., c. xviii.)

His disciple, Tsang Tze, thus imposes upon every man who occupies high station the obligation to guard his demeanour, deportment, speech, and conduct to the end that none of those who look up to him shall be corrupted thereby: "There are three principles of conduct which the man of high rank should consider specially important: that in his deportment and manner he keep from violence and heedlessness; that in regulating his countenance he keep near to sincerity; and that in word and tone he keep far from lowness and impropriety." (Analects, bk. viii., c. iv., v. 3.)

Upon the chief ruler of China, the leader and exemplar for all the people, this responsibility is so made to rest that, were it fully realized in actual government, every emperor would present the touching and edifying picture of an Abraham Lincoln, bending beneath the heavy burdens of the people whom he so loved and so served with conscientious reverence. For these words the sage puts into the prayer of him whom imperial sway makes the servant of all his people: "If, in my own person, I commit offences, they are not to be attributed to you, ye people of the myriad regions. If ye in the myriad regions commit offences, the guilt must rest upon my head." (Analects, bk. xx., c. i., v. 3.)

Universal Education. "When the man of high station is well instructed, he loves men; when the man of low station is well instructed, he is easily ruled." (Analects, bk. xvii., c. iv., v. 3.)

Thus Confucius sets forth the necessity for general education of all classes of the people and the benefits in respect of government which flow from it. In another place, he says, even more significantly, of the levelling power of education: "There being instruction, there will be no distinction of classes." (Analects, bk. xv., c. xxxviii.)

This levelling extended also to those of the highest rank and beyond school-days into official life, determining the fitness and title to public office. Thus the "Hsun Tse" (bk. ix.) says of this: "Even among the sons of the emperor, the princes, and the great officials, if they were not qualified to rites and justice, they should be put down to the class of common people; even among the sons of the common people, if they have good education and character and are qualified to rites and justice, they should be elevated to the class of minister. and nobles."

According to the "Li Ching," the education of the child commences with its conception, and accordingly explicit instructions are given to secure proper prenatal influences and ward off evil influences. The instructions are as to physical, mental, and moral conduct of the mother during gestation, with the direct object of producing a strong, intelligent, and moral human being.

The value and potency of education are set forth in the same work (bk. xlviii.) as follows: "When a child is trained completely, his education is just as strong as his nature; and when he practises anything constantly, he will do it naturally as a permanent habit."

Mencius made the following sage and practical remark concerning another aspect of the relation of education to government: "Good government is feared by the people, while good instruction is loved by them. Good government gets the people's wealth, while good instruction wins their hearts." (Bk. vii., pt. i., c. xiv., v. 3.)

In this, of course the expression "good government" means much the same as in modern politics, *i.e.*, "business men's government," bent upon securing order and economy only, but often utterly disregarding the desires and even the essential well-being of the lowly and oppressed. Real "good government" necessarily includes instruction; and that Mencius fully understood this, the following penetrating remark from his book fully substantiates: "Men possess a moral nature; but if they are well fed, warmly clad, and comfortably lodged, without at the same time being instructed, they become like unto beasts." (Bk. iii., pt. i., c. iv., v. 8.)

This principle, that education is the great and constant need of all minds and most especially of the mind of him who would lead others, Mencius also applied remorselessly to the princes of his day, as a paramount duty resting upon them, in this passage: "Now, throughout the empire, the jurisdictions of the princes are of equal extent and none excels his fellows in achievement. Not one is able to go beyond the others. This is from no other reason than that they love to make ministers of those whom they teach rather than to make ministers of those by whom they might themselves be taught." (Bk. ii., pt. ii., c. ii., v. 9.)

And to the burden of this responsibility, i.e., at all times to be earnestly and humbly seeking instruction themselves, he thus added the duty of providing for the education of the people, coupled with the promise of such fulfilment of ambitions as naturally flows from excellence in the performance of obligations already assumed: "Let careful attention be paid to education in schools, inculcating in it especially the filial and fraternal duties, and grey-haired men will not be seen upon the roads, bearing burdens on their backs or on their heads. It never has been that the ruler of a state where such results were seen, persons of seventy wearing silks and eating flesh and the black-haired people suffering neither from hunger nor cold—did not attain to the Imperial dignity." (Mencius, bk. i., pt. i., c. iii., v. 4.)

That these were not intended as mere platitudes is shown, not merely by the result that in China for thousands of years education has been the test, on a strictly competitive basis, without regard to wealth, social position, and influence of forbears, by which political preferment has been determined; but also by the strictly practical statements concerning popular instruction, such as this from the "Li Ki": "If he wish to transform the people and to perfect their manners and customs, must he not start with the lessons of the school?" (Bk. xvi., 1.)

The established public means of education are thus described in the same book: "According to the system of ancient teaching, for the families of a hamlet (25) there was the village school; for a neighbourhood (500 families) there was the academy; for a larger district (2500 families), the college; and in the capitals, a university." (Bk. xvi., 4.)

That there may be no question that the competitive examination was already the essential for political appointment or advancement, this is also quoted from the "Li Ki": "Every year some entered the college and every second year there was a competitive examination." (Bk. xvi., 5.)

The accepted and approved purpose of instruction, as laid down in the "Li Ki," is also most progressive and may to advantage, perhaps, be contrasted with the insistence, now happily subsiding, in Occidental nations that "the three R's," i.e., reading, writing, and arithmetic, if indeed so much as that, are quite sufficient and all that, or more than, the government should concern itself to secure for the people. This passage illustrates the view in China, even before Confucius came to instruct his people for all time: "Teaching should be directed to develop that in which the pupil excels, and correct the defects to which he is prone." (Li Ki, bk. xvi., 14.)

Modern courses in psychology for the instruction of teachers were anticipated also in the olden times, centuries before the Christian era; and the whole matter had been clearly and discriminatingly put, as in this from the "Li Ki": "Among pupils there are four defects with which the teacher must make himself acquainted. Some err by assuming too many branches of study; some, too few; some in over-facility; some, in want of persistence. These four defects arise from the differences of their minds. When the teacher understands the character of his pupil's mind, he can rescue him from the fault to which he is prone." (Bk. xvi., 14.)

It is also said upon this interesting topic: "When a man of talents and virtue understands the stupidity of one pupil and the precocity of another in the attainment of knowledge and also comprehends the good and bad qualities of his pupils, he can vary his methods of teaching accordingly. When he can vary his methods of teaching, he is indeed a master. When so fitted to be a teacher, he is qualified for administrative office; and when so qualified for administrative office, he is even fitted to be chosen as ruler of the state. Therefore is it that from a teacher one learns how to be a ruler; and therefore that in the choice of a teacher the greatest care should be exercised. As it is said in the History: 'The three kings and the four dynasties were what they were, by reason of their teachers.'" (Li Ki, bk. xvi., 16.)

This also, from the same source, bears upon the psychology of the problem of teaching and also shows that the true meaning of "to educate" was already apprehended: "When a superior man knows the causes which make instruction successful and those which make it of no effect, he can become a teacher of others. Thus, in his teaching, he draws out and does not merely carry along; he encourages and does not discourage; he opens up the subject but does not exhaust it, leaving the student nothing to do. Drawing out and not merely dragging along produces concert of effort. Encouraging and not restraining makes it easy to go forward. Opening up the subject and not exhausting it forces the student himself to think. He who brings about this concert of action, this ready advancement, and this independent initiative of thought may be pronounced a skilful teacher." (Bk. xvi., 13.)

Confucius, in the "Analects," twice gives expression to the same fundamental principle: "With one like Tsze, I can commence talking about the Odes. I told him one point and he knew its proper sequence." (Bk. vii., c. viii.) "I do not open up the truth to one who is not eager for knowledge, nor help out any one who is not himself anxious to explore causes. When I have presented one corner of a subject to any one and he cannot learn from it the other three, I do not repeat my lesson." (Bk. xii., c. viii.)

In its entirety this was a course necessary for Confucius with his great work to do, but scarcely practicable for all teachers for the reason that all must be instructed, whether bright or dull, whether studious or indolent; the sage's impatience with sluggishness and dulness, the ordinary teacher could not imitate, except by utterly destroying his usefulness. In consequence, therefore, the sage nowhere recommends such procedure to teachers, whether of the young or of the mature.

In the "Li Ki," the correct view of this aspect of teaching is thus set forth with considerable fulness: "The skilful student, though his teacher seems indifferent, yet attains double as much as another and in the sequel ascribes the credit to his teacher. The unskilful, though his teacher be diligent with him, makes but half the progress and in the sequel blames his teacher. The skilful inquirer is like a workman addressing himself to deal with a hard log: first he attacks the easy parts and then the knotty. After applying himself a good while, he talks with his teacher and all is plain. The unskilful does the contrary." (Bk. xvi., 18.)

The popular impression among Occidental peoples—so far as they have any impression—concerning the instruction of Chinese children is well illustrated by what the "Li Ki" condemns in this passage: "Under the system of instruction now in use the teachers hum over the tablets which they have before them and ask many questions. They then speak of their pupils making rapid progress but pay no attention to whether they retain what they have been taught. They are not earnest in imposing burdens upon their pupils nor do they put forth all their power to instruct them. The habits they thus cause the pupils to form are not good and the students are disappointed about attaining what they seek. Accordingly, they find their studies onerous and despise their teachers; they are embittered by the difficulties they encounter and realize but poor results of their toil. They may appear to do their work but they quickly lose what they acquire. That there are no stable results of their instruction, is it not due to these defects in their teacher?" (Bk. xvi., 10.)

That the good teacher is to be regarded as an important member of the community and must be treated with respect and veneration, in order that he may best perform his useful function, is inculcated also in the "Li Ki" in these terms: "In providing a system of education, one trouble is to secure proper respect for the teacher; when such is assured, what he teaches will also be regarded with respect; when that is done, the people will know how to respect learning. Therefore is it that there are two of his subjects whom the ruler does not treat as such: him who is personating his ancestor at the sacrifice, he does not so treat, nor yet his own teacher." (Bk. xvi., 17.)

The same book names the following as the objects to be sought in education: "In all learning, for him who would be an officer, the first thing is the knowledge of business; for scholars, the first thing is the directing of the mind." (Bk. xvi., 6.)

And it thus urges the desirability of class-work, as affording abundant opportunity for companionship, a just estimate of one's acquirements and true culture: "To study alone and without friends makes one feel solitary, uncultivated, and but little informed." (Bk. xvi., 12.)

In the same book, this brief description of the method of Confucius is to be found: "The Master taught them by means of current events; and made them understand what was virtuous." (Bk. vi., sect. i., 17.)

The following are a few of the passages in the "Analects," some of which have already been quoted in other connections, that shed light upon the methods of teaching followed by Confucius and the subjects which he taught:

"The subjects on which the Master did not talk were extraordinary things, feats of strength, disorder, and spiritual beings." (Bk. vii., c. xx.)

"There are four things which the Master taught: letters, ethics, devotion of soul, and truthfulness." (Bk. vii., c. xxiv.)

"The Master said, 'Hwuy gives me no assistance. There is nothing that I say in which he does not delight.'" (Bk. xi., c. iii.)

"The Master said, To those whose talents are above mediocrity the highest subjects may be announced. To those who are below mediocrity the highest subjects may not be announced.' (Bk. vi., c. xvii.)

"There was Yen Hwuy; he loved to learn. He did not transfer his anger; he did not repeat a fault." (Bk. vi., c. ii.)

"I have talked with Hwuy for a whole day and he has not made any objection—quite as if he were stupid. He has retired and I have examined his conduct while out of my sight and found him able to illustrate my teaching. Hwuy? He is not stupid." (Bk. ii., c. ix.)

"The Master said to Tsze-Kung, 'Which do you consider superior, yourself or Hwuy?' Tsze-Kung replied, 'How dare I compare myself with Hwuy? Hwuy hears one point and understands the whole subject; I hear one point and understand the next.' The Master said, 'You are not equal to him. I grant you, you are not equal to him.' (Bk. v., c. viii.)

"The Master's frequent themes of discourse were the Odes, the History, and the observance of the rules of propriety. On all these he frequently discoursed." (Bk. vii., c. xvii.)

The importance and indeed the necessity of popular education Confucius often dwelt upon, placing it next after mere physical sustenance for the people, as in this passage:

"When the Master went to Wei, Yen Yew acted as driver of his carriage.

"The Master observed, 'How numerous are the people!'

"Yew said, 'Since they are thus numerous, what more shall be done for them?' 'Make them prosperous' was the reply.

"'And when they are prosperous, what then shall be done?' The Master said, Instruct them.'" (Analects, bk. xiii., c. ix.)

Law and Order. "The Duke King, of Ts'e, asked Confucius about government. Confucius replied, 'It is when the prince is prince, the minister is minister, the father is father, the son is son.'" (Analects, bk. xii., c. xi.)

Thus Confucius in the "Analects" enjoins the necessity for order in the state. Both the things requisite for the maintenance of good order and the conditions that lead to disorder, he thus describes in another place: "When good government prevails in the empire, ceremonies, music, and punitive military expeditions proceed from the emperor. When bad government prevails in the empire, ceremonies, music, and punitive expeditions proceed from the princes. When they proceed from the princes, as a rule the cases will be few in which they do not lose their power in ten generations. When they proceed from the great officers of the princes, as a rule the cases will be few in which they do not lose their power in five generations. When the subsidiary ministers of the great officers hold in their grasp the orders of the kingdom, as a rule the cases will be few in which they do not lose their power in three generations." (Analects, bk. xvi., c. ii., v. 1.)

The peril to the state within which, in the words of the English poet, "wealth accumulates and men decay" was vividly present in the sage's mind, as this saying from the "Li Ki" abundantly witnesses: "The Master said, 'Under heaven the cases are few in which the poor have enjoyment, the rich love the rules of propriety, and families that are powerful remain quiet and orderly.'" (Bk. xxvii., c. iii.)

In the "Shu King," the following declaration of King Khang is to be found: "Families which have for generations enjoyed places of emolument seldom observe the rules of propriety." (Pt. v., bk. xxiv., 3.)

And, also in the "Shu King," the Duke of Kau is represented as saying of the evil effects sometimes witnessed, when even a moderate amount of unearned wealth passes to untutored youth: "I have observed among the lower people that, where the parents have diligently laboured in sowing and reaping, their sons often do not understand this painful toil, but abandon themselves to ease and to village slang and become quite disorderly." (Pt. v., bk. xv., 1.)

King Wu, however, one of the almost mythical monarchs and heroes of the earlier period of Chinese history, yet more powerfully portrays in the same book the depths to which disorder and demoralization may descend: "All who themselves commit crimes, robbing, stealing, practising villainy and treachery, and who kill men or violently assault them to take their property, being reckless and defiant of death—these are abhorred by all." (Pt. v., bk. ix., 3.)

The course of one who restored order in the kingdom was thus warmly commended by Confucius in the "Analects": "He carefully attended to the weights and measures, examined the body of the laws, restored those who had been unjustly removed from office; and the good government of the empire took its course." (Bk. xx., c. i., v. 6.)

The duty of care in the selection of administrative officers is particularly enjoined by him as in the following: "Employ first the services of your various officers, pardon small faults, and raise to office men of virtue and talents. Chung-kung said, 'How shall I know the men of virtue and talents, so that I may raise them to office?' He was answered, 'Raise to office those whom you know. As to those whom you do not know, will others neglect them?'" (Analects, bk. xiii., c. ii., v. 2.)

This is the sage's characterization of the course of a wise king in the selection and discharge of officers: "He does not cause the great ministers to repine at his not employing them. Without some great cause, he does not dismiss from their offices the members of old families. He does not seek in one man talents for every employment." (Analects, bk. xviii., c. x.)

Due consideration of whether one's friends and even, indeed especially, one's relatives may not be fit for office, is not discouraged but instead insisted upon in the same passage: "The Duke of Chow addressed his son, the Duke of Loo, saying, 'The virtuous prince does not neglect his relatives.'" (Analects, bk. xviii., c. x.)

In favour of this course, he urges the following arguments: "When those who are in high stations perform well their duties to their relatives, the people are aroused to virtue. When old friends are not neglected by them, the people are preserved from meanness." (Analects, bk. viii., c. ii., v. 2.)

The acceptance of office for "what there is in it" or otherwise than as a sacred trust, he thus denounces: "Heen asked what is shameful. The Master said, 'When good government prevails in a state, to be thinking only of one's salary; and when bad government prevails, to be thinking, in the same way, only of one's salary. This is shameful.'" (Analects, bk. xiv., c. i.)

In the "Li Ki," Confucius is quoted as saying that it is safer and better in every way to wait until a man's death to confer any special honour upon him, thus: "The Master said, 'When honours and rewards are first conferred upon the dead and afterward upon the living, people will not depart from the course of the honoured dead.'" (Bk. xxvii., 10.)

That both the ruler and his ministers are subject to and should be governed by the elemental principles of right and wrong, which are of universal obligation, he here affirms: "A prince should employ his ministers according to the rules of propriety; ministers should serve their prince with faithfulness." (Analects, bk. iii., c. xix.)

In the "Li Ki," this caution to ministers and public officers is given: "Affairs of state should not be privately discussed." (Bk. i., sect. iii., pt. i.)

In the "Shu King" are found these instructions, among others, for the judges of the criminal courts: "It is not persons with crafty tongues who should try criminal cases, but persons who are really good, whose judgments will exemplify the due mean. Watch carefully for discrepancies in statements; the view you intended not to adopt, you may find reason to adopt. With pity and reverence determine the issues; painstakingly consult the penal code; give ear to all respecting the matter—to the end that your judgment may exemplify the due mean, whether in imposing a fine or another punishment, by careful investigation and the solution of every difficulty. When the trial has such an event, all will acknowledge that the judgment is just; and so likewise will the sovereign do, when the report reaches him." (Pt. v., bk. xxvii., 5.)

The same book lays down this discriminating fundamental for the administration of justice, recognizing that criminality consists in intent: "You pardon inadvertent faults, however great; and punish purposed crimes, however small." (Pt. ii., bk. ii., 2.)

Another passage of this ancient book asserts in words ascribed to Kau-Yau, speaking to Shun, a maxim of criminal justice which many suppose to be peculiar to its administration in Anglo-Saxon countries: "Rather than put an innocent person to death, you will run the risk of irregularity and error." (Pt. ii., bk. ii., 2.)

In the "Li Ki," the following passage describes the emoluments of public officers, indicating the use of "standards of value" much less subject to fluctuation than the precious metals: "The officers of the lowest grade in the feudal states received salary sufficient to feed nine individuals; those of the second grade, enough to feed eighteen; and those of the highest, enough for thirty-six. A great officer could feed 72 individuals, a minister 288, and the ruler 2880. In a state of the second class, a minister could feed 216, and the ruler 2160. A minister of a small state could feed 44. individuals and the ruler 1440." (Bk. iii., sect. v., 24.)

There were also restrictions in those days upon the military defence and equipment of states and cities, intended to keep down the spirit of domination and to avoid revolt. The "Li Ki" thus describes these laws: "Hence it was made the rule that no state should have more than 1000 chariots, no chief city's wall more than 100 embrasures, no family more than 100 chariots, however opulent. These regulations were intended for the protection of the people; yet some of the governors of states rebelled against them." (Bk. xxvii., 3.)

The foregoing are some of the more important of the things which Confucius and the ancients before him deemed prerequisite to the maintenance of good order throughout the nation. The breadth and depth of statesmanship required are even better set forth in this saying of Confucius: "The superior man governs men according to their nature, with what is proper to them." (Doctrine of the Mean, c. xiii., v. 21.)

With greater circumstantiality, yet in a very brief compass, he sets forth the prerequisites anew in this sentence: "To rule a country of a thousand chariots, there must be reverent attention to business, and sincerity; economy in expenditure, and love for men; and the employment of the people at the proper seasons." (Analects, bk. i., c. v.)

The course of wisdom when there is not good government, he marks out as follows: "When good government prevails in a state, language may be lofty and bold, and actions the same. When bad government prevails, the actions may be lofty and bold, but the language may be with some reserve." (Analects, bk. xiv., c. iv.)

The manner in which a state may crumble ands decay and therefore succumb to superior force and pass away, Mencius thus describes: "A man must first despise himself and then others will despise him. A family must first destroy itself and then others will destroy it. A kingdom must first strike down itself and then others will strike it down." (Bk. iv., pt. i., c. viii., v. 4.)

Duty Respecting Acceptance of Office. "When right principles of government prevail in the empire, he will show himself; when they are prostrated, he will keep retired." (Analects, bk. viii., c. xiii., v. 2.)

In the "Analects," Confucius thus described the duty of the superior man as regards accepting office and retiring from it. The following, to like effect, is attributed, in the "Analects," to Tsze-chang: "The minister, Tsze-wan, thrice took office and manifested no joy in his countenance. Thrice he retired from office and manifested no displeasure. He made it a point to inform the new minister of the way in which he had conducted the government." (Bk. v., c. xviii., v. I.)

Confucius again gave voice to the same sentiment in this: "When good government prevails in the state, he is to be found in office. When bad government prevails, he can roll his principles up and keep them in his breast." (Analects, bk. xv., c. xi., v. 2.)

Indeed, he proclaimed it the part of a wise and prudent man to quit a badly governed state forthwith: "Such an one will not enter a tottering state nor dwell in a disorganized one." (Analects, bk. viii., c. xiii., v. 2.)

Yet he quoted with warm approval the following reply of Hwuy, when reproved for remaining in a state which had dismissed him for acting the part of a righteous judge: "Hwuy of Lew-hea, being chief criminal judge, was thrice dismissed from office. Someone said to him, 'Is it not time for you, sir, to quit the country?' He replied, 'Serving men in an upright way, where shall I go and not experience such a thrice-repeated dismissal? If I chose to serve men in a crooked way, what need would there be that I leave the country of my parents?'" (Analects, bk. xviii., c. ii.)

The border-warden at E, having interviewed Confucius after the latter had been deprived of office, announced: "My friends, why are you distressed by your Master's loss of office? The empire has long been without principles; Heaven is going to use your Master as a wooden-tongued bell." (Analects, bk. iii., c. xxiv.)

Confucius, however, held it to be no part of the duty of an officer who has been discharged, to air his grievances and criticize his successor, as witness these words, spoken to Yen Yuen: "The Master said to Yen Yuen, 'When called to office, to undertake its duties; when not so called, to lie retired,—it is only I and you who have attained to this!'" (Analects, bk. vii., c. x., v. i.)

And at another time he spoke even more to the point in this fashion: "He who is not in a particular office has nothing to do with the plan for the administration of its duties." (Analects, bk. viii., c. xiv.)

Acceptance of retirement from office, absolute acquiescence in it, even warm welcome of it and refusal to accept even the most exalted official station were warmly commended, as in this: "The Master said, 'T'ao-pih may be said to have reached the highest point in virtuous action. Thrice he declined the empire, and the people could not express their approbation of his conduct.'" (Analects, bk. viii., c. i.)

Yet service and even ambition to be called to public service were recommended to his disciples, as in this: "When you are living in any state, take service with the most worthy among its great officers and make friends with the most virtuous among its scholars." (Analects, bk. xv., c. ix.)

And his disciple, Tsze-Loo, holds that, when called to office and conscious of ability to render valuable service, the superior man is obliged to respond, albeit both against his inclination and against his judgment, in that the conditions will not permit thorough reform: "Not to take office is wrong. If the relations between old and young may not be neglected, how is it that he sets aside the duties that should be observed between the sovereign and the minister? Wishing to maintain his personal purity, he allows that great relation to come to confusion. A superior man takes office and performs the righteous duties belonging to it. As to the failure of right principles to make progress, he is aware of that." (Analects, bk. xviii., c. vii., v. 5.)

Government Is by the Consent of the Governed. " By winning the people, the kingdom is won; by losing the people, the kingdom is lost." (Great Learning, c. x., v. 5.)

This statement taken from "The Great Learning" is characteristic of the view of Confucius concerning government. It was already old in his time, however; for in the "Shu King," the following is quoted among the most ancient "Cautions of the Great Yu": "The people are the root of a country." (Pt. iii., bk. iii.)

And in the same book, the great ruler, Shun, is reported as saying: "Of all who are to be feared, are not the people the chief?" (Pt. ii., bk. ii., 2.)

Mencius gives much fuller and more detailed expression to the view in this passage: "That Kee and Chow lost the empire arose from their losing the people; to lose the people means to lose their hearts. There is a way to get the empire—get the people and it is yours. There is a way to get the people—win their hearts and they are yours. There is a way to win their hearts—simply procure for them what they like and lay not upon them what they do not like. The people turn to a benevolent government as water flows down hill and as wild beasts flee to the wilderness." (Bk. iv., pt. i., c. ix., v. 1, 2.)

The following concerning the truly royal ruler is quoted in "The Great Learning": "When he loves what the people love and hates what the people hate, then is a ruler what is called the parent of his people." (C. x., v. 3.)

That the sage did not mean thereby to commend the acts of the demagogue, which are also vain, Mencius indicates in this brief saying: "If a governor will please everyone, he will find the days not sufficient." (Bk. iv., pt. ii., c. ii., v. 5.)

Yet to King Hwuy, of Leang, he thus presents the reward for protecting and serving the people: "Those rulers, as it were, drive their people into pitfalls and drown them. Your Majesty will go to punish them. In such a case, who will oppose Your Majesty?" (Bk. i., pt. i., c. v., v. 5.)

Ch'êng Tang, in the "Shu King," thus attributes all wisdom to the people and invariable correctness to their deliberate choice: "The great God has conferred on the common people a moral sense, compliance with which would show their nature invariably right." (Pt. iv., bk. iii., 2.)

In the "Shi King" the same view is expressed in these words: "Heaven, in giving birth to the multitude of the people, to every faculty and relationship annexed its law. The people possess this normal nature, and they love normal virtue." (Major Odes, ode 6, decade iii.)

And in the "Shu King" I Yin expatiates upon it more at length as follows: "There is no invariable model of virtue; a supreme regard for what is good makes a model for it. There is no invariable characteristic of what is good that is to be supremely regarded; it is found where there is a conformity with the common consciousness as to what is good." (Pt. iv., bk. vi., 3.)

Mencius unhesitatingly applied this in the most democratic manner, as in this: "If the people of Yen will be pleased at your taking possession of it, do so. Among the ancients one acted upon this principle, King Wu. If the people of Yen will not be pleased at your taking possession of it, do not do so. Among the ancients one acted upon this principle, King Wan." (Bk. i., pt. i., c. x., v. 3.)

But he does not content himself merely with citing precedents in the conduct of the half-mythical fathers; instead, as in his conversation with King Seang, of Leang, he boldly affirmed the fundamental principle that the people are the sole source of power:

"'How can the empire be settled?'

"'It will be settled by being united under one sway.'

"'Who can so unite it?'

"'He who has no pleasure in killing men can so unite it.'

"'Who can give it to him?'

"'All the people of the empire will unanimously give it to him.'" (Mencius, bk. i., c. vi., v. 2, 3, 4, 5, 6.)

That merit produces the confidence of the people in their ruler and thereby secures for him his throne, Mencius asserts in this conversation, which has come down to us:

"Wan Chang asked, 'Is it true that Yaou gave the empire to Shun?'

"Mencius answered: 'No. The emperor cannot give the empire to another.'

"'Yes, but Shun got the empire. Who gave it to him?'

"'Heaven gave it to him.'

"'Heaven gave it to him? Did Heaven confer this appointment upon him in express terms?'

"'No. No. Heaven does not speak. It simply showed its will by his personal behaviour and his management of affairs.'" (Bk. v., pt. i., c. v., v. 1, 2, 3, 4.)

The divine right of kings he did not deny; instead he proclaimed it, but only with this explanation, taken from an ancient source: "This sentiment is expressed in the words of the Great Declaration: 'Heaven sees as my people see; Heaven hears as my people hear.'" (Bk. v., pt i., c. v., v. 8.)

In the "Li Ki," it is even related that in earlier days all was democratic, thus: "There was nowhere such a thing as being born noble. . . . Anciently, there was no rank in birth and no honorary title after death." (Bk. ix., sect. iii., 5.)

In the same book, the existence of a hereditary monarchy is deplored as a sign of degeneration, in these words: "Now that the Grand Course has fallen into disuse and obscurity, the kingdom is a family inheritance." (Bk. vii., sect. i., 3.)

The Right to Depose the Ruler. "Tsze-loo asked how a sovereign should be served. The Master said: 'Do not impose on him, and, moreover, withstand him to his face.'" (Analects, bk. xiv., c. xxiii.)

In another place in the "Analects," however, the disciple, Tsze-hea, explains the requisite foundation for such boldness of conduct, thus: "Having obtained the confidence of his prince, he may then remonstrate with him. If he have not gained his confidence, the prince will think that he is vilifying him." (Bk. xix., c. x.)

Mencius thus characterizes this friendly, though perilous action: "It was then that the Che-shaou and Keo-shaou were made, in the poetry of which it was said: 'What blame is there for restraining one's prince? He who restrains his prince is his friend.'" (Bk. i., pt. ii., c. iv., v. 10.)

In the "Li Ki" this duty of the minister is yet more circumstantially described, as follows: "One in the position of a minister and inferior might remonstrate with his ruler, but not speak ill of him; might withdraw but not remain and hate; might praise but not flatter; might remonstrate but not give himself haughty airs when his advice is followed. If the ruler were idle and indifferent, he might arouse and assist him; if the government were going to wreck, he might sweep it away and institute a new one." (Bk. xv., 21.)

Neither Confucius nor Mencius avoided this duty of protest and of rebuke. The following from Mencius is an instance:

"'Suppose the chief criminal judge could not regulate the officers; how would you deal with him?'

"The king said: 'Dismiss him.'

"'If within the four borders of your kingdom there is not good government, what is to be done?'

"The king looked to the right and left, and spoke of other matters." (Bk. i., pt. ii., c. vi., v. 2, 3.)

Yet in the "Analects" this is found, by way of warning: "Tsze-Yew said: 'In serving one's prince, frequent remonstrances lead to disgrace.'" (Bk. iv., c. xxvi.)

The estimate which the people, however, place upon the contrary course is well set forth in this: "The Master said: "The full observance of the rules of propriety in serving one's prince [*i.e.*, by himself, Confucius] is accounted by the people to be flattery.'" (Analects, bk. iii., c. xviii.)

Confucius offers this counsel to the great minister who finds his mild persuasion and counsel rejected: "What is called a great minister is one who serves his prince according to what is right, and when he finds he cannot do so, retires." (Analects, bk. xi., c. xxiii., v. 3.)

Mencius advises a more Spartan course on the part of a monarch's relatives if he proves impracticable, thus:

"The king said: 'I beg to ask about the chief ministers who are noble and related to the prince."

"Mencius answered: 'If the prince have great faults, they ought to remonstrate with him; and, if he do not listen to them after they have done so again and again, they ought to depose him.' (Bk. v., pt. ii., c. ix., v. I.)

Mencius thus justified even regicide, when the circumstances call for it:

"King Seuen of Ts'e asked: "Is it true that Tang banished Kee and that King Wu slew Chow?'" Mencius replied: 'History tells us so.'

"The king asked: 'May a minister put his sovereign to death?'

"Mencius said; 'He who outrages benevolence is called a robber; he who outrages righteousness, is called a ruffian. The robber and ruffian we call a mere fellow. I have heard of the execution of the fellow, Chow, but I have not so heard of one's sovereign being put to death.'" (Bk. i., pt. ii., c. viii.)

Chapter Six - Cultivation of the Fine Arts

CONFUCIUS held that the encouragement of the fine arts was no less a duty of the state than the protection of the people from foreign foes and the suppression of internal disorder.

The Fine Arts in General. "When good government prevails in the empire, ceremonies, music, and punitive military expeditions proceed from the emperor." (Analects, bk. xvi., c. ii., v. i.)

This saying of Confucius, recorded in the "Analects" and suggesting that wise patronage and encouragement of art by the government which has distinguished the most enlightened governments of ancient and of modern times, was re-enforced without ceasing by Mencius when he rebuked princes who indulged themselves, but failed to share their pleasures with the meanest citizen. Thus he said: "If the people are not able to enjoy themselves, they condemn them that are over them. Thus to condemn their superiors when they cannot enjoy themselves is wrong; but when they that are over the people do not make pleasure a thing common to all as to themselves, they also do wrong." (Bk. i., pt. ii., c. iv., v. 1, 2.)

And again, speaking of beauty in woman: "If Your Majesty loves beauty, let the people be able to gratify the same feeling!" (Bk. i., pt. ii., c. v., v. 5.)

Confucius repeatedly emphasized the importance of the cultivation of the arts, as when he said of himself: "When I had no official employment, I acquired many arts." (Analects, bk. ix., c. vi., v. 4.) Among these were, of course, letters in which he excelled all others, ceremonies in which he had no peer, and music in which he was also trained, both as a critic and as a performer.

To others he gave this counsel: "Let relaxation and enjoyment be found in the polite arts!" (Analects, bk. vii., c. vi., v. 4.) "It is by the Odes that the mind is aroused. It is by the rules of propriety that the character is established." (Analects, bk. viii., c. viii., v. 1, 2.)

In the "Li Ki" is this admonition: "A scholar should constantly pursue what is virtuous and find recreation in the arts." (Bk. xv., v. 22.)

His disciples' related of him: "The Master's frequent themes of discourse were: the Odes, History, and the maintenance of the rules of propriety." (Analects, bk. vii., c. xvii.) "There were four things which the Master taught: letters, ethics, devotion of soul, and truthfulness." (Analects, bk. vii., c. xxiv.)

The following disjointed passages, apropos of nothing else in common, indicate the appreciation by the sage of æsthetic values of the most varied character: "I have not seen one who loves virtue as he loves beauty." (Analects, bk. ix., c. xvii., and bk. xv., c. xii.)" The Master, standing by a stream, remarked: 'It flows on like this, never ceasing, day and night!'" (Analects, bk. ix., c. xvi.) "Is it not delightful to have friends coming from distant quarters?" (Analects, bk. i., c. i., v. 2.) "The wise find pleasure in water, the virtuous find pleasure in hills." (Analects, bk. vi., c. xxi.) "I hate the manner in which purple takes away the lustre of vermilion. I hate the way in which the songs of Ch'ing confound the music of the Gna." (Analects, bk. xvii., c. xviii.)

The foregoing reference to colour implies appreciation of painting which, however, is seldom, if ever, referred to and seems to have been in an undeveloped state, compared, for instance, with poetry or music. The following from the "Analects" appears to refer to it, however: "Tsze-hea asked, saying, 'What is the meaning of the passage: "The pretty dimples of her artful smile! The well-defined black and white of her eye! The plain ground for the colours!"?' The Master answered: 'The business of laying on the colours follows the preparation of the plain ground." (Bk. iii., c. viii., v. 1, 2.)

The value of beauty for beauty's sake, even though it be but the beauty of ornament or of accomplishments, was enforced by Tsze-kung, one of his disciples, in this colloquy: "Kih Tsze-shing asked: 'In a superior man it is only the substantial qualities that are wanted; why should we seek for ornamental accomplishments?' Tsze-kung replied: 'Alas! your words, sir, show you to be a superior man; but four horses cannot overtake the tongue. Ornament is as substance; substance is as ornament. The hide of a tiger or leopard stripped of its hair is like the hide of a dog or goat stripped of its hair.'" (Analects, bk. xii., c. vii.)

That it will be beneficial for a state to encourage and foster the arts, because of their civilizing effect upon the people, these words from the "Li Ki" may be quoted to illustrate: "Confucius said: 'When you enter a state you can know what subjects have been taught. If they show themselves men who are mild and gentle, sincere and good, they have been taught from the Book of Poetry. . . . If they be big-hearted and generous, bland and honest, they have been taught from the Book of Music.'" (Bk. xxiii., 1.)

Poetry and Letters. "In the Book of Poetry are three hundred pieces, but the design of them all may be embraced in one sentence: 'Have no depraved thoughts!'" (Analects, bk. ii., c. ii.)

The importance of poetry and of good literature in general was frequently emphasized as in this passage from the "Analects" by Confucius who on one occasion addressed his disciples, saying: "My children, why do you not study the Book of Poetry? The Odes serve to stimulate the mind, They may be used

123

for purposes of self-contemplation. They teach the art of companionship. They show how to moderate feelings of resentment. From them you learn the more immediate duty of serving one's father and the remoter duty of serving one's prince." (Bk. xvii., c. ix.)

Mencius seems to have been the earliest to make use of this metaphor in describing the delights and benefits of reading: "When a scholar feels that his friendship with all the virtuous scholars of the empire is not sufficient, he proceeds to ascend to consider the men of antiquity. He repeats their poems and reads their books and, as he does not know what they were as men, to ascertain this, he considers the conditions of their time. This is to ascend and make them his friends." (Bk. v., pt. ii., c. viii., v. 2.)

The manner in which Confucius enjoined the study of poetry upon his eldest son is told in this conversation with Chin K'ang: "Ch'in K'ang asked Pih-yu, saying, 'Have you had any lessons from your father different from what we have all heard?' Pih-yu replied: 'No. He was standing alone once, when I passed below the hall with hasty steps, and said to me: "Have you learned the Odes?" On my replying, "Not yet," he added: "If you do not learn the Odes, you will not be fit to converse with." I retired and studied the Odes.'" (Analects, bk. xvi., c. xiii., v. 1, 2.)

That learning should not be merely by rote, that the sentiments and thoughts of the poet must be made a part of a man's self, and that all training should be with a view to use as well as ornament, Confucius set forth in these words: "Though a man may be able to recite the three hundred Odes, yet if, when intrusted with a governmental charge, he knows not how to act or if, when sent to any quarter on a mission, he cannot give his replies unassisted, then notwithstanding the extent of his learning, of what practical use is it?" (Analects, bk. xiii., c. v.)

The finely discriminating literary taste of Confucius was the marvel of his time and his canons are yet generally accepted. He is even represented as saying of himself, in all modesty: "In letters I am perhaps equal to other men." (Analects, bk. vii., c. xxxii.) Still his views were of the simplest, the most naïve. Thus, for instance, he says, tersely: "Of language, it is sufficient that it convey the meaning." (Analects, bk., xv., c. xl.)

Yet, well pondered, this saying is both true and discerning; for comprehensive and accurate conveyance of the precise meaning in its every shade and distinction is the office of the most consummate literary art.

When Confucius was in Wei and was asked, by Tsze-loo, his pupil, what he would consider the first thing to do in administering the government of Wei, he replied: "What is first necessary is to correct names," i.e., the names of things, and said in explanation: "If names be not correct, language is not in accordance with the truth of things." (Analects, bk. viii., c. iii.)

The mischiefs which arise from miscomprehension, due to the inexact use of language, he painted in strong colours, and then said: "Therefore the superior man considers it necessary that the names he uses may be rightly spoken, so that what he says may be fulfilled to the letter. What the superior man requires is just that in his language there may be nothing inaccurate." (Analects, bk. xiii., c. iii., v. 7.)

That a man's diction should also be guarded against inelegance and coarseness, the disciple Tsang declares in this: "There are three principles of conduct which the man of high rank should consider especially important: that in his deportment and manner he keep from violence and heedlessness; that in regulating his countenance he keep near to sincerity; that in his words and tones he keep far from lowness and impropriety." (Analects, bk. viii., c. iv., v. 3.)

The emphasis upon "far" is worthy of special note.

Certainly Confucius was so completely removed from ignoring the beauties and even the subtleties of style, that he was the most eminent of all the Chinese ancients for simplicity, purity, elegance, and exactitude of language, both spoken and written. He had, also, the conception that it is only he who can discriminate finely between expressions that can divine the thought from the spoken or written word or even from the act, fully, accurately, and clearly; and therefore he says: "Without knowing words, it is impossible to know men." (Analects, bk. xx., c. iii., v. 3.)

In the "Li Ki" is thus described the accepted manner of elegant speech: "The style prized in conversation is that it should be grave and distinct." (Bk. xv., 23.)

The usefulness of letters and of association with men of literary taste, in forming character and confirming it, the disciple Tsang set forth as follows: "The superior man on literary grounds meets with his friends and by their friendship helps his virtue." (Analects, bk. xii., c. xxiii.)

And the inadequacy of both the written and the spoken word to express the highest, noblest, and sublimest thought, is set forth in this saying of Confucius, taken from the "Yi King" (appendix iii., sect. i., c. xii., 76): "The written characters are not the full exponent of speech and speech is not the full expression of ideas."

Music. "Music produces pleasure which human nature cannot be without." (Li Ki, bk. xvii., sect. iii.) "Virtue is the strong stem of human nature and music is the blossoming of virtue." (Li Ki, bk. xvii., sect. ii., 21.)

These eloquent tributes to both the charm and the usefulness of music are from the "Li Ki," in which much attention is given to this fascinating art, which seems to have been developed in ancient China far beyond any other of the fine arts.

This is the more remarkable since in these days Chinese music is rightly regarded of a poor sort. The disappearance of the old, worthy, classical music is ascribed, singularly enough, to the Chinese scholastics. The work of Confucius, "The Book of Music," was wholly lost during the Han dynasty together with the old operas, choruses, songs, and instrumental pieces. Later, the antiquarian scholars found it impossible to discover and restore these; and, influenced by the word but not by the spirit of Confucius, they ignored the music of the common people which, accordingly, became and continues degraded.

This is the tradition offered to explain the absence of noble melodies and harmonies in a country where, by the testimony of one of the world's greatest, it was in full development more than two thousand years ago.

In the "Analects," also, Confucius has said: "If a man be without the virtues proper to humanity, what has he to do with music?" (Analects, bk. iii., c. iii.)

Its development was already ancient in his day; and, according to the "Li Ki," the tradition ran: "It was by music that the ancient kings gave appropriate expression to their joy." (Bk. xvii., sect. iii., 30.) It was also said in this book of the olden days: "He [the emperor] had music at his meals." But the most significant of the traditions there found was this: "In music the sages found pleasure and that it could be used to make the hearts of the people good. Because of the deep influence which it exerts on a man and the change which it produces in manners and customs, the ancient kings appointed it as one of the subjects of instruction." (Bk. xvii., sect. ii., 7.)

Of singing it was there said: "All the modulations of the voice arise from the mind, and the various affections of the mind are produced by things external to it. . . . Music is the production of the modulations of the voice and its source is in the affections of the mind as it is influenced by external things." (Bk. xvii., sect. i., 1, 2.)

That music is not merely an expression of what may be in the mind, be it good or bad, but also a powerful influence upon it, for weal or ill, is affirmed by Tsze-hsia in the "Li Ki" in these words: "The airs of Kang go to wild excess and debauch the mind; those of Sung speak of slothful indulgence and of women, and submerge the mind; those of Wei are strenuous and fast and perplex the mind; and those of Khi are violent and depraved and make the mind arrogant. The airs of these four states all stimulate libidinous desire and are injurious to virtue." (Bk. xvii., sect. iii., 11.) That such may be is accounted for by ascribing to music the property of universal speech open to all the intelligences of the universe, as follows: "Whenever notes that are evil and depraved affect men, a corresponding evil spirit responds to them; and when this evil spirit accomplishes its manifestations, licentious music is the result. Whenever notes that are correct affect men, a corresponding good spirit responds to them; and when this good spirit accomplishes its manifestations, sublime music is the result." (Li Ki, bk. xvii., sect. ii., 14.)

The labours of Confucius in editing, pruning, and perfecting the poetry and music extant in his day were among his most celebrated feats. Of it he himself says: "I returned from Wei to Loo, and then the music was reformed and the pieces in the Imperial Songs and Songs of Praise all found their proper places." (Analects, bk. ix., c. xiv.)

In the "Li Ki" it is also said: "In an age of disorder, ceremonies and music are forgotten and neglected, and music becomes licentious." (Bk. xvii., sect. ii., 12.)

But this need for reform did not apply to all music. "The Shaou" was famous in his day as a noble piece of music, and "The Woo" scarcely second to it. Between these he is said to have distinguished, discriminatingly, thus: "The Master said of 'The Shaou' that it was perfectly beautiful and also perfectly good.

He said of 'The Woo' that it was perfectly beautiful but not perfectly good." (Analects, bk. iii., c. xxv.)

Of his appreciation of "The Shaou" this is related: "When the Master was in Ts'e, he heard 'The Shaou'; and for three months he did not know the taste of flesh. 'I did not think,' he said, 'that music could have been made so excellent as this!'" (Analects, bk. vii., c. xiii.)

Of the performance of another piece, "The Kwan Ts'eu," he said: "When the music-master, Che, first entered upon his office, the finish of 'The Kwan Ts'eu' was magnificent. How it filled the ears!" (Analects, bk. viii., c. xv.)

Of this piece he elsewhere said: "The Kwan Ts'eu is expressive of enjoyment without being licentious and of grief without being hurtfully excessive." (Analects, bk. iii., c. xx.)

Obviously there were already performances of the oratorio or even the opera type, for in the "Li Ki" this is found: "Poetry gives the thought expression; singing prolongs the notes of the voice; pantomime puts the body into action. These three spring from the mind and musical instruments accompany them." (Bk. xvii., sect. ii., 21.)

"The Shaou" was evidently something akin to opera. Confucius indicates as much when he speaks its praise in the following, commingled with dispraise of certain other songs: "Let the music be Shaou with its pantomimes! Banish the songs of Ch'ing and keep aloof from specious orators! The songs of Ch'ing are licentious; specious orators are dangerous." (Analects, bk. xv., c. x., v. 5, 6.)

That "The Woo" was operatic is plainly shown by this description of it, given in the "Li Ki": "Regarding the music of Woo, in the first scene, the pantomimes proceed towards the north to imitate the marching of Wu Wang against Shang (or the Yin dynasty). In the second scene, they show the extinction of Shang. In the third scene, they exhibit the victorious return to the south, In the fourth scene, they play the annexation of the southern states. In the fifth scene, they manifest the division of labour of the dukes of Chou and Shao, one on the left and the other on the right, in charge of the empire. In the sixth scene, they return to the point of starting to show that the work of the emperor is complete and that the whole empire recognizes him as the supreme ruler." (Bk. xvii., sect. iii., 18.)

The condemnation of the sage was visited in action as well as in words upon the following occasion: "The people of Ts'e sent to Loo a present of female musicians, which Ke Hwan Tze accepted; and for three days no court was held. Confucius took his departure." (Analects, bk. xviii., c. iv.)

Loo, it is to be recalled, was the very state where Confucius afterwards revised and harmonized the music of the realm. Of mere jingle, he spoke disparagingly, thus: "'It is music!' they say, 'It is music!' Are bells and drums all that is meant by music?" (Analects, bk. xvii., c. xi.)

In the "Li Ki" it is said, likewise: "What you ask about is music, what you like is sound. Now music and sound are akin but they are not the same." (Bk. xvii., sect. iii., 9.)

And yet greater purity of taste is indicated by this saying from the same book: "In music, more than aught else, there should be nothing showy or false." (Bk. xvii., sect. ii., 22.)

To his eldest son, Pih-yu, he said: "Give yourself to the Chow-nan and the Chaou-nan. The man who has not studied the Chow-nan and the Chaou-nan is like one who stands with his face against a wall." (Analects, bk. xvii., c. x.)

Confucius was himself a musical performer upon many instruments, according to tradition. In the "Analects" is found this account of his skill upon "the musical stone": "The Master was playing one day on a musical stone in Wei, when a man carrying a straw basket passed the door of the house where Confucius was and said, 'His heart is full who beats the musical stone!'" (Analects, bk. xiv., c. xlii., v. i.)

That he had comprehensive knowledge of the art is obvious, not merely from what he did for the music of Loo but also from the fact that this saying of his was deemed worthy to be handed down: "How to play music may be known. At the commencement of the piece, all the parts should sound together. As it proceeds, they should be in harmony, severally distinct and flowing, without break, and thus on to the conclusion." (Analects, bk. iii., c. xxiii.)

That Chinese music had already progressed far beyond mere melodies is sufficiently plain, no doubt, from what has already been said. Yet it is germane to quote this from the "Li Ki": "Harmony is the thing principally sought in music." (Bk. xvii., sect. i., 29.)

The following also indicates the reverence and respect in which Confucius was held even by the most accomplished singers of his time, both as a man and an expert on matters of taste, and perhaps as a musician also: "When the Master was in company with a person who was singing, if he sang well, he would make him repeat the song while he accompanied it with his own voice." (Analects, bk. vii., c. xxxi.)

His preference for classical music is voiced in this saying: "The men of former times, in the matters of ceremonies and music, were rustics, it is said, while the men of these later times, in ceremonies and music, are accomplished artists. If I have occasion to use those things, I follow the men of former times!" (Analects, bk. xi., c. i.)

He included among the " three things men find enjoyment in, which are advantageous," this: "The discriminating study of ceremonies and music." (Analects, bk. xvi., c. v.)

The method by which music is conceived of, as profoundly affecting the moral nature of man, is thus circumstantially and persuasively delineated in the "Li Ki": "Hence the superior man returns to the good affections proper to his nature, in order to bring his will into harmony with them, and compares the different qualities of actions in order to perfect his conduct. Notes that are evil and depraved and sights leading to disorder and licentiousness are not allowed to affect his ears and eyes. Licentious music and corrupted ceremonies are not admitted into the mind to affect its powers. The spirit of idleness, indifference, depravity, and perversity finds no exhibition in his person." (Bk. xvii., sect. ii., 15.)

These most desirable results, however, by no means exhaust the conception of Confucius, of the benefits to the heart and mind which a full knowledge and appreciation of music can impart. The highest possibilities are set forth in these words of most enthusiastic eloquence, also in the pages of the "Li Ki": "When one has mastered music completely and regulates his heart and mind accordingly, the natural, correct, gentle, and sincere heart is easily developed and joy attends its development. This joy proceeds into a feeling of calm. This calm continues long. In this unbroken calm the man is Heaven within himself. Like unto Heaven, he is spiritual. Like unto Heaven, though he speak not, he is accepted. Spiritual, he commands awe, without displaying anger." (Bk. xvii., sect. iii., 23.)

Ceremonies. "Ceremonies and music should not for a moment be neglected by any one." (Li Ki, bk. xvii., sect. iii., v. 23.)

In this passage from the "Li Ki" and in many other sayings of Confucius and his followers, music and ceremonies are mentioned together. This is particularly true in the "Li Ki" in which both subjects are most discussed and from which all the quotations under this head have been taken.

It is partly explained, as follows: "The sphere in which music manifests, is within; the sphere of ceremonies is without." (Li Ki, bk. xvii., sect. iii., v. 25.)

This is repeated in another place with emphasis and with apposite deductions therefrom, thus: "Music springs from the inner motions of the soul; ceremonies are the outward motions of the body. Therefore do men make ceremonies as few and short as possible but give free range to music." (Li Ki, bk. xvii., sect. iii., v. 26.)

That Chinese ceremonies are, or were, few and short, none will perhaps credit, especially after looking through the portions relating to them in the works of Confucius. But it must be recalled—and it requires a distinct effort for the Occidental mind to conceive and to realize the thought—that ceremonies constitute a language,—a language, also, very erudite, richly expressive, ornate and comprehensive when developed as in China. This language, indeed, in its difficulties, as in many other respects, no doubt, is comparable only with a written language such as the ideographs of China constitute; and perhaps, like them, has within it the possibilities of a universal means of symbolical communication as by a printed text, entirely independent of the speech of men.

It must have been with somewhat of this sentiment that the ancient sage viewed ceremonies, else his praise would be extravagant, indeed. It is said of those whose work was even then traditional: "The sages made music in response to Heaven and framed ceremonies in correspondence with Earth." (Li Ki, bk. xvii., sect. i., v. 29.)

Of good taste in manners as in music, the "Li Ki" well says: "The highest style of music is sure to be distinguished by its ease; the highest style of elegance, by its undemonstrativeness." (Bk. xvii., sect. i., v. 17.)

And it unites them with the real things of character and of life in these words: "Benevolence is akin to music and righteousness to ceremonies." (Bk. xvii., sect. i., v. 28.)

This also, is not a mere commonplace or abstraction in the mind of this wisest of the Orientals; for the book returns to it as follows: "He who has understood both ceremonies and music may be pronounced to be a possessor of virtue; virtue means self-realization." (Li Ki, bk. xvii., sect. i., v. 8.)

This work even indicates the method by which these practical results may flow from an art so simple and apparently so void of deep significance: "Perform ceremonies and music perfectly in all their outward manifestation and application, and all else under heaven will be easy." (Li Ki, bk. xvii., sect. iii., v. 25.)

This is more definitely and clearly said in the following: "The instructive and transforming power of ceremonies is subtle. They check depravity before it has taken form, causing men daily to move toward what is good and to keep themselves far from wrong-doing, without being conscious of it. It was on this account that the ancient kings set so high a value on them." (Li Ki, bk. xxiii., 9.)

Confucius, however, does not think of music as merely a human art, but also as the common speech of all intelligences of the universe; and he desires that ceremonies become and be to the eyes of men just such a delicate, graceful, and expressive mode of communication. Therefore their interrelationship with the seen and the unseen is asserted in the "Li Ki" in these terms, in no respect uncertain: "In music of the grandest style there is the same harmony that prevails between Heaven and Earth; in ceremonies of the grandest form there is the same graduation that exists between Heaven and Earth." (Bk. xvii., sect. i., v. 19.)

Yet more explicit is this language, all the more significant in that Confucius did not often discuss, or even refer to, spiritual beings: "In the visible there are ceremonies and music; in the invisible, the spiritual agencies." (Li Ki, bk. xvii., sect. i., v. 19.)

And in the same book he even asserted the psychical power of ceremonies, as of music,—of both of these, united—to summon the intelligences of the universe for communion with minds imprisoned in human bodies, in these burning phrases: "Ceremonies and music in their nature resemble Heaven and Earth, penetrate the virtues of the spiritual intelligences, bring down spirits from above and lift the souls that are abased." (Bk. xvii., sect. iii., v. 2.)

Chapter Seven - Universal Relations

THE views of Confucius on man's relations to the universe are singularly in line with the cosmic philosophy of the ancient Greeks and Romans.

Death and Immortality. "The body and the animal soul go downwards; and the intelligent spirit is on high." (Li Ki, bk. vii., sect. i., 7.)

Thus in the "Li Ki" is voiced the belief of the ancient Chinese, which was accepted by Confucius and his disciples, not as a saving article of creed, but merely as a fact. It is again stated in the "Li Ki" in this manner: "That the bones and flesh should return to earth is what is appointed. But the soul in its energy can go everywhere; it can go everywhere." (Bk. ii., sect. ii., pt. iii., 13.)

How fully this was accepted by Confucius, may be seen, not merely from the fact that by editing the "Li Ki" and permitting these apothegms to stand, he gave them his approval, but by this saying, much more explicit on this point, attributed to him by the same book: "The Master said: 'The intelligent spirit is of the Shan nature and shows that in fullest measure; the animal soul is of the Kwei nature and shows that in fullest measure...All who live, must die and, dying, return to the earth; this is what is called Kwei. The bones and flesh moulder below and, hidden away, become the earth of the fields. But the spirit issues forth and is displayed on high in a condition of glorious brightness.'" (Bk. xxi., sect. ii., I.)

That scientific investigation would show this to be true, is indicated by the "Yi King" (appendix iii., sect. i., c. iv., v. 2) thus: "He traces things to their beginning and follows them to their end; thus he knows what can be said about death and life."

His disciple, Tsang, in speaking thus of a man about to die, signified his view that death is but an awakening: "When a bird is about to die, its notes are mournful; when a man is about to die, his words are good." (Analects, bk. viii., c. iv., v. 2.)

The following account of the sanitary precautions to be taken when one is about to die, is given in the "Li Ki": "When the illness was extreme, all about the establishment was swept clean, inside and out." (Bk. xix., sect. i., 1.)

And this of the precaution to assure that death has really taken place: "Fine floss was laid over to make sure that breathing had stopped." (Bk. xix., sect. i., 1.),

And yet another passage exhibits the same care which has long been taken in Occidental countries to avoid the possibility of burial alive: "Therefore when it is said that the body is not clothed in its last raiment until after three days, it signifies that it is so delayed to see if the father may not come to life." (Li Ki, bk. xxxii., 4.)

The following from the same book which devotes more attention to the subject than any other of the books upon which Confucius wrought or in which his sayings are recorded, is an apt and even illuminating statement of the peculiar horror with which the dead body has ever been regarded: "When a man dies, there arises a feeling of repugnance; the impotence of his body causes one to revolt from it." (Bk. ii., sect. ii., pt. ii., 8.)

Khang-Tsze Kâo, in the "Li Ki," is reported as saying the following upon the ethics of burial, urging that the disposition of the bodies of the dead should not interfere with the welfare of the living: "I have heard that in life we should be useful to others and in death do them no harm. Though I may not have

131

been useful to others in life, shall I in death do them harm? When I am dead, choose a piece of barren ground and bury me there." (Bk. ii., sect. i., pt. iii.)

In the same book Confucius is credited with having inaugurated, or, if not, with having confirmed, a departure from the ancient custom of levelling the earth over the grave, so that it would become indistinguishable: "When Confucius had buried his mother in the same grave [i.e., in which his father was interred], he said: 'I have heard that the ancients, in making graves, raised no mound over them. But I am a man who will be east, west, south, and north.' On this he raised a mound, four feet high." (Bk. ii., sect. i., pt. i., 6.)

After the fact of death is assured, however, and before any other ceremony or duty relative to the departed is performed, there is the "calling back" of the soul to reoccupy the garments he has quitted. The "Li Ki" describes it thus: "At calling back the soul . . . an officer of low rank performed the ceremony. All who co-operated, used court robes of the deceased. . . . In all cases they ascended the east wing to the middle of the roof, where the footing was perilous. Facing the north, they gave three loud calls for the deceased; after which they rolled up the garment they had used and cast it down in front where the wardrobe-keeper received it." (Bk. xix., sect. i., 3.)

The garments used in calling back the soul were not available to array the corpse; upon this the same book says: "The robe which was used in calling the soul back was not used to cover or to clothe the corpse." (Bk. xix., sect. i., 4.)

The appellation used in summoning the soul to return appears from this passage: "In all cases of calling back the soul, a man was called by his name and a woman by her designation." (Li Ki, bk. xix., sect. i., 4.)

The levelling of rank by the unrelenting hand of death is typified by this feature of this ancient ceremony: "In summoning the dead to return and in writing the inscription, the language was the same for all, from the son of Heaven to the ordinary officer." (Li Ki, bk. xiii., sect. ii., 7.)

The purpose and significance of the ceremony, which, when the dead is a parent, is but the commencement of lifelong veneration for his spirit and attempted communion with it, are revealed in this passage from the same book: "Calling the soul back is the way love receives its consummation, and contains the expression of the mind in prayer." (Bk. ii., sect. ii., pt. i., 22.)

Communion with Departed Ancestors. "They served the dead as they would have served them when living; they served the departed as they would have served them, had they continued with them." (Doctrine of the Mean, c. xix., v. 5.)

In these words from the "Doctrine of the Mean" Confucius set forth the conception of the observances of filial piety toward parents and other nearly related ancestors which should be continued unbroken throughout life, even after they depart this life—a conception which pervaded his own conduct, as is thus described in the "Analects": "He sacrificed to the dead as if they were present. He sacrificed to the spirits, as if the spirits were present." (Bk. iii., c. xii.)

The central idea is that the disembodied soul of this ancestor is yet interested in the conduct of his family in the world of flesh and, if given an opportunity to do so by the due observance of sacrificial rites, watches over and communes with his descendants, in order to warn, counsel, rebuke, and even to correct them. This he does, not merely for their sake but also for his own, to the end that the good name of the family may become more illustrious, thus redounding to his own credit, as well as to the credit of the living.

This idea of "accumulating goodness" by means of serried generations of men who acquit themselves well in all the offices of life, is an important feature of the sanction which the pious reverence for ancestors, both when living and after death, gives for correct moral conduct throughout life.

Upon this, the "Yi King" (appendix iv., sect. ii., w. iii., 5) says: "The family that accumulates goodness is sure to have superabundant happiness, and the family that accumulates evil, to have superabundant misery. The murder of a ruler by his minister or of a father by his son, is not the result of the events of one morning or one evening. The causes of it have gradually accumulated, through the absence of early discrimination."

And it thus presents yet another view of the lamentable consequences of neglect of this law of what we moderns term "heredity": "If acts of goodness be not accumulated, they are not sufficient to give its finish to one's name; if acts of evil be not accumulated, they are not sufficient to destroy one's life. The inferior man thinks that small acts of goodness are of no benefit and does not do them, and that small deeds of evil, do no harm and does not abstain from them. Hence his wickedness becomes great till it cannot be covered and his guilt becomes great till it cannot be pardoned." (Yi King, appendix iii., sect. ii., c. v., 38.)

The general view of the filial duty of the progeny both toward living ancestors and toward the dead, so far as concerns avoiding acts which will disgrace them and cultivating conduct which will do them credit, has, however, been fully set forth in the chapters upon the subject of filial piety. Here we have to do only with the reverent ceremonies in the ancestral temples, by means of which veneration for the souls of the departed was exhibited and communion with them was sought. To these ceremonies the "Hsiâo King" (c. viii.) thus refers: "In such a state of things, parents while living reposed in their sons; and when dead and offered sacrifices, their disembodied spirits enjoyed the offerings."

The mode of effecting this was by offering sacrifices of food and drink, accompanied with ceremonies, more or less elaborate according to the rank and estate of the son. The eldest living son in these august ceremonies impersonated the deceased father and presided at the sacrifice.

Only the emperor sacrifices to his ancestors generally; the king, only to ancestors to the fourth removal; feudal princes and great officers to those of the third degree; high officers to parents and grandparents; subordinate administrative officers and the common people to the immediate parent only. All ancestors further removed were said to "remain in the ghostly state," *i.e.*, presumably, to interest themselves not at all in matters of this earth. In the "Li Ki," this is described thus: "The death of all creatures is spoken of, as their dissolution; but man, when dead, is said to be in the ghostly state." (Bk. xx., 4.)

Recurring to the statement that sacrifices should be offered to the dead as if they were living, we find that the "Li Ki" offers a necessary qualification of this in the following caution: "In dealing with the dead, if we treat them as if they were entirely dead, that would show want of affection and should not be done; if we treat them as if they were entirely living, that would show want of wisdom and should not be done." (Bk. ii., sect. i., pt. iii., 3.)

Something of the manner of offering these sacrifices and also of the purpose of it is set forth in this passage from the same book: "The ruler and his wife take alternate parts in presenting these offerings, all being done to please the souls of the departed _ and constituting a union with the disembodied and unseen." (Bk. vii., sect. i., II.)

And the purpose, spiritual communion, in this: "It was thus that they maintained their intercourse with spiritual intelligences." (Bk. ix., sect. i., 5.)

Confucius thus rebukes attempts to secure free communion with spirits of men with whom one is not connected by ancestral ties: "For a man to sacrifice to a spirit which does not belong to him, is flattery." (Analects, bk. ii., c. xxiv., v. i.)

The mischief of such miscellaneous seeking after communications from departed spirits is so familiar a thing in all ages that it is both a relief and also reassuring to find it thus set forth by the sage who apparently fully recognized both the continuance of conscious life after the change, called death, and the possibility of intercommunication between intelligences yet in this world and intelligences that have departed from it.

In view of his primary injunction to investigate all phenomena, it seems improbable that he would have condemned scientific research in such matters; but mere idle promiscuity of such communion was to his mind an impertinence, a peril, and even an act of impiety; yet in "Shuo Yüan," he is reported as saying: "If I were to say that the dead have consciousness, I am afraid that filial sons and dutiful grandsons would impair their substance in paying their last offices to the departed; and if I were to say that the dead have not consciousness, I am afraid that unfilial sons and undutiful grandsons would leave their parents unburied. If you wish to know whether the dead have consciousness or not, you will know it when you die. There is no need to speculate upon it now." (Bk. xviii.)

This, however, appears to be of dubious authenticity as a statement by Confucius, and certainly is not in harmony with his general teaching upon this subject.

General sacrifices, also inviting such communion, might however be offered, according to the prescriptions of the "Li Ki," to a few who had served their fellow-men with thoroughness and distinction. The following passage illustrates the nature of these exceptions: "According to the institutes of the sage kings about sacrifices, they should be offered to him who gave just laws to the people; to him who laboured unto death in the discharge of his duties; to him who by indefatigable industry strengthened the state; to him who with courage and success faced great calamities; and to him who warded off great evils." (Bk. xx., 9.)

It was not in the least the ancient conception of sacrifice to ancestors that it should be a season of recreation or often be repeated. It should take place at least once each year, upon the anniversary of the departure of the ancestor, and sacrifices might also be held in the spring and autumn, in accordance with these instructions in the "Li Ki": "Sacrifices should not be frequently repeated. Such frequency is indicative of importunateness, and importunateness is inconsistent with reverence. Nor should they be at distant intervals. Such infrequency is indicative of indifference; and indifference leads to forgetting them altogether. Therefore, the superior man, in harmony with the course of Heaven, offers the spring and autumn sacrifices. When he treads the dew which has descended as hoar-frost, he cannot help a feeling of sadness which arises in his mind and cannot be ascribed to the cold. In spring, when he treads upon the ground, wet with the rains and dews that have fallen heavily, he cannot avoid being moved by a feeling as if he were seeing his departed friends. We greet the approach of our friends with music and escort them away with sadness, and hence at the spring sacrifice we use music but not at the autumn sacrifice." (Bk. xxi., sect. i., 1.)

This, from the same book, cautions against over-indulgence in this regard: "Do not take liberties with or weary spiritual beings!" (Li Ki, bk. xv., 22.)

The following injunctions against attempting to make of the sacrifice a time of rest or recreation are also from the "Li Ki": "In maintaining intercourse with spiritual, intelligent beings, there should be nothing like an extreme desire for rest and ease for our personal gratification." (Bk. ix., sect. ii., 16.)

"The idea which leads to intercourse with spiritual beings is not interchangeable with that which finds its realization in rest and pleasure." (Bk. ix., sect. ii., i5.)

And earnest efforts to attain the purposes of the sacrifice are pronounced indispensable in the following passage: "When they had reverently done their utmost, they could serve the spiritual intelligences." (Li Ki, bk. xxii., 5.)

The following more particularly describes what is necessary in this regard: "Therefore there was the milder discipline of the mind for seven days, to bring it to a state of singleness of purpose; and the fuller discipline of it for three days, to concentrate all the thoughts. That concentration is called purification; its final attainment is when the highest order of pure intelligence is reached. Then only is it possible to enter into communion with the spiritual intelligences." (Li Ki, bk. xxii., 6.)

The nature of this earnest concentration is sufficiently indicated in the following account of the procedure of the ancients: "When the time came for offering a sacrifice, the man wisely gave himself to the work of purification. That purification meant concentration and singleness, rendering all uniform until the thoughts were all focussed upon one object." (Li Ki, bk. xxii., 6.)

Or as more briefly said in another place, thus: "Sacrificing means 'directing one's self to.' The son directs his thoughts and then he can offer up the sacrifice." (Li Ki, bk. xxi., 6.)

The absolute necessity for this single-minded sincerity is asserted in these words ascribed by the "Shu King" to I Yin: "The spirits do not always accept the sacrifices that are offered to them; they accept only the sacrifices of the sincere." (Pt. iv., bk. v., sect. iii., I.)

In the "Li Ki" the subjective character of true sacrifice or seeking for spiritual communion is thus set forth: "Sacrifice comes not to a man from without; it issues from him and flows from his heart." (Bk. xxii., I.)

Its subjective benefits are also thus portrayed: "Only men of ability and character can give complete expression to the concept of sacrifice. The sacrifices of such men have their reward, not indeed what the world calls reward. Their reward is the perfecting of self; this also means the full and normal discharge of all one's duties." (Li Ki, bk. xxii., 2.)

It must not for a moment be supposed, however, that such was the only or indeed the chief purpose in performing the arduous ceremonies of devotion for departed ancestors. Instead, actual, perceptible, realized communion and communication, resulting in counsel, warning, commendation, or reproof, and, in general, assistance in directing his course so that it will be creditable both to his ancestors and to himself, were expected and intended. The "Li Ki" does not leave this for a moment in doubt; for it says: "The object of all the ceremonies is to bring down the spirits from above, even their ancestors." (Bk. vii., sect. i., 10.)

It will be recalled that in the following passage regarding the influence of ceremonies and music, already quoted from the "Li Ki," this idea of summoning the spirits of the departed is involved: "Ceremonies and music in their nature resemble Heaven and Earth, penetrate the virtues of spiritual intelligences, bring down spirits from above, and lift the souls that are abased." (Bk. xvii., sect. iii., 2.)

And also pertinent to the subject, is this passage: "In the visible sphere, there are ceremonies and music; in the invisible, the spiritual agencies." (Li Ki, bk. xvii., sect. i., 19.)

And of one who is completely under the spell of music, this, also, already quoted: "In this unbroken calm the man is Heaven within himself. Like unto Heaven, he is spiritual. Like unto Heaven, though he speaks not, he is accepted. Spiritual, he commands awe, without displaying anger." (Li Ki, bk. xvii., sect. iii., 23.)

These are recognized means of producing psychical phenomena in these days of scientific investigation, as also are the following, likewise from the "Li Ki," save that fixing the mind upon that which it desires to behold would be shunned as tending to self-delusion: "The severest vigil and purification are maintained and carried on inwardly, while a scarcely looser vigil is maintained outwardly. During the days of such vigil, the mourner thinks of his departed, how and where they sat, how they smiled and spoke, what were their aims and views, what they delighted in, what they desired and enjoyed. On the third day of such discipline, he will see those for whom it has been exercised." (Bk. xxi., sect. i., 2.)

Spiritual Beings and Spiritual Power. "The rites to be observed by all under heaven were intended to promote the return of the mind to the source of all things, the honouring of spiritual beings, the harmonious utilization of government, righteousness, and humility." (Li Ki, bk. xxi., sect. i., 20.)

The broader purpose of sacrifices to ancestors, viz.: to make men conscious and aware at all times of the existences of spiritual beings and of their powers, is well set forth in the foregoing, from the "Li Ki."

The following passage from the "Yi King," already quoted in another connection, refers to the same process of scientific inquiry: "When we minutely investigate the nature and reasons of things till we have entered into the inscrutable and spiritual in them, we attain to the largest practical application of them; when that application becomes quickest and readiest and personal poise is secured, our virtue is thereby exalted. Proceeding beyond this, we reach a point which it is hardly possible to comprehend; we have thoroughly mastered the inscrutable and spiritual and understand the processes of transformation. This is the fulness of virtue." (Appendix iii., sect. ii., c. v., 33, 34.)

Yet, in order to enforce the very necessary lesson that in this life it is the duties here and now with which a man should concern himself, Confucius often rebuked over-insistent curiosity concerning disembodied spirits and the future life. Several of these sayings have been quoted elsewhere; and of them these only are reproduced here: "To give one's self earnestly to the duties due to men, and while respecting spiritual beings to keep aloof from them, may be called wisdom." (Analects, bk. vi., c. xx.)

"Ke Loo asked about serving the spirits of the dead. The Master said: 'While you are not able to serve men, how can you serve their spirits?' Ke Loo then said: 'I venture to ask about death.' He was answered: 'While you do not know life, how can you know about death?'" (Analects, bk. xi., c. xi.)

In the "Analects," it is also related of Confucius by his disciples: "The subjects on which the Master did not talk, were: extraordinary things, feats of strength, disorder, and spiritual beings." (Bk. vii., c. x.)

Yet in the "Doctrine of the Mean" he is quoted as declaring: "How abundantly do spiritual beings display the powers that belong to them! We look for them but we do not see them; we listen but we do not hear them. Yet they permeate all things and there is nothing without them." (C. xvi., v. 1, 2.)

In the "Yi King" much more is said about the general subject and this definition of spirit is given: "When we speak of spirit, we mean the subtle element of all things." (Appendix v., c. vi., 10.)

The author of this conceived of the universe as the field of operations and the result of operations of force and substance, of static and dynamic powers, in the phenomena produced by which he recognized the activities of spirit, thus: "That which is unfathomable in the movement of the passive and active operations, is the presence of a spiritual power." (Yi King, appendix iii., sect. i., c. v., 32.)

The close similarity of this view with the most recent views of modern scientists is illustrated yet more startlingly in this passage, also from the "Yi King" (appendix iii., c. v., 24): "The successive interaction of the passive and active forces constitutes what is called the flow of phenomena."

The "Yi King" is a book, written for the most part in highly symbolical language,—it is often utilized by the Chinese for purposes of divination as will be seen,—which had even for Confucius himself already become so difficult to master and at the same time so fascinating, that the sage once said of it: "If some years were added to my life, I would give fifty to the study of the Yi and then I might come to be without great faults." (Analects, bk. vii., c. xvi.)

In this book, *i.e.*, the "Yi King," Confucius said of the clear perception of the spiritual activities underlying phenomena: "He who knows the method of change and transformation, may be said to know what is done by spiritual power." (Appendix iii., sect. i., c. ix., 58.)

And again, in this illustrative manner: "Does not he who knows the causes of things, possess spirit-like wisdom? The superior man, in his intercourse with the exalted, uses no flattery; and in his intercourse with the humble, no coarse freedom—does not this show that he knows the causes of things?" (Appendix iii., sect. ii., c. v., 41.)

And yet more eloquently in this passage of the "Li Ki" are the essential spirituality and prescience of the pure and sincere mind set forth: "When the personal character is pure and clean, the spirit and mind are like those of a spiritual being. When what such an one desires is about to come to pass, he is sure to have premonitions of it, as when Heaven sends down the rains in due season and the hills condense the vapours into clouds." (Li Ki, bk. xxvi., 8.)

This is yet more concisely said in this passage from the "Doctrine of the Mean" (c. xxiv.), already quoted: "When calamities or blessings are about to befall, the good or the evil will surely be foreknown to him. He, therefore, who is possessed of the completest sincerity, is like a spirit."

Heaven. "In order to know men, he may not dispense with a knowledge of Heaven." (Doctrine of the Mean, c. xx., v. 7.)

In the foregoing from the "Doctrine of the Mean" is announced both the view of the disciples of Confucius that there is a divinity " that shapes our ends, rough hew them how we will," and also that, through His works, He may be known of men. This saying is only another version of this passage of the "Yi King" (appendix i., c. liv., 1): "If Heaven and Earth were to have no intercommunication, things would not grow and flourish as they do."

The expression "Heaven" seems to stand rather for all the spiritual beings, if more than one, that hold sway over the universe. Earlier, it undoubtedly signified this; for in the "Shu King," Mu is credited with this most extraordinary statement: "Then he [*i.e.*, Yao] commissioned Khung and Li to make an end of the communications between Earth and Heaven; and the descents of spirits ceased." (Pt. v., bk. xxvii., 2.)

By the days of Confucius in any event, the recognition of an unimaginably great universe of spirit was firmly coupled in the minds of sages with the principle that man's duties here are with his fellow-men and that he will but fail in their performance if he continually seeks communion with intelligences of the spirit universe.

Confucius does not present the view that Heaven so communicates with Earth that there may be complete revelation of its purposes and processes, by verbal inspiration or otherwise. Instead, he says: "Does Heaven speak? The four seasons pursue their courses, and all things are continually being produced; but does Heaven say anything?" (Analects, bk. xvii., c. xix., v. 3.)

This is further expatiated upon in " The Doctrine of the Mean" (c. xvi., v. 1, 2) as follows: "The Master said: 'How abundantly do spiritual beings display the powers that belong to them! We look for them but do not see them; we listen for them but do not hear them. Yet they enter into all things and there is nothing without them.'"

And in the "Shi King" the continual presence of these invisible witnesses is thus cited as abundant reason for virtuous conduct when in the privacy of one's chamber: "Looked at in your chamber, you ought to be equally free from shame before the light which shines in. Do not say: 'This place is not public; no one can see me here.' The approaches of spiritual beings cannot be foretold; the more, therefore, should they not be left out of the account." (Major Odes, decade iii., ode 2.)

Confucius also says: "But there is Heaven—it knows me!" (Analects, bk. xiv., c. xxxvii., v. 2.)

The "Yi King" thus describes the greatest of the joint offices of Heaven and Earth: "The great attribute of Heaven and Earth is the giving and maintaining life." (Appendix iii., c. i., 10.)

And again in the following, already quoted in another connection: "Heaven and Earth are separate and apart, but the work which they do is the, same. Male and female are separate and apart, but with a common will they seek the same object." (Appendix i., c. xxxviii., v. 3.)

This idea is again put forward in the "Li Ki" in this fashion: "Man is the product of the attributes of Heaven and of Earth through the interaction of the dual forces of nature, the union of animal and intelligence, the finest and most subtle matter of the five elements." (Bk. vii., sect. iii., 1.)

This theory is developed further in this passage from the same book: "This [i.e., the Grand Unity] separated and became Heaven and Earth. It revolved and became the dual force in nature. It changed and became the four seasons. It was distributed and became the breathings, thrilling in the universal frame. Its lessons, transmitted to men, are called its orders; the law and authority of them are in Heaven." (Bk. vii., sect. iv., 4.)

Thinking of Heaven as the creator of man apparently caused it soon to be addressed in prayer by poor humanity; and accordingly we find this in the "Yi King" (appendix ii., sect. ii., c. xlii., 6): "There is the misery of having none upon whom to call."

Confucius stated it in even stronger terms, when he said: "He who offends against Heaven, has none to whom he can pray." (Analects, bk. iii., c. xiii., v. 2.)

Such prayer, continually offered by means of a virtuous and useful life, Confucius commended and practised. As much appears from this: "The Master being very sick, Tsze-loo asked leave to pray for him. He said: 'May such a thing be done?' Tsze-loo replied: 'It may. In the Prayers it is said: "Prayer has been made to the spirits of the upper and lower worlds."' The Master said: 'My prayer has been for a long time.'" (Analects, bk. vii., c. xxxiv.)

That man, even before his transition, may become the co-worker, however, with the spiritual forces which constitute Heaven and even of equal dignity with them, the "Doctrine of the Mean" (c. xxii.,) thus declares: "Able to assist the transforming and nourishing powers of Heaven and Earth, he may with Heaven and Earth form a ternion."

And again of the man of the completest sincerity, *i.e.*, Chinese scholars assert, Confucius: "Hence it is said: 'He is the peer of Heaven!'" (Doctrine of the Mean, c. xxxi., v. 3.)

This is much more explicitly set forth in this passage from the same book; also considered by Chinese scholars to refer to Confucius: "It is only the individual possessed of the most entire sincerity that can exist under Heaven, who can adjust the great, unvarying relations of mankind, establish the great, fundamental virtues of humanity, and comprehend the transforming and nourishing processes of Heaven and Earth. Shall such an one have any being or anything beyond himself on which he depends?" (Doctrine of the Mean, e. xxxii., v. 1.)

Providence. "Without recognizing the ordinances of Heaven, it is impossible to be a superior man." (Analects, bk. xx., c. iii., v. 1.)

Thus in the "Analects" Confucius gives expression to the necessity for full recognition of the unchanging laws of the universe and their operation.

In the "Yi King," the blessed consequences of knowledge of these laws and of trust in the beneficent purposes of the powers that are the universe, are thus portrayed: "He acts according to the exigency of circumstances without being carried away by their current. He rejoices in Heaven and knows its ordinances; and hence he has no anxieties." (Appendix iii., sect. i., c. v., 22.)

The same sentiment and conception are voiced in these words from the "Doctrine of the Mean" (c. xiv., v. 4): "Thus it is that the superior man is grave and calm, waiting for the appointments of Heaven, while the inferior man walks in dangerous paths, looking for lucky occurrences."

The ancients of China had evolved from this, the idea of a just Providence, rewarding for good deeds and punishing for evil. Thus in the "Shu King," I Yin is represented as saying: "Good and evil do not wrongly befall men, but Heaven sends down misery or happiness according to their conduct." (Pt. iv., bk. vi., 2.)

And Ch'êng Tang in the same book, as follows: "The way of Heaven is to bless the good and make the bad miserable." (Pt. iv., bk. iii., 2.)

And the Duke of Kau also in the same book: "Heaven gives length of days to the just and the intelligent." (Pt. v., bk. xvi., 2.)

And King Wu: "I clearly consider that, severe as are the inflictions of Heaven on me, I dare not murmur." (Pt. v., bk. ix., 4.)

The "Doctrine of the Mean" says of the superior man: "He does not murmur against Heaven." (C. xiv., v. 3.)

Confucius also said of himself in the "Analects": "I do not murmur against Heaven." (Bk. xiv., c. xxxvii., v. 2.)

That this is a universe of law, however, and not of special interpositions of Providence, is everywhere insisted on.

In the "Li Ki," Confucius is recorded as saying: "Heaven covers all without partiality; earth sustains and embraces all without partiality; the sun and the moon shine upon all without partiality." (Bk. xxvi., 6.)

In the "Shu King," Mu is reported to have said: "It is not Heaven that does not deal impartially with men, but men ruin themselves." (Pt. v., bk. xxvii., 6.)

And Zu Ki, as speaking in this fashion: "It is not Heaven that cuts short men's lives; they themselves bring them to an end." (Shu King, pt. iv., bk. ix.)

This saying of Tai Chai in the same book certainly has a most modern sound: "Calamities sent by Heaven may be avoided, but from calamities brought on by one's self there is no escape." (Shu King, pt. iv., bk. v., sect. ii., 2.)

Confucius himself sets forth the conception of the protection of Providence, thus: "Heaven produced the virtue that is in me. Hwan Tuy—what can he do to me?" (Analects, bk. vii., c. xxii.)

And this, also from the "Analects," is yet more to the point: "The Master was put in apprehension in K'wang. He said: 'Since the death of King Wan, has not the cause of truth been lodged here in me? If Heaven had wished to let this cause of truth perish, then I, a mortal yet to be born, should not have got such a relation to that cause. While Heaven does not let this cause of truth perish, what can the people of K'wang do to me?'" (Analects, bk. ix., c. v.)

This subject is so extremely important and all that is found in the Confucian classics so little, relatively, that the following passages, which have already been quoted in other connexions, are again given: "Riches and honours depend upon Heaven." (Analects, bk. xii., c. v., v. 3.)

"What Heaven confers, when once lost, will not be regained." (Shi King, Minor Odes of the Kingdom, decade v., ode 2.)

"When Heaven is about to confer a great office on any man, it first disciplines his mind with suffering and his bones and sinews with toil. It exposes him to want and subjects him to extreme poverty. It confounds his undertakings. By all these methods, it stimulates his mind, hardens him, and supplies his shortcomings." (Mencius, bk. vi., pt. ii., c. xv., v. 2.)

"Filial piety is the constant requirement of Heaven." (Hsiâo King, c. vii.)

"Sincerity is the path of Heaven." (Doctrine of the Mean, c. xx., v. 18.)

"Awful though Heaven be, it yet helps the sincere." (Shu King, pt. v., bk. ix., 2.)

In the "Doctrine of the Mean" this last thought is much more thoroughly worked out—indeed into a theory of intimate co-operation with Heaven, actually of ability to transform. This, to which reference has already been made in the preceding section, is set forth with some fulness in this passage, deemed by Chinese scholars to refer to Confucius: "It is only he who is possessed of the completest sincerity that can exist under Heaven, who can give its full development to his nature. Able to give its full development to his own nature, he can do the same to the nature of other men. Able to give its full development to the nature of other men, he can give their full development to the natures of animals and things. Able to give their full development to the natures of animals and things, he can assist the transforming and nourishing powers of Heaven and Earth." (Doctrine of the Mean, c. xxii.)

One of the most fervent commendations of music and ceremonies, already quoted from the "Li Ki," runs: "In music of the grandest style, there is the same harmony that prevails between Heaven and Earth; in ceremonies of the grandest form there is the same graduation that exists between Heaven and Earth." (Bk. xvii., sect, i,, 19.)

The following somewhat cryptic passage from the "Yi King" illustrates the view of Confucius concerning the opposite tendencies of things spiritual and of things material: "Notes of the same pitch respond to one another; creatures of the same nature seek one another; water flows toward the marsh; fire catches upon what is dry; . . . the sage makes his appearance and all men look to him. Things that have their origin in Heaven, tend upward; things that have their origin in Earth, cling to what is below." (Appendix iv., sect. i., c. ii., 8.)

The following from the same great book of mystery, relative to the harmony that must subsist in order that man be truly great, is perhaps more clearly and surely comprehensible: "The great man is he who is in harmony, in his attributes, with Heaven and Earth; in his brightness, with sun and moon; in his orderly procedure, with the four seasons; in his relations with good and evil fortune, with the spiritual operations of Providence." (Yi King, appendix iv., sect. i., c. vi.)

God. "There is the great God; does He hate any one?" (Shi King, Minor Odes, decade iv., ode 8.)

The number of times in all the Confucian classics that the appellation for Deity occurs which indicates personality and not something impersonal or multi-personal, like Heaven, and which may accordingly properly be translated, "God," instead of "Heaven," is exceedingly few. The similarity of the use of words, one singular and the other plural in form, to the "Jehovah" and "Elohim" of the Hebrews is worthy of remark. The foregoing saying, Christian, even Christ-like in its spirit, occurs in one of the Odes of the "Shi King." In the same book are found the only passages in all these classics which affirm that God has spoken to any man. There are three of them, of which this is the only one of general application: "God said to King Wan: 'Be not like them who reject this and cling to that. Be not like them who are ruled by their likes and desires.'" (Shi King, Major Odes, decade i., ode 7.)

If this were indeed the word of God and His only revelation to man, this command to be free and impartial and not to be ruled by mere desire could not be deemed unworthy.

In the "Li Ki" the following circumstantial account is given of the rise from primitive barbarity, reaching its acme in the worship—not of gods—but of God: "Formerly the ancient kings had no houses. In winter they lived in caves which they had excavated, and in summer in nests which they had framed. They knew not the transforming power of fire, but ate the fruit of plants and trees and the flesh of birds and beasts, drinking their blood and swallowing hair and feathers. They knew not yet the use of flax and silk, but clothed themselves with feathers and skins.

"The later sages then arose, and men learned to utilize the blessing of fire. They moulded metals and fashioned clay, so as to rear towers with structures on them and houses with windows and doors. They toasted, grilled, broiled, and roasted. They produced must and sauces. They dealt with the flax and silk, so as to form linen and silken fabrics. They were thus able to nourish the living and to make offerings to the dead, to serve the spirits of the departed and God." (Li Ki, bk. vii., sect. i., 9.)

The exalted conception which these ancients, so chary about using His name or claiming a knowledge of Him which mortal may not attain, really had of God, and of the qualifications required in order to worship Him in spirit and in truth, is indicated in this text from the "Li Ki": "It is only the sage who can sacrifice to God." (Bk. xxi., sect. i., 6.)

To this, also, may be referred with greatest emphasis this other saying in the "Li Ki": "Do not take liberties with or weary spiritual beings." (Bk. xv., 22.)

The shock with which this idea of remoteness and even exclusiveness must needs be received by a people who have so lately emerged—if, indeed, we have emerged—from the most violent controversies as to which man or group of men knew all about the Almighty, His designs, His will, His purposes with His creature, man, may possibly be relieved a little by the reflection that this aloofness would at least be unfavourable to the development of that levity and jocose blasphemy concerning the Great Spirit to which somehow our over-familiarity has conduced.

The ancient Chinese had the same conception of the possibility of ascertaining the future from the Divine Mind, by oracular utterances or divination, which was also common to the Greeks, the Romans, and other peoples in ancient times. The following passage from the "Yi King" charges the superior man to engage in no important undertaking without thus seeking Divine enlightenment and guidance: "Therefore, when a superior man is about to take action of a more private or of a public character, he asks the Yi, making his inquiry in words. It receives his order and the answer comes as the echo's response. Be the subject remote or near, mysterious or deep, he forthwith knows of what kind will be the coming result." (Appendix iii., sect. i., c. x., 60.)

The foregoing has striking similarity to the consultation of the oracle in the days of classic Greece. The "Li Ki" gives the following description, however, of divining by the use of the "Yi King," which shows that a most peculiar and indeed singular custom of divining had sprung up among the Chinese: "Anciently the sages, having determined the phenomena of Heaven and Earth in states of rest and activity, made them the basis for the Yi. The diviner held the tortoise-shell in his arms, with his face toward the south, while the son of Heaven, in his dragon-robe and square-topped cap, stood with his face toward the north. The latter, however, discerning his mind, felt it necessary to proceed to obtain a decision upon what he purposed, thus showing that he dared not pursue his own course and deferred to the will of Heaven." (Li Ki, bk. xxi., sect. ii., 25.)

Though nowhere in the "Analects" or "The Great Learning," all or most of the text of which is attributed to Confucius though handed down by his disciples, is there mention of the personal name, God, as distinguished from the impersonal one, Heaven, which is several times used, in the "Li Ki" the following is found: "These were the words of the Master, 'The ancient and wise kings of the three dynasties served the spiritual intelligences of Heaven and Earth. They invariably consulted the tortoise-shells and divining stalks; and did not presume to use their private judgment in serving God.'" (Bk. xxix., 52.)

And in the "Doctrine of the Mean," the following: "By the ceremonies of the sacrifices to Heaven and Earth they served God."

It is but a step, to be sure,—and one which was frequently taken in all parts of the world,—from trust in Providence to a belief that God determines all fortuitous events and accordingly that by observation of them His will may be known.

In another place, however, the "Li Ki" seems pointedly to disapprove attempts to penetrate the mysteries of the future: "Do not try ... to fathom what has not yet arrived." (Bk. xv., 22.)

It is, perhaps, sufficiently obvious from all that is in this book—and yet more from all of the text of the Confucian classics, that is ascribed to Confucius, or apparently emanates from him—that the sage did not intend to dogmatize concerning the personality, the identity, the nature, the purposes of God, nor to limit the earnest seekers after Him, whatever path they were destined to pursue in this so bootless quest for that which is unknowable. He was but a sage, seeking to make of his fellow-men spiritual seers, apprehending clearly and sincerely the truths that would guide them aright along the simple, but far from easy, path which mortals should tread. Should he guide them, indeed, into the mental morass of mere theological speculation upon the unknown and unknowable?

Yet withal his own view was once clearly enunciated: "I seek unity, all pervading." (Analects, bk. xv., c. ii., v. 2.)

Appendix - The "Great Principle" of Confucius

DR. CHEN HUAN CHANG in his work "The Economic Principles of Confucius and His School" gives the following version of a passage in the "Li Ki" (bk. vii., sect. 1, 2, 3):

"When the Great Principle (of the Great Similarity) prevails, the whole world becomes a republic; they elect men of talents, virtue, and ability; they talk about sincere agreement, and cultivate universal peace. Thus men do not regard as their parents only their own parents, nor treat as their children only their own children. A competent provision is secured for the aged till their death, employment for the middle-aged, and the means of growing up for the young. The widowers, widows, orphans, childless men, and those who are disabled by disease, are all sufficiently maintained. Each man has his rights, and each woman her individuality safeguarded. They produce wealth, disliking that it should be thrown away upon the ground, but not wishing to keep it for their own gratification. Disliking idleness, they labour, but not alone with a view to their own advantage. In this way selfish schemings are repressed and find no way to arise. Robbers, filchers, and rebellious traitors do not exist. Hence the outer doors remain open, and are not shut. This is the state of what I call the Great Similarity.

"Now that the Great Principle has not yet been developed, the world is inherited through family. Each one regards as his parents only his own parents, and treats as his children only his own children. The wealth of each and his labour are only for his self-interest. Great men imagine it is the rule that their estates should descend in their own families. Their object is to make the walls of their cities and suburbs strong and their ditches and moats secure. Rites and justice are regarded as the threads by which they seek to maintain in its correctness the relation between ruler and minister; in its generous regard that between father and son; in its harmony that between elder brother and younger; and in a community of sentiment that between husband and wife; and in accordance with them they regulate consumption, distribute land and dwellings, distinguish the men of military ability and cunning, and achieve their work with a view to their own advantage. Thus it is that selfish schemes and enterprises are constantly taking their rise, and war is inevitably forthcoming. In this course of rites and justice, Yü, T'ang, Wên, Wu, Ch'êng Wang, and the Duke of Chou are the best examples of good government. Of these six superior men, every one was attentive to the rites, thus to secure the display of justice, the realization of sincerity, the exhibition of errors, the exemplification of benevolence, and the discussion of courtesy, showing the people all the constant virtues. If any ruler, having power and position, would not follow this course, he should be driven away by the multitude who regard him as a public enemy. This is the state of what I call the Small Tranquillity."

Dr. Chen identifies "The Small Tranquillity" with "The Advancing Peace Stage," into which men proceed in the form of nations out of the primitive "Disorderly Stage," and "The Great Similarity" with "The Extreme Peace Stage," *i.e.*, with what Tennyson meant in "Locksley Hall":

"When the war drums throb no longer and the battle-flags are furled
In the parliament of man, the federation of the world."

Proceeding with this interpretation, Dr. Chen says: "This is the most important statement of all Confucius' teachings. The stage of Great Similarity or Extreme Peace is the final aim of Confucius; it is the golden age of Confucianism. If we make a comparison between the Great Similarity and the Small Tranquillity, we may get a clear view. Everyone knows that Confucianism has five social relations and five moral constants: ruler and subject, father and son, elder and younger brothers, husband and wife, friend and friend, make up the five social relations; love, justice, rite, wisdom, and sincerity make up the five moral constants. But, according to the statement of Confucius himself, they belong only to the Small Tranquillity. Everyone knows that Confucianism is in favour of monarchical government and of filial piety. But they are good only in the Small Tranquillity. In the Great Similarity, the whole world is the only social organization, and the individual is the independent unit; both socialistic and individualistic characters reach the highest point. There is no national state, so that there is no war, no need of defence, nor of men of military ability and cunning. Men of talents, virtue, and ability are chosen by the people, so that the people themselves are the sovereign, and the relation between ruler and subject does not exist. Man and woman are not bound by the tie of marriage, so that the relations between husband and wife, between father and son, and between brothers do not exist. The only relation that remains is friendship. There is no family, so that there is no inheritance, no private property, no selfish scheme. There is no class, so that the only classification is made either by age or by sex; but whether old, middle-aged, or young, whether man or woman, each satisfies his needs. The Great Principle of the Great Similarity prevails, so that everyone is naturally as good as everyone else and the distinction of the five moral constants is gone. Each has only natural love toward others, regardless of artificial rites and justice. Speaking of the Small Tranquillity, Confucius gives six superior men as examples, but for the Great Similarity, he does not mention any one, because it has never existed. In the Canon of History, Confucius takes up Yao and Shun to represent the stage of Great Similarity as they did not hand down their thrones to their sons, yet he does not mention them here. The principle of the Three Stages is the principle of progress; we must look for the golden age in the future; the Extreme Peace or the Great Similarity is the goal."

The similarity of this conception to the social scheme of Socrates, as set forth in Plato's "Republic," is remarkable, as also its similarity to the views of advanced socialists nowadays. It is indeed significant and weighty if these two greatest intellects of the ancients and perhaps of all mankind saw this ultimate goal alike. But the interpretation may in some regards be deemed doubtful; and certainly others have interpreted it otherwise. Thus Legge translates the passage, using the past tense throughout, as follows:

"When the Grand Course was pursued, a public and common spirit ruled all under the sky; they chose men of talents, virtue, and ability; their words were sincere, and what they cultivated was harmony. Thus men did not love their parents only, nor treat as children only their own sons. A competent provision was secured for the aged till their death, employment for the able-bodied, and the means of growing up to the young. They showed kindness and compassion to widows, orphans, childless men, and those who were disabled by disease, so that they were all sufficiently maintained. Males had their proper work, and females had their homes. (They accumulated) articles (of value) disliking that they should be thrown away upon the ground, but not wishing to keep them for their own gratification. (They laboured) with their strength, disliking that it should not be exerted, but not exerting it (only) with a view to their own advantage. In this way (selfish) schemings were repressed and found no development. Robbers, filchers, and rebellious traitors did not show themselves, and hence the outer doors remained open, and were not shut. This was (the period of) what we call the Grand Union.

"Now that the Grand Course has fallen into disuse and obscurity, the kingdom is a family inheritance. Everyone loves (above all others) his own parents and cherishes (as) children (only) his own sons. People accumulate goods and exert their strength for their own advantage. Great men imagine it is the rule that their estates should descend in their own families. Their object is to make the walls of their cities and suburbs strong and their ditches and moats secure. The rules of propriety and of what is right are regarded as the threads by which they seek to maintain in its correctness the relation between ruler and minister; in its generous regard that between father and son; in its harmony that between elder brother and younger; and in a community of sentiment that between husband and wife; and in accordance with them they frame buildings and measures; lay out the fields and hamlets (for the dwellings of the husbandmen); adjudge the superiority to men of valour and knowledge; and regulate their achievements with a view to their own advantage. Thus it is that (selfish) schemes and enterprises are constantly taking their rise, and recourse is had to arms; and thus it was (also) that Yü, Thang, Wan, and Wu, King Khâng, and the Duke of Kau obtained their distinction. Of these six great men everyone was very attentive to the rules of propriety, thus to secure the display of righteousness, the realization of sincerity, the exhibition of errors, the exemplification of benevolence, and the discussion of courtesy, showing the people all the normal virtues. Any rulers who did not follow this course were driven away by those who possessed power and position, and all regarded them as pests. This is the period of what we call Small Tranquillity."

But whether past or future is intended, undoubtedly it is the "golden age," or ideal state, which is meant. The open question as to whether the Grand Course is past or yet to come, is of course due to the ideographic form of the language; owing to his standing as a Confucian scholar, Dr. Chen is certainly entitled to have his interpretation preferred, if all else is equal.

The statement concerning safeguarding the individuality of women would perhaps scarcely seem to warrant the notion that the idea of the family, upon which Confucius built his entire superstructure of personal and governmental relations, should be abandoned; Legge translated this, it should be noted, "Males had their proper work, and females had their homes."

www.ingramcontent.com/pod-product-compliance
Lightning Source LLC
Chambersburg PA
CBHW031319040426
42443CB00005B/148